Programmable
Pocket Calculators

Programmable Pocket Calculators

HENRY MULLISH and STEPHEN KOCHAN

HAYDEN BOOK COMPANY, INC.
Rochelle Park, New Jersey

Library of Congress Cataloging in Publication Data

Mullish, Henry.
   Programmable pocket calculators.

   SUMMARY: Examines in detail programmable pocket
calculators, pointing out their architecture, special features,
and programming techniques for the reader with no
previous knowledge of programming.
   1. Programmable calculators. [1. Programmable
calculators. 2. Calculating machines] I. Kochan, Stephen,
joint author. II. Title.
QA75.M79   001.64'2   80-11088
ISBN 0-8104-5175-1

1	2	3	4	5	6	7	8	9	PRINTING
80	81	82	83	84	85	86	87	88	YEAR

PREFACE

A veritable calculator revolution erupted in 1971 when a million pocket calculators were sold in the United States alone. Overnight, the slide rule became obsolete and gave way to these electronic marvels which, in 1971, could do no more than add, subtract, multiply, and divide—albeit with phenomenal speed and accuracy.

Since then, the prices of pocket calculators have fallen from their initial $400 to the low price of $10, which some four-function calculators command today.

On the heels of the pocket calculator revolution now emerges yet another revolution—the programmable pocket calculator.

The origin of the programmable pocket calculator revolution dates back to December 1973 when Hewlett-Packard, a leading United States computer and calculator manufacturer, introduced to the world its stunning HP-65 "superstar" programmable calculator in pocket size. In addition to its programmability, the HP-65 provided the user with almost all the mathematical and scientific functions he could use. There were two reasons this particular model had such an impact on the calculator world. It made its mark in technological history by being the first pocket calculator produced that was *programmable*. Secondly, it permitted the user to record the program on a thin strip of metal-oxide coated plastic. Although the HP-65 opened up a completely new market, it was restricted by its somewhat prohibitive cost of $800, the price it commanded until the model was finally superseded in 1976 by its successor, the HP-67.

Apparently in an effort to capture an even greater share of the market, Hewlett-Packard introduced in December 1974 yet another programmable pocket calculator, the HP-55. Though not nearly so versatile as the HP-65, it was programmable and sold for half the price of the HP-65.

Inevitably, other leading manufacturers such as National Semiconductor entered the field of programmable pocket calculators and in January 1975 announced four different models: the 4515, the "Programmable Mathematician"; the 4524, the "Programmable Scientist"; the 1625, the "Programmable Financier"; and the 6035, the "Programmable Statistician." Although these four Novus brand models represented a somewhat lower level of sophistication than the Hewlett-Packard or Texas Instruments machines of their day, their price range of around $100 made them extremely attractive for students and professionals in education, science, and business.

In June 1975, a British calculator manufacturer, Sinclair Radionics, introduced its 19-key, 24-step scientific programmable calculator, selling initially for $80.

Once again, in July 1975, Hewlett-Packard astounded the calculator world with its introduction of the HP-25, a programmable pocket calculator weighing a mere 6 ounces and selling initially for $195.

In July 1976, Hewlett-Packard announced a successor to its HP-65. The name given to their new 224-step card-programmable calculator was the HP-67. This feature-packed calculator was released with a price tag of $450. At this time Hewlett-Packard also announced a novel improvement to their highly popular HP-25. The model was called the HP-25C and it distinguished itself by being the first programmable calculator with a "continuous memory."

In December 1977, Hewlett-Packard introduced the HP-19C and the HP-29C. The HP-19C was the first programmable pocket calculator to become commercially available with a built-in thermal printer, which partially accounted for its retail price of $325. Its companion model, the HP-29C, similar in functions except for the printer, sold for $185.

At this point Hewlett-Packard changed gears slightly and made an attempt to capture the lower end of the pocket calculator market. In April 1978 they released their Series E calculators. The HP-33E, retailing for $100, and the HP-38E, retailing for $120, are the two programmable models of this series.

The purpose of this book is to examine in detail these programmable pocket calculators and to point out their architecture, special features, and programming techniques designed to maximize their use. At no time will it be assumed that the reader has any previous knowledge of programming, since to do so would put him at the mercy of the calculator manuals that all too often leave so much to be desired.

Today it is not unusual to find a wide range of assorted programmable and nonprogrammable calculators on sale. Making a sensible selection is difficult because of the bewildering variety of calculator features available. But this is only part of the problem—from the consumer's point of view. The salesman has his problems, too. He is expected to be conversant on all the various models, many of which differ from each other in subtle ways. How is he supposed to know the advantages and disadvantages of so many machines, particularly the programmable models, since he probably has never had the training or experience necessary to understand the principles of programmables, let alone to answer intelligently incisive questions on the subject?

It is an interesting commentary on our times that the state of the art has progressed so far and so rapidly in so short a period of time that many department store calculator counters now provide a free telephone connection directly to the manufacturer, of whom technical questions may be asked.

This book has been written to assist both the consumer and the salesman. Every program for each calculator is incorporated in a schematic showing *precisely* how to enter the program and to put the calculator to work. In this way the salesman and consumer alike will be at liberty to key in any program step by step, watch it calculate and display the final results without having to get involved with the various programming philosophies, logic, or the particular calculator architecture.

HENRY MULLISH
STEPHEN KOCHAN

CONTENTS

CHAPTER ONE
THE ART OF PROGRAMMING

Computer programming is not only a well-paid profession demanding considerable expertise of the individual but is also one of the most satisfying and challenging of professions. The profession itself is a mere child in terms of its beginning, but since the 1950s when computers came on the scene, it has grown by leaps and bounds. Universities around the world now offer a plethora of courses on the subject, and it is becoming increasingly common for high schools to offer courses in computer languages such as FORTRAN, ALGOL, PL/I, BASIC, COBOL, and so on.

Why are computers so much in demand? The reason is that for the first time in our history we are able to solve problems with the speed of electricity. These electronic marvels have no inherent intelligence of their own. It is up to us to write appropriate instructions for them in order to arrive at the solutions. Such a sequence of instructions is called a *program* for the simple reason that the sequence is a planned one, exactly like a theatrical dramatic presentation follows its program in terms of acts and scenes.

Does one have to be a genius to be a programmer? Certainly not. Anybody with a modicum of intelligence and a slight sense of logic can program, without any previous training whatever. Of course, the greater one's sense of logic the easier it will be. It seems that certain people—particularly those who excel at puzzle solving and game playing—prove to be excellent programmers. What's more, such people tend to get "turned on" to programming almost with a passion. Programming is, like so many other things in life, improved by success. Once one has written a program, no matter how elementary it is, it seems to provide the kind of thrust to propel one to greater heights. The success feeds on itself. For some people, programming becomes a kind of addiction—happily one without any known negative effects, however.

Some Fundamental Programming Concepts

One is often faced with the problem of evaluating a complicated, perhaps lengthy mathematical expression using any one of the many available calculators. A sequence of keystrokes is then decided upon, and each individual step is performed until the final solution is reached and displayed. Now, if there is a need to evaluate the same mathematical expression, one would have to physically repeat each one of the steps in the sequence as used to find the first solution. If this whole sequence of instructions must be repeated hundreds or even thousands of times, this would become a formidable chore. Ideally one would want some method by which the calculator could "remember" the sequence of instructions used in evaluating the expression the first time, permitting the user to reinitiate the sequence of instructions in the calculator's "memory" for each new set of data to be operated upon.

The basic feature of the modern programmable ·calculator provides precisely this ability: to store and execute a sequence of instructions known as a *program* in the calculator's memory and to have those stored instructions process as many data sets as are necessary.

An important variation of this sequential operation is the ability to automatically repeat a group of instructions when a particular part of the program is reached. This provides what is known as a *loop,* one of the fundamental properties of programming. This ability to alter normal

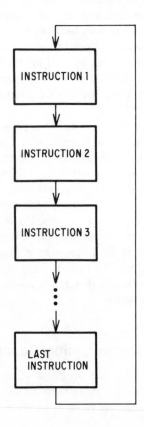

Fig. 1-1

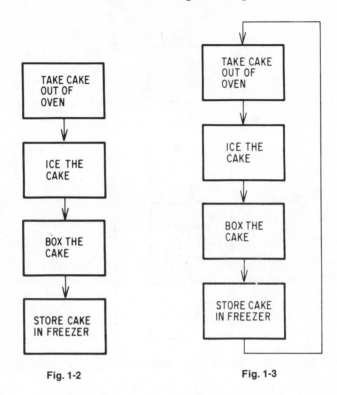

Fig. 1-2   Fig. 1-3

sequential flow of a program is accomplished by what is referred to as an *unconditional jump,* as illustrated in Fig. 1-1.

Another important dimension is added to this sequential operation (Fig. 1-1) when a jump is made to another point in the program when a *special condition is met.* This is known as a *conditional jump* and provides the means for highly sophisticated decisions to be made within a program.

As an analogy to both these different types of situations, imagine that a baker apprentice has a job of taking cakes out of the oven. He must then ice the cake, place it in a box, and store it in the freezer. The individual steps may be represented simply, as shown in Fig. 1-2.

Naturally there are many cakes that are produced by a bakery, and our apprentice's job is to repeat the same sequence of operations for each cake.

This may be represented schematically, as shown in Fig. 1-3. Here we have the concept of the loop connecting the end of the sequence of operations with the beginning.

Suppose now that the apprentice ends his day at 5:00 P.M. and has no wish to work overtime. After storing each cake in the freezer, he might ask himself whether it is 5:00 P.M. yet. If it is, he puts on his coat and leaves work. Otherwise he takes out the next cake, completing the sequence once

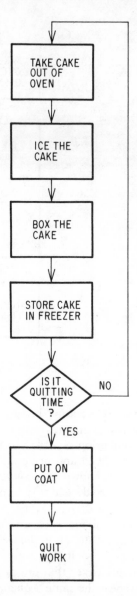

Fig. 1-4

again. It will be noticed that in this situation a decision is being made each time the process is executed; namely, is it quitting time or not? This may be represented schematically, as shown in Fig. 1-4.

This kind of schematic is usually referred to in programming as a *flowchart* and can be an extremely useful method of indicating the flow of control through a program.

Let us now amend our baker analogy so that we can illustrate further important principles of programming. Let us assume that in accordance with union rules our apprentice finishes his workday after he has processed 200 cakes, regardless of what time of the day it happens to be. If he finishes at 3:00 P.M., then he leaves at 3:00 P.M., but if he does not finish until 7:00 P.M., then he works until 7:00 P.M. without further remuneration.

This new situation implies that a count of the number of cakes processed must be kept throughout the working day. At the beginning of the day, of course, this count is zero. As soon as a cake is stored in the freezer, he adds one to the count. Since we may assume that he is anxious to quit work as soon as possible, each time he adds a cake, he checks the count to see whether it has yet reached 200. If it has, he puts on his coat and quits work. If the count has not yet reached 200, he stays to process the next cake. The flowchart in Fig. 1-5 represents this new situation.

The concept of keeping a counter is of primary importance in programming. Here, the counter is the only means by which we know when to exit from the loop. In other words, a critical decision is being made based upon the value of the counter.

Notice that in Fig. 1-5 where the question, "Does count equal 200?" is asked (it is customary to write such questions within diamond-shaped "decision" boxes) if the answer is NO we do not go back to the very beginning, where the counter is set to zero, but rather to the following step.

Flowcharting a Mathematical Problem

Let us now take a simple problem in which a basic decision has to be made. We shall examine a series of integer numbers and determine how many of them are even and how many of them are odd.

By definition, an integer number is even if it is divisible by two with no remainder. If there is a remainder, that number is considered to be odd. In this particular problem there are two counters involved: one to keep a tally of the even numbers and the other to count the number of odd integers.

The input data to the flowchart in Fig. 1-6 are the individual numbers themselves. Each number is examined to determine if it is odd or even, and one is added to the appropriate counter. Once all the numbers have been examined, the contents of the odd counter and that of the even counter are displayed. This represents the output to the problem.

With few exceptions, the concepts of *input* and *output* are common to all programs.

Debugging and Editing Programs

When examining programs such as those included in this book, one should not be misled into thinking that they were written this way the first time. Few programs work the first time. Moreover, even if a program appears to be working the first time, the chances are that it will not work for

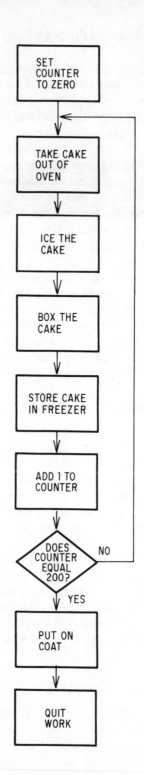

Fig. 1-5

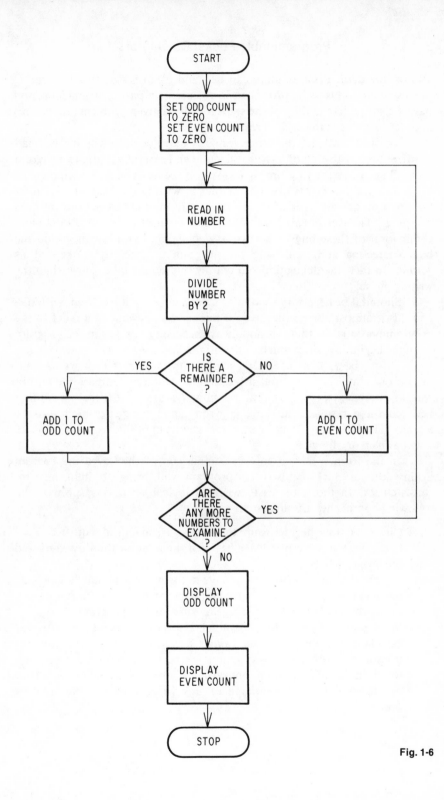

START

SET ODD COUNT
TO ZERO
SET EVEN COUNT
TO ZERO

READ IN
NUMBER

DIVIDE
NUMBER
BY 2

IS
THERE A
REMAINDER
?

YES   NO

ADD 1 TO
ODD COUNT

ADD 1 TO
EVEN COUNT

ARE
THERE
ANY MORE
NUMBERS TO
EXAMINE
?

YES

NO

DISPLAY
ODD COUNT

DISPLAY
EVEN COUNT

STOP

Fig. 1-6

all possible data. Programming can be—and often is—quite a frustrating process. One needs to be proficient in the use of a particular machine and have a clear understanding of the steps to solve a given problem (algorithm) in order to arrive at the desired result.

To our knowledge the programmer is yet to be born who has not had to suffer the frustration of having diligently and carefully written a program that did not work the first time it was run. It seems to be a characteristic of programming that errors are made either in writing the program—that is, the program has an error of logic—or in entering the instructions into the computer. These errors are traditionally known as *bugs* and the finding and elimination of these bugs is known as *debugging*. Once having found the bug, correcting and modifying the program is generally spoken of as *editing*. In fact, the debugging and editing phase may take longer than the writing phase!

Should it be necessary to modify a program once it has been written—and this is almost always the case—it might be somewhat of a relief to the programmer to know that it is not always necessary to rekey in the program from the beginning, since much of the original program may be salvaged.

Before being convinced that a program is in perfect working condition, one should check it out using sample data and compare the output with known results, if this is at all possible. Naturally, if there is a conflict between these results something is wrong, and the program has to be suspect. The fault may lie in the incorrect keying in of the program, or there may be an error of logic.

In the former case, a careful comparison of the keyed in program against the original handwritten program will bring to light any inconsistencies. In the latter case, where a logical error is suspected, the following approaches are suggested:

1. Check the flowchart to insure that blocks are in logical sequence.
2. Compare the correspondence between the logic of the flowchart and the program itself.
3. Be sure that the instructions behave in the manner planned. This may mean going through the program on paper step-by-step, keeping track of the contents of each of the registers used by the program.
4. Make use of any additional debugging aids available on the particular calculator. This may include a *single step* key, which permits the user to proceed through the program one instruction at a time; a *pause* key, which halts the program temporarily to permit intermediate results to be viewed; or take advantage of any listed features that may be present.

CHAPTER TWO
AN OVERVIEW OF PROGRAMMABLE POCKET CALCULATORS

The Logic Used in Programmable Pocket Calculators

A large number of programmable pocket calculators use what has now become known as Reverse Polish Notation. This is not some kind of an ethnic slur but a name to describe a system of logic originally conceived in 1949 by a Polish mathematician named Jan Lucasiewicz. He invented a parenthesis-free but unambiguous mathematical language that came to be known as Polish Notation, in which the arithmetic operator preceded the two operands. For example, the algebraic expression

$$(a + b)$$

was written

$$+ a b$$

This same principle is still used except that the arithmetic operator, instead of being pre-fixed, has become post-fixed in modern times. As a result, the system is now called Reverse Polish Notation. It is often abbreviated to RPN, and it has become a standard language of computer science. Thus the above expression would be written in RPN as

$$a b +$$

RPN is wedded to a four-register memory stack in all Hewlett-Packard programmable pocket calculators and to usually fewer than four registers in other companies' models. RPN permits the solution of complex algebraic equations without recourse to either parentheses or an equals key. In fact, a calculator that uses RPN logic can be readily identified by the absence of an equals key. Moreover, in RPN calculators all internal partial answers are displayed automatically as the calculation proceeds. They are automatically saved and retrieved as needed during the course of the calculation. The manner in which the stack works is treated in great detail in Chaps. 3 and 4, in which the Novus and Hewlett-Packard programmable models are described.

In order to familiarize the reader with RPN, we present below a succession of algebraic expressions, their representations in Reverse Polish Notation, and the keystrokes needed to evaluate these expressions. The symbol ↑ is an abbreviation for the ENTER key found on the various calculators.

	Algebraic Expression	*Reverse Polish Notation*	*Keystrokes*
1.	a + b	a b +	a ↑ b +
2.	a − b	a b −	a ↑ b −
3.	a × b	a b ×	a ↑ b ×
4.	a ÷ b	a b ÷	a ↑ b ÷
5.	a + (b × c)	a b c × +	a ↑ b ↑ c × +
6.	a − (b × c)	a b c × −	a ↑ b ↑ c × −
7.	a (b + c)	a b c + ×	a ↑ b ↑ c + ×
8.	a/(b + c)	a b c + ÷	a ↑ b ↑ c + ÷
9.	a + (b/c)	a b c ÷ +	a ↑ b ↑ c ÷ +
10.	a − (b/c)	a b c ÷ −	a ↑ b ↑ c ÷ −
11.	(a × b) + (c × d)	a b × c d × +	a ↑ b × c ↑ d × +
12.	(a + b) × (c + d)	a b + c d + ×	a ↑ b + c ↑ d + ×
13.	a + [b × (c + d)]	a b c d + × +	a ↑ b ↑ c ↑ d + × +
14.	a × [b + (c/d − e)]	a b c d ÷ e − + ×	a ↑ b ↑ c ↑ d ÷ e − + ×

Here are some general rules for evaluating algebraic expressions in Reverse Polish Notation:

1. Algebraic expressions may always be keyed in from left to right, regardless of parentheses.
2. There is never a need for a parenthesis key.
3. There is never a need for an equals key.
4. When in doubt as to whether to press the [↑] key, ask yourself the question, "Can I perform an operation?" If the answer to this question is YES, go ahead and perform the operation. If NO, press the [↑] key and key in the next number.

In September 1975 Texas Instruments announced its SR-52 programmable pocket calculator. Without exception, the Texas Instruments nonprogrammable calculators do not use RPN, but operate by what has come to be called *algebraic logic*. Their more advanced scientific calculators such as the SR-50, SR-50A, SR-51, SR51-A, and SR51-I use a modified form of algebraic logic called AOS (Algebraic Operating System).

All the Texas Instruments programmable models use modified algebraic logic, and they overcome the problem of a stack by having multi-levels of parentheses. Modified algebraic logic means that expressions are evaluated in accordance with the hierarchical rules of algebra.

The manner in which arithmetic expressions are keyed into the Texas Instrument programmable models is illustrated in the chart that follows.

	Algebraic Expression	Keystrokes
1.	a + b	a + b =
2.	a − b	a − b =
3.	a × b	a × b =
4.	a ÷ b	a ÷ b =
5.	a + (b × c)	a + (b × c) = or simply a + b × c =
6.	a − (b × c)	a − (b × c) = or simply a − b × c =
7.	a (b + c)	a × (b + c) =
8.	a/(b + c)	a ÷ (b + c) =
9.	a + (b/c)	a + (b ÷ c) = or simply a + b ÷ c =
10.	a − (b/c)	a − (b ÷ c) = a − b ÷ c =
11.	(a × b) + (c × d)	(a × b) + (c × d) = or simply a × b + c × d =
12.	(a + b) × (c + d)	(a + b) × (c + d) =
13.	a + [b × (c + d)]	a + [b × (c + d)] = or a + b × (c + d) =
14.	a × [b + (c/d − e)]	a × [b + (c ÷ d − e)] =

Here are some points worth noting about AOS calculators:

1. There is a more or less one-to-one correspondence between the algebraic expression to be evaluated and the sequence of keystrokes required. This means that it is not necessary to learn any kind of new notation.
2. The final answer is always obtained by pressing the equals key.
3. In expressions such as in example 8 above, it is essential to treat the denominator b + c as if it were enclosed within parentheses when keying it in, so that the numerator a is divided by the *entire* denominator b + c.

Manufacturers of calculators using RPN and AOS both claim that their way is the way you normally think. Few people will argue the fact that RPN requires some "getting used to." However, once it has been mastered, calculations can be done swiftly and with a high degree of confidence. There are some who feel so strongly about RPN that they would refuse to handle a calculator that did not use this form of logic.

The controversy as to whether RPN or AOS is the better system will probably never be resolved. Most likely it is a question of personal preference on the one hand and the particular kind of problems one customarily has to solve on the other. It seems that certain kinds of problems are better solved in RPN, while others require fewer keystrokes in AOS.

Calculator Displays

By far the most common type of display found in pocket calculators is the red colored light-emitting diode (LED). LEDs are not miniaturized hot-wire lamps but rather exploit a new kind of semiconductor technology. All light-emitting diodes are composed of two semiconducting compounds, gallium arsenide phosphide (GaAsP) and gallium phosphide (GaP). Although it is unusual to see any but red LEDs in calculator displays, the technology now also offers green, orange, and yellow. The commercial LED consists of a tiny chip of a light-emitting semiconductor with a plastic lens, giving it a magnification of between 10 to 20 times.

These tiny LEDs are used to illuminate the vertical and horizontal bars of the seven-segment display be means of which all the decimal digits, minus sign, and certain letters of the alphabet may be constructed.

The Seven-Segment Display

The standard method of forming the digits of the display using the seven-segment scheme is shown in Fig. 2-1. Note that each of the segments is used in the digit 8. Figure 2-2 shows how the minus sign and the rest of the digits are formed.

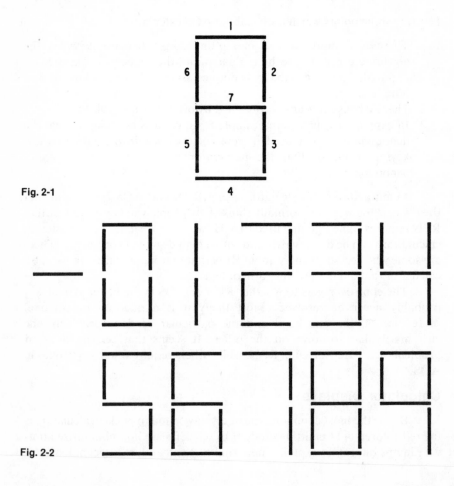

Fig. 2-1

Fig. 2-2

One of the interesting innovations first introduced by the Hewlett-Packard HP-25 is that upon attempting certain invalid operations the word *error* is flashed on the display. This too is done by means of the seven-segment display, as shown in Fig. 2-3.

Fig. 2-3

Gas Discharge Displays

Another popular device for illuminating numeric displays is by tubes containing an inert gas such as neon. For each digit of the display is a separate tube, each containing a seven-segment matrix. When a digit is to be displayed the appropriate segments are energized and the surrounding gas causes the digit to glow with either a green or orange color, depending upon the gas used.

The Sinclair Scientific Programmable uses a green gas discharge display that is easy on the eye and whose digits are particularly large.

Liquid-Crystal Displays

The liquid-crystal display (LCD) is popular in nonprogrammable pocket calculators. It is particularly suitable to calculators because of its low power requirements. In view of the fact that it reflects only the light in the surrounding environment, it is not very useful in the dark.

The method by which LCDs operate is rather technical, but suffice it to say that it also uses the seven-segment structure. LCDs rest on the phenomenon that certain liquid crystals change their opacity when activated by an electric current. So far no programmable pocket calculators have liquid-crystal displays.

Programmable Pocket Calculator Features

Program Memory

One of the primary considerations in selecting a programmable pocket calculator is the size of the program memory. This will determine, in many cases, whether a particular program can or cannot be written to solve a specific problem on the calculator. Thus it emerges that the amount of memory space available is a critical factor. Typically the program memory of the calculator is a sequence of consecutive storage locations capable of holding instructions. Usually, each instruction on the calculator is stored in separate consecutive locations in program memory. Here is a conceptual diagram of a 24-step program that does not occupy all of the calculator's program memory area.

Location Number	Instruction
1	Instruction 1
2	Instruction 2
3	Instruction 3
.	.
.	.
.	.
24	Last instruction
.	.
.	.
.	.

The numbers written to the left of the locations are known as *addresses* and provide a convenient means of referencing any particular instruction in the calculator's memory. The instructions are normally executed in sequence, but more often than not, and especially in more complicated programs, branching is performed either unconditionally or conditionally to a specific location in memory.

Another factor to be considered in selecting a programmable pocket calculator is that the length of a program may depend upon the number and manner of the branching facilities that a particular calculator offers. There is no absolute consistency about this even among calculators produced by the same manufacturer, to say nothing of those models produced by different manufacturers. There are also several calculators available that are programmable only to the extent that they are capable of "learning" a sequence of instructions. These calculators do not provide any branching facilities. In other words, programs may be executed only in a sequential manner, and hence such models would perhaps be better described as sequential programmable calculators. Although these lower level programmable calculators lack the sophisticated features of their fully programmable counterparts, they serve a useful function and also have their place.

Indirect Addressing

There is a feature known as *indirect addressing,* which has been borrowed from modern electronic computers. This feature is proving increasingly important in programmable pocket calculators, since it not only lends itself to sophisticated programming but also permits more concise programs. Indirect addressing capability is found on the Hewlett-Packard HP-19C/29C and HP-67.

Subroutines

We have already seen that there are various factors that bear upon the size of the memory available to the user. Among them we must include the subject of subroutines, an extremely important feature that allows for both conservation of memory space and a style of programming known as structured programming.

Subroutines may be visualized in the following way. Imagine that we have a long sequence of program instructions. At various points along the program we want to treat a certain value in a particular manner but each time in the *same* manner. The set of instructions that accomplishes this task could be regarded as a "package." Transfer would have to be made to the package, and once the processing was completed control would have to be sent back to the instruction *following* the one that branched off to the package.

Couldn't this be done by means of unconditional branching? Yes, but only for the first occasion. The second time transfer to the package is made, control would have to go back to a different location. This situation is made very easy by resorting to subroutines, where our package is, in fact, a subroutine. The "calls" to the subroutine and the "returns" to the "main" program are part of a system that ensures that these transfers are made correctly. The reader is advised that this concept of subroutines sounds more complex than it really is.

In Fig. 2-4 the subroutine is called from two different places in the main program. When a subroutine is invoked by a main routine and returns to that main routine, this is described as *one-level subroutining.* Should the subroutine itself invoke a second subroutine (which returns to the first subroutine) we have an example of a *second-level* subroutine structure. Generally speaking, if subroutine A calls subroutine B which in turn calls subroutine C, subroutine C is spoken of as a *third-level* subroutine.

In view of the fact that the presence of a subroutine facility on a particular calculator is an indication of its programming power, needless to say, not all programmable calculators are equipped with this feature. In some calculators the subroutine feature is absent, while in others one or more levels are permitted.

Merged Codes

As mentioned earlier, on some programmable calculators each keystroke is stored in a separate location in program memory. Other models permit the merging of shift keys with their associated function key so that they occupy a single location, thereby resulting in a considerable saving of memory space. Some models permit the merging of register arithmetic instructions and even branch instructions.

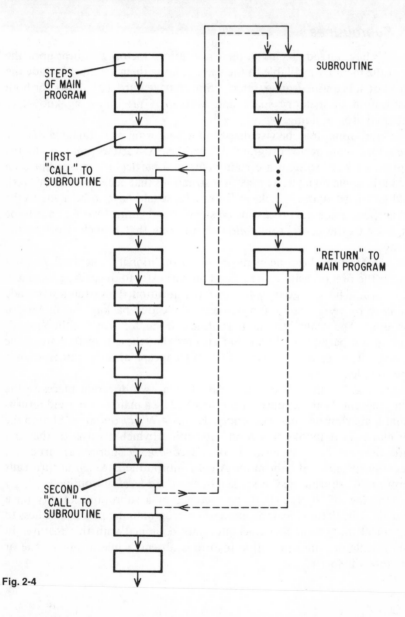

Fig. 2-4

Data Registers

Since one of the most common causes of error is the incorrect writing down of intermediate results or the subsequent incorrect keying in of these intermediate results, it became necessary to make provision for minimizing or eliminating these errors. The most popular strategy employed was to provide a bank of data registers, each of which could be accessed separately when required. Displayed values could be stored in these registers by means of a *store* instruction and recalled to the display either for viewing or for computational purposes. On some calculators the *store* and *recall* instructions are merged together with their related register address in the same instruction, thereby lending itself to a more compact program. In the case of one of the more sophisticated calculators to be described, there is a method to "protect" data stored in these registers.

Depending upon the problem being solved, the question of the number of data registers available on a particular calculator could also be a major consideration. On some later models the user has the option to specify up to a given maximum how many data registers he wants, depending upon the needs of the particular problem.

Programmable Calculator Modes

One intriguing feature of programmable pocket calculators is their ability to remember a sequence of keystrokes once it has been keyed in. This sets the programmable calculators apart from their nonprogrammable predecessors.

Programmable pocket calculators normally operate in two distinct modes: (1) program or learn mode and (2) run mode.

When the calculator is operating in program mode, keystrokes are automatically retained in the program memory. It is in this mode that the program is entered into the calculator.

In order to execute the program—that is, to perform this sequence of steps with some specific data—it is necessary to switch to RUN mode. Incidentally, in RUN mode the calculator may be used without a program, just as if it were a nonprogrammable calculator.

Recording Programs

Under ordinary circumstances, once a program has been keyed into a calculator and the calculator is switched off, the program is lost. If the program were needed on a subsequent occasion it would have to be keyed in afresh. For short programs this perhaps is no particular chore, just mildly bothersome. However, for longer programs this can prove to be quite a tedious task and one which invites errors in the rekeying in of the instructions.

This situation is partially alleviated by the so-called continuous memory calculators in which a trickle of electrical current keeps the keyed in program "alive" even when the calculator is switched off. This continuous memory feature is a distinct advantage but is restrictive in the sense that only the program currently contained in memory can be saved for subsequent use. As a matter of fact, it is impossible not to have the memory alive in continuous memory calculators. Perhaps later versions of such calculators will provide an optional switch, permitting the user to decide whether or not he or she wishes to take advantage of this feature.

A feature that vastly increases the versatility of a programmable pocket calculator is the magnetic card. This is a strip of metal-oxide coated plastic that plays the role of the punched card in computer systems. In fact, the magnetic card is superior to the punched card in that it may be reused for other programs as often as is necessary. By means of a magnetic card a program may be recorded directly from the calculator. When that program is to be run on a future occasion, all that is necessary is for the magnetic card to be read by the calculator. The complete program is then stored in the memory of the calculator, and the possibility of errors that may occur when rekeying in the program is totally obviated. By means of these magnetic cards, an extensive library of programs may be written and stored by the user, thereby saving him considerable time and effort when running the programs on subsequent occasions. In computer jargon, a system of such "routines" is generally referred to as a *software* library, in contrast to the physical parts of the computer, which are known as the *hardware* of the system.

Plug-In ROM Modules

One of the more recent innovations in programmable pocket calculators is the introduction of so-called solid state software in the form of a plug-in module the size of a postage stamp. Despite their small size, these modules can contain up to 5,000 additional program steps in the form of a library of subroutines. Each module is geared to a particular type user, and one is therefore at liberty to purchase other plug-in modules tailor-made for a particular discipline. As opposed to magnetic cards, the routines contained in the modules cannot be altered by the user. In other words, they are available on a "read only" basis, and, in fact, are referred to as ROMs (Read Only Memories).

Thus it is clear that when purchasing a programmable pocket calculator one has to consider a wide range of options. A decision about which calculator to purchase will have to be based on the expertise of the individual involved, the price range, particular applications, as well as the many features described in this chapter. Admittedly, this may not be an easy choice.

CHAPTER THREE
THE ECONOMY-LEVEL PROGRAMMABLE POCKET CALCULATORS

The Novus Programmable Calculators

National Semiconductor's Novus line of calculators are highly competitive in price. In January 1975 National Semiconductor introduced four programmable models differing considerably in operation from most other programmable calculators. These are the Programmable Mathematician (Model 4515), the Programmable Statistician (Model 6035), the Programmable Financier (Model 6025), and the Programmable Scientist (Model 4525). Each of these four calculators permits the keying-in of a program of up to 100 steps with the option that several separate programs, whose total does not exceed 100 steps, may be stored simultaneously in the calculator's memory. Each of the four Novus programmable calculators operates in Reverse Polish Notation, has a stack of three registers, and has a rechargeable battery. A typical full charge takes about four hours, and the calculator may even be used while it is charging. In order to save battery life, the display automatically shuts off if no key has been pressed for approximately 35 seconds. In this case a string of decimal points is displayed to notify the user of the fade out. However, a display fade out in no way changes the program or the data that has been keyed in, and further entries or operations will bring back the display. At any given point in a calculation after the display has faded, it may be recalled by merely pressing the change sign key twice.

For reasons of space we have restricted our description of the Novus line of programmable pocket calculators to the Programmable Mathematician (Model 4515). All the programming features on the Novus calculators are identical so that a familiarity with this machine will benefit a user of any of them.

The Programmable Novus Mathematician

The Programmable Novus Mathematician, labeled Mathematician PR, comes in an attractive, slim-lined casing with color-coded keys, some of which have a dual role. It contains a host of important mathematical functions including sine, cosine, tangent and their inverses, y^x, e^x, ln, log, $1/x, \pi, \sqrt{x}$, x to y interchange, and a change sign key. It has a memory into which numbers may be stored using the key labeled [MS], and recalled using the [MR] key. In the top left-hand corner of the keyboard is a prominent yellow key labeled [F], which must be pressed before any of the yellow printed functions can be accessed. These include the arc sine, arc cosine, and arc tangent, memory plus, memory minus, and memory plus x^2. Also present are keys for radians and degrees, which are also initiated by first pressing the [F] key. Since this calculator operates in RPN, provision is made to enter numbers using the white key labeled [ENT↑].

A picture of the Novus Mathematician PR is shown in Fig. 3-1.

Manual Operation of the Mathematician PR

The ON/OFF switch is located on the top left-hand side of the Novus Mathematician and is recessed for protection. With the LOAD/ STEP/RUN switch in RUN mode, the calculator may be used as any nonprogrammable pocket calculator.

Example 1: Evaluate $\sqrt{\pi \times (5.986)^2}$

*S	1	2	3	4
K	π	ENT↑	5.986	F
D	3.1415926	3.1415926	5.986	5.986

S	5	6	7
K	x^2	×	$\sqrt{}$
D	35.832196	112.57016	10.609908

Example 2: Evaluate $(\sin 22.9°)^{4.1}/\log 38.7$

S	1	2	3	4
K	22.9	sin	4.1	y^x
D	22.9	.389124	4.1	.0208623

S	5	6	7
K	38.7	log	÷
D	38.7	1.587711	.01313985

---

*In this and all schematics that follow, the sequence numbers are indicated by the letter *S,* the keyed in values by the letter *K,* and the displayed values by the letter *D.*

Fig. 3-1 Novus Mathematician PR (*Courtesy* National Semiconductors, Inc.)

Example 3:   Evaluate $\sin 2\,(\pi/2)\,e^{\sqrt{.3}}/(-15.68 + \ln 3.7)$

S	1	2	3	4	5
K	π	2	÷	F	deg
D	3.1415926	2	1.5707963	1.5707963	89.999999

S	6	7	8	9	10
K	sin	.3	$\sqrt{}$	e^x	X
D	1.	.3	.54772255	1.729309	1.729309

S	11	12	13	14	15
K	MS	15.68	CHS	ENT↑	3.7
D	1.729309	15.68	−15.68	−15.68	3.7

S	16	17	18	19	20
K	ln	+	MR	x ↔ y	÷
D	1.308333	−14.371667	1.729309	−14.371667	−.12032765

Example 3 above uses many of the powerful mathematical features available on the Novus Mathematician PR, and though we have not as yet covered each of the available functions on the keyboard, we shall use them in the programming mode. Since this is the *raison d'être* for the calculator, we shall proceed immediately to illustrate the power of the calculator in its programming mode.

Programming the Novus Mathematician PR

The Average of Two Numbers. For our first problem we shall set up a program to find the average of two numbers. The sequence of steps to accomplish this manually (with the LOAD/STEP/RUN switch in RUN mode) for the two numbers 3 and 4 follows:

$$3$$
$$\text{ENT}\uparrow$$
$$4$$
$$+$$
$$2$$
$$\div$$

This is almost identical to the sequence of instructions that constitute the program to find the average of an infinite number of pairs.

There would be no point in repeating the above sequence of instructions time and again because we would merely be calculating the average of 3 and 4 each time. What we want is to interrupt the sequence to enable us to key in the next pair of numbers at the appropriate time. The Novus Mathematician provides the user with a key labeled [halt] to permit the program to be interrupted for the entry of new data. Therefore, whenever data is to be keyed in, replace that step of the program with a [halt]. The program to compute the average of any pair of numbers is shown directly.

Program Novus-1: The Average of Two Numbers

Step Number	Instruction	Comments
1	halt	Stop program to permit keying in of first number
2	ENT↑	Copy number from x to y register
3	halt	Stop program again to permit keying in of second number
4	+	Add two numbers together
5	2	Puts 2 into x register, lifting stack
6	÷	Calculate average

Keying in the Program

1. Move the mode switch to the LOAD position.
2. Press the [start] key.
3. Key in the six instructions of Program Novus-1, as indicated above, starting with [halt] and ending with [÷].

Running the Program

1. Move the mode switch to RUN.
2. Press the [start] key.
3. Key in the first number of the pair to be averaged.
4. Press the [start] key.
5. Key in the second number of the pair.
6. Press the [start] key. The average of the two numbers will be displayed.
7. Go to step 2 to process the next pair of numbers.

Suppose we wanted the average of each of the following four pairs of numbers:

29	37
3.289	4.1
–10.7	16.82
138.3	5.6

Here is a schematic showing each step of the procedure required to process each pair.

Schematic Novus-1

S	1	2	3	4	5	6	7
K	start	29	start	37	start	start	3.289
D	0.	29	29.	37	33.	33.	3.289

S	8	9	10	11	12	13	14
K	start	4.1	start	start	10.7	CHS	start
D	3.289	4.1	3.6945	3.6945	10.7	−10.7	−10.7

S	15	16	17	18	19	20	21
K	16.82	start	start	138.3	start	5.6	start
D	16.82	3.06	3.06	138.3	138.3	5.6	71.95

A careful examination of this schematic will show that the first pair of numbers, 29 and 37, is keyed in in steps 2 and 4. Pressing [start] in step 5 immediately displays the average of these numbers, namely 33. In steps 7 and 9 the second pair of numbers is keyed in, and its average is displayed in step 10. This process is repeated until all of the pairs of numbers have been averaged.

Finding the nth Root of a Series of Numbers. Although the square root function is readily available on the Mathematician PR calculator, provision is not made for finding a root other than the square root. We notice, however, that there is a [y^x] key, and this may be used to calculate the nth root of a number based on the following mathematical concept:

$$\sqrt[n]{y} = y^{1/n}$$

To find the cube root of 8, for example, we can raise the number 8 to the power 1/3, advantage being taken of the reciprocal button. Using the calculator in the manual mode, the sequence of instructions is as follows:

$$8$$
$$ENT\uparrow$$
$$3$$
$$1/x$$
$$y^x$$

This yields a result of 1.999998, rather than the 2 that we expected. Sometimes we have to settle for these close approximations when using calculators.

Here is a program for computing the nth root (where n can be any positive integer) of any keyed in number.

Program Novus-2: Computing the nth Root

Step Number	Instruction	Comments
1	halt	Stops program to allow keying in of number to be "rooted"
2	ENT↑	Copies number into y register
3	halt	Stops program to allow the desired root to to be entered
4	1/x	Takes the reciprocal of the x register
5	y^x	Computes the nth root

Using this program we shall solve the following problems:

$$\sqrt[3]{8} \qquad \sqrt[5]{68} \qquad \sqrt[9]{272}$$

Remember, before keying in the above program, switch the calculator into LOAD mode and press [start]. When the program has been keyed in, switch to RUN mode.

Schematic Novus-2

S	1	2	3	4	5
K	start	8	start	3	start
D	0.	8	8.	3	1.999998

S	6	7	8	9	10
K	start	68	start	5	start
D	1.999998	68	68.	5	2.325421

S	11	12	13	14	15
K	start	272	start	9	start
D	2.325421	272	272.	9	1.864263

Thus from this schematic we find that the cube root of 8 is the same approximation to 2 that we calculated in manual mode. The fifth root of 68 is found to be equal to 2.325421 (step 10) and the ninth root of 272 is 1.864263, as shown in step 15.

A Program Using the Memory

The following three equations are probably quite familiar:

1. Area of a circle $= \pi r^2$
2. Circumference of a circle $= 2\pi r$
3. Volume of a sphere $= (4/3)\pi r^3$

We shall now write a program to compute each of these three values for a given value of the radius r.

Program Novus-3

Step Number	Instruction	Comments
1	halt	Stops program to allow value for r to be keyed in
2	MS	Stores value of r into memory
3	F x^2	r^2
4	π	Puts 3.1415926 into x register
5	X	πr^2
6	halt	Stops program to display area
7	MR	Recalls value of r from memory into x register
8	2	
9	X	2r
10	π	
11	X	2πr
12	halt	Stops program to display circumference
13	MR	Recalls value of r again
14	3	
15	y^x	r^3
16	π	
17	X	πr^3
18	4	
19	X	4πr^3
20	3	
21	$\div$	(4/3) πr^3

Assuming that this program has been keyed in correctly, we shall calculate the area, circumference, and volume for values of r equal to 1 and 4.98. Here is the schematic illustrating the procedure at each step.

Schematic Novus-3

S	1	2	3	4	5
K	start	1	start	start	start
D	0.	1	3.1415926	6.2831852	4.18879
*C		r = 1	area	circumference	volume

S	6	7	8	9	10
K	start	4.98	start	start	start
D	4.18879	4.98	77.912753	31.290262	517.34026
C		r = 4.98	area	circumference	volume

---

*In this and all schematics that follow, the letter *C* stands for comments.

The Mathematician PR has two additional keys to aid the programmer. The key marked [del], when pressed in LOAD mode, deletes the last step entered in a program. In this way, the [del] key can be used to delete portions of a program that may then be replaced by the correct keystrokes. For example, suppose a program has been keyed in as follows, where a division has inadvertently been keyed in rather than a multiplication:

> halt
> $F x^2$
> π
> ÷   (oops! I meant ×)

With the calculator still switched in the LOAD position, pressing the [del] key followed by the [×] key will delete the division and substitute in its place the required multiplication. A succession of deletes will erase consecutively a sequence of instructions. The key labeled [skip] permits more than one program to be stored and accessed independently in the calculator's 100-step memory. For example, suppose we had the following two independent programs for calculating the circumference and area, respectively of a circle:

> halt   halt
> π $F x^2$
> × π
> 2   ×
> ×

The two programs can be entered simultaneously into the calculator by inserting a [skip] between the two programs. The skip instruction tells the calculator where one program ends and another begins. The two programs can then be keyed in as one large program as follows:

> halt
> π
> ×
> 2
> ×
> skip
> halt
> $F x^2$
> π
> ×

One may then selectively execute either of the two programs by using the [skip] key when the calculator is in RUN mode.

For example, to calculate the circumference of a circle whose radius is 5 inches, we proceed as usual: press [start] to initiate the program, key in 5, and then press [start] again to compute the circumference. If we then wished to compute the area of the same circle, pressing [skip] would bypass the first program that computes the circumference and would begin execution at the *instruction immediately following the skip instruction that was keyed in.* In this case, the calculator executes a [halt], permitting the user to enter his value for r. Pressing [start] will reinitiate the program, and the calculator will stop with the correct area displayed. After the second program is completed, the calculator will be ready to execute the first program again.

The use of the [skip] key should become clear from the following schematic.

Schematic Novus-4

1. Find the circumference and area of a circle whose radius is 5 inches.
2. Find the area of a circle whose radius is 3.2 inches.
3. Find the circumference of a circle whose radius is 15.6 inches.

S	1	2	3	4
K	start	5	start	skip
D	0.	5	31.415926	31.415926
C	initiate	first	circumference	"skip" to area
	program	radius		program

S	5	6	7	8
K	5	start	skip	3.2
D	5	78.539815	78.539815	3.2
C		area	"skip" past	
			circumference	
			program to	
			area program	

S	9	10	11
K	start	15.6	start
D	32.169908	15.6	98.017689
C	area		circumference

One must be cautious when using the [skip] key. In this schematic where two programs were resident in memory, separated by a skip, termination of the second program *automatically* brings the calculator to the beginning of the first program. Therefore, if the [skip] key were pressed after the second program were terminated, it would skip over the first program and, in effect, would begin executing the second program again.

A diagram of the flow of control using the [skip] key is shown in Fig. 3-2.

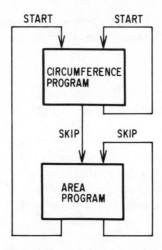

Fig. 3-2

The Sinclair Scientific Programmable

The Sinclair Scientific Programmable comes in an attractive black casing. An ac adapter permits the calculator to be plugged directly into a wall socket, but the Sinclair Programmable can also be powered from a single 9-volt, disposable battery. The 19 keys of the Sinclair Programmable enable the user to calculate the trigonometric functions sine, cosine, and arc tangent of an angle expressed in radians. Other functions that are readily accessible include a change sign key, x^2, $1/x$, $\sqrt{x}$, log, and antilog (base e). A memory is also available on the Sinclair Programmable for storing intermediate results or saving a value for future use. Operations on the memory include store, recall, and memory-display interchange key.

The absence of the equals key on the Sinclair Scientific Programmable is an indication that this calculator operates in Reverse Polish Notation. Numbers are displayed in scientific notation with a five-digit mantissa and a two-digit exponent, thus enabling the user to deal easily with both very small and very large numbers.

Manual Operation of the Sinclair Scientific Programmable

To turn the machine on, the switch located on the upper right-hand corner of the calculator is moved downward. The digits 0.0000 will appear automatically in the display.

Example 4:   Evaluate 2.3 + 3.9

S	1	2	3	4	5
K	2.3	Δ	enter	3.9	+
D	2.3	2.3	2.3000	3.9	6.2000

The schematic in Example 4 requires some explanation. As is the case with Reverse Polish Notation, the addition of 2.3 and 3.9 is actually calculated as

$$2.3 \quad 3.9 +$$

where the addition operation is keyed in *after* the two operands have been entered into the calculator. However, in order to tell the calculator where the first number ends and where the second one begins, it is necessary to enter the first number into the "stack" before keying in the second number. This is done in steps 2 and 3 of the schematic in Example 4. The key marked [Δ] is actually a shift key in that it tells the calculator that the function of the next key pressed is the one that is written *above* that particular key.

For example, a glance at the keyboard will show that "enter" actually appears *above* the key marked [0]. Pressing the [Δ] key informs the calculator that when the key marked $^{enter}_{[0]}$ is next pressed, it is the enter operation that is to be performed, and not the entry of the digit zero.

Another point worth noting is that the key marked [•/EE/__] serves *three* purposes. The first role of this key is to enter a decimal point when keying in the mantissa of a number. For example, in step 1 of the schematic in Example 4, the key sequence

$$[2] \; [•/EE/\_\_] \; [3]$$

correctly inserts the decimal point between the digits 2 and 3 and displays the number 2.3. The two additional functions of this key will be described shortly, when we work with numbers expressed in scientific notation.

Example 5: Evaluate 15.82 − 28.7

S	1	2	3	4	5
K	15.82	Δ	enter	28.7	—
D	15.82	15.82	1.5820 1	28.7	−1.2880 1

It will be noticed from this schematic that when the number 15.82 is ENTERed into the machine (in step 3) that it is converted into scientific notation. The display shows

$$1.5820 \quad 1 \quad .$$

This should be read as

$$1.5820 \times 10^1$$

which is, of course, equivalent to 15.82.

As a rule, all numbers are automatically converted into scientific notation by the Sinclair Scientific Programmable. They are displayed in the form

$$x.yyyy \quad dd$$

where dd represents the exponent of the mantissa (x.yyyy), and can range from –99 to 99.

Example 6:   Evaluate 2.97 × 20.9

S	1	2	3	4	5
K	2.97	Δ	enter	20.9	×
D	2.97	2.97	2.9700	20.9	6.2073 1

This yields a result of 62.073.

Example 7:   Evaluate 40.982/0.35

S	1	2	3	4	5
K	40.982	Δ	enter	.35	÷
D	40.982	40.982	4.0982 1	0.35	1.1709 2

Thus we see that the result of the above division is 1.1709×10^2 or 117.09.

Example 8:   Evaluate (12.345 + 15.98)/3.5 × 10^9

S	1	2	3	4	5
K	12.345	Δ	enter	15.98	+
D	12.345	12.345	1.2345 1	15.98	2.8325 1

S	6	7	8	9
K	3.5	EE	9	÷
D	3.5	3.5	3.5 9	8.0928 –9

The result of the above calculation is 8.0928×10^{-9}.

The schematic in Example 8 illustrates the second role of the [°/EE/__] key. When the [°/EE/__] key is pressed the *first* time (as it must be to key in the number 3.5 in step 6) it has the effect, as mentioned earlier, of entering a decimal point into the mantissa of the number in the display.

Pressing the [°/EE/__] key the *second* time has the effect of activating the EE function of this button—that is, the calculator is now ready to accept the entry of an exponent, which in this case is 9.

As might have been guessed by now, pressing this triple function key the *third* time brings the negation feature into play. It changes the sign of the *exponent*. Repeatedly pressing this key merely alternates the sign of the exponent.

Table 3-1 has been compiled to summarize the various uses of this most unique key.

Table 3-1 The Three–Function [*/EE/_] Key

To Enter	Press
13.982	[1] [3] [*/EE/_] [9] [8] [2]
5.67×10^3	[5] [*/EE/_] [6] [7] [*/EE/_] [3]
20.2×10^{15}	[2] [0] [*/EE/_] [2] [*/EE/_] [1] [5]
20×10^{15}	[2] [0] [*/EE/_] [*/EE/_] [1] [5]
5.67×10^{-3}	[5] [*/EE/_] [6] [7] [*/EE/_] [3] [*/EE/_]
5×10^{-3}	[5] [*/EE/_] [*/EE/_] [3] [*/EE/_]

Example 9: Evaluate $(1.3 \times 10^{-7})(15 \times 10^{12})$

S	1	2	3	4	5	6
K	1.3	*/EE/_	7	*/EE/_	Δ	enter
D	1.3	1.3	1.3 7	1.3 − 7	1.3 − 7	1.3000 − 7

S	7	8	9	10	11
K	15	*/EE/_	*/EE/_	12	×
D	15.	15.	15.	15. 12	1.9500 6

Example 10: Evaluate $\sqrt{12.3} \times (1.29)^2$

S	1	2	3	4	5	6	7
K	12.3	Δ	$\sqrt{x}$	Δ	sto	c/ce	1.29
D	12.3	12.3	3.5071	3.5071	3.5071	0.0000	1.29

S	8	9	10	11	12	13
K	Δ	enter	x^2	Δ	rcl	×
D	1.29	1.2900	1.6641	1.6641	3.5071	5.8362

A detailed explanation of the schematic in Example 10 seems appropriate. Steps 1 through 3 merely compute the square root of 12.3, which turns out to be 3.5071. Steps 4 and 5 copy the value in the display (3.5071) into the memory of the calculator, leaving the display unaltered. Pressing the [C/CE] key in step 6 was necessary due to the particular way in which the memory operates. Whenever one of the three keys dealing with the memory on the Sinclair Programmable is activated, the number left in the display after the memory key has been pressed remains in the display as if it has *just been keyed in and not yet entered.*

Therefore, the [C/CE] key is pressed in step 6 to clear the display and permit the keying in of the number 1.29.

Steps 8 through 10 illustrate another unique feature of the Sinclair Scientific Programmable. It will be noticed upon close examination of the Sinclair's keyboard that the three functions $1/x$, x^2, and $-x$ are printed *alongside* the keys marked [÷], [×], and [−], respectively. If a number is keyed into the calculator and then entered into the machine's stack (by using the [Δ] and [enter] keys), pressing the [÷], [×], or [−] keys will have the effect of calculating $1/x$, x^2, or $-x$, respectively. Thus, if we wish to take the reciprocal of a number in the display, the key sequence

$$[\Delta] \text{ [enter] } [1/x]$$

will calculate and display the desired result. These three keys will have the same effect when used directly on a number in the display that is the result of a previous calculation. For example, $1/(2 + 3.5)$ can be calculated by the following key sequence:

$$[2] \text{ [enter] } [3.5] \text{ } [+] \text{ } [1/x]$$

Steps 11 and 12 recall the value 3.5071 from the memory into the display, "pushing" the previous value in the display (1.6641) into the calculator's stack. Step 13 completes the required multiplication, displaying the final result of 5.8362.

Example 11:   Evaluate sin 0.385 radians

S	1	2	3
K	.385	Δ	sin
D	0.385	0.385	3.7556 −1

Thus we see from this schematic that the sine of 0.385 radians is 0.37556.

When using either the sine or cosine functions, it is important to note that the angles must be expressed in radians and must lie between 0 and $\pi/2$ (approximately 1.5707).

Example 12:   Evaluate $(\cos 0.293/\sin 0.187) + \sqrt{58.7}$

S	1	2	3	4	5	6
K	.187	Δ	sin	Δ	sto	C/CE
D	0.187	0.187	1.8591 −1	1.8591 −1	1.8591 −1	0.0000

S	7	8	9	10	11	12
K	.293	Δ	cos	Δ	rcl	÷
D	0.293	0.293	9.5737 −1	9.5737 −1	1.8591 −1	5.1496

S	13	14	15	16	17	18
K	Δ	sto	C/CE	58.7	Δ	$\sqrt{x}$
D	5.1496	5.1496	0.0000	58.7	58.7	7.6615

S	19	20	21
K	Δ	rcl	+
D	7.6615	5.1496	1.2811 1

Thus we find that the result of the above calculation is 12.811. It will be noticed that the denominator is calculated first and then stored into the memory of the calculator. This is done so that once the numerator is calculated, the denominator can be recalled from the memory and the required division performed immediately.

The reader will once again note the use of the [C/CE] key in steps 6 and 15. These steps were necessary due to the particular operation of the memory on the Sinclair Programmable.

Example 13: Evaluate (arc tan 23.7)^2

S	1	2	3	4
K	23.7	Δ	arctan	x^2
D	23.7	23.7	1.5286	2.3366

Thus we see that the result is 2.3366, as shown in step 4 of the above schematic. The arc tangent function can be applied to any number between the range of 0 and 49.9, with the resulting angle expressed in radians.

It will be noticed that the trigonometric functions tangent, arc-sine, and arc-cosine are not available on the Sinclair Programmable. However, these functions can be readily calculated by referring to Table 3-2.

Table 3-2 Trig Functions Not Found on the Sinclair Programmable

Function	Formula	Keystrokes			
tan x	$\sqrt{(1/\cos^2 x)-1}$	Key in x	cos	X	÷
		1	−	$\sqrt{x}$	
Arc sine x	$\text{Arctan}\left[1/\sqrt{(1/x^2)-1}\right]$	Key in x	enter	X	÷
		1	−	$\sqrt{x}$	÷ Arctan
Arc cosine x	$\text{Arctan}\left[\sqrt{(1/x^2)-1}\right]$	Key in x	enter	X	÷
		1	−	$\sqrt{x}$	Arctan

Example 14: Evaluate tan 0.687

S	1	2	3	4	5
K	.687	Δ	cos	X	÷
D	0.687	0.687	7.7314 −1	5.9774 −1	1.6729
C			cos x	cos^2 x	1/cos^2 x

S	6	7	8	9
K	1	−	Δ	$\sqrt{x}$
D	1.	6.7290 −1	6.7290 −1	8.2030 −1
C		(1/cos^2 x) −1		tan x = $\sqrt{(1/\cos^2 x)-1}$

Thus we see from the above schematic that the tangent of 0.687 radians is 0.82030. Of course, an alternate way to compute the tangent of an angle is to divide the sine of that angle by its cosine, according to the identity:

$$\tan x = \sin x/\cos x$$

If the reader usually deals with degrees rather than radians, an angle expressed in degrees can be converted easily into its radian equivalent by the following formula:

$$R = D/57.3$$

where

D = angle expressed in degrees
R = angle expressed in radians

Example 15:   Evaluate sin 30°

S	1	2	3	4	5	6	7
K	30	Δ	enter	57.3	÷	Δ	sin
D	30.	30.	3.0000 1	57.3	5.2356 −1	5.2356 −1	5.0000 −1

Thus we find that the sine of 30° is 0.50000.

Example 16:   Evaluate log 28.7 + antilog 1.28

S	1	2	3	4	5	6	7
K	28.7	Δ	log	Δ	sto	C/CE	1.28
D	28.7	28.7	1.4579	1.4579	1.4579	0.0000	1.28

S	8	9	10	11	12
K	Δ	antilog	Δ	rcl	+
D	1.28	1.9054 1	1.9054 1	1.4579	2.0512 1

Programming the Sinclair Scientific

The Sinclair Scientific Programmable is capable of "remembering" or "learning" up to 24 calculator steps. In other words, it is capable of accepting data that may be operated upon by a maximum of 24 programming steps. Once a particular problem is solved, different data for the same program can be keyed in and the sequence reinitiated. In this way, the user is spared the time-consuming chore of having to key in the same instructions for each different set of data. Not only would this be time-consuming, but it also would leave open the possibility that an error might be made in keying in the sequence of instructions on subsequent occasions. Naturally, the longer the program, the greater the likelihood of an error occurring.

To assist the user in writing efficient and useful programs, the manufacturer provides a packet of literally hundreds of programs, ranging in scope from general arithmetic to geometry, statistics, finance, electronics, radiation and propagation, electrostatics and electromagnetics, mechanics, structures, gravity, thermodynamics, and fluid mechanics. Each of these programs is printed on a 5-by-5 3/4-inch plastic coated card and contains not only the pertinent equations but also the exact program steps and the method of executing the program.

If, however, this package of programs does not contain those that the user needs, he will have to resort to writing his own. What we plan to do in this section is to teach precisely that—how to write programs of one's own design.

When writing a program for the Sinclair Scientific Programmable, one is, of course, restricted to the functions and operations on the keyboard. But when combined with a healthy sprinkling of human ingenuity, the calculator's power can be extended considerably.

Computation of $\sqrt{x^3}$. For our first illustration we shall write a program to cube a number keyed into the display and then take its square root. Forgetting for the time being how the calculator may be programmed to solve this problem, let us first address ourselves to the question of how this problem may be solved manually, that is, in the nonprogrammable mode.

Suppose it were desired to compute the square root of 4^3. The following schematic would accomplish this task.

Example 17

S	1	2	3	4	5	6
K	4	Δ	sto	Δ	enter	x
D	4.	4.	4.0000	4.0000	4.0000	1.6000 1
C			stores 4 in memory register			computes 4^2

S	7	8	9	10	11
K	Δ	rcl	x	Δ	$\sqrt{x}$
D	1.6000 1	4.0000	6.40000 1	6.4000 1	8.0000
C			computes 4^3		$\sqrt{4^3}$

If we had a need for computing the square root of the cubes of many such numbers, it would not be necessary to key in the sequence for each. Instead—and herein lies the virtue of the programmable calculator— we can switch the calculator to programming mode and have it "learn" the required sequence. The program may then be executed as often as is necessary, thereby minimizing considerably the human effort involved.

To initiate programming mode the [B/E] key must be pressed. The sequence of instructions may now be keyed in individually, and they will be retained within the calculator's program memory for future use. To signal the end of the program and to exit from programming mode, the [C/CE] key is pressed. It is pointed out that when instructions are keyed in in programming mode, the uppercase shift key [ ] should not be used since the uppercase functions only are automatically referenced. In other words, uppercase functions should not be prefixed by the uppercase shift key.

Program SSP-1: Computation of $\sqrt{x^3}$

Step Number	Instruction	Comments
1	sto	Stores x into memory register
2	enter	
3	x	Computes x^2
4	rcl	
5	x	Computes x^3
6	$\sqrt{x}$	Computes $\sqrt{x^3}$

Schematic SSP-1

S	1	2	3	4	5
K	B/E	[key in steps of Program SSP-1]	C/CE	4	EXEC
D	0.		0.0000	4.	8.0000

S	6	7	8	9	
K	3	EXEC	1.234	EXEC	. . . etc.
D	3.	5.1961	1.234	1.3708	

As shown in Schematic SSP-1, once the particular value for x is keyed in (as it is in steps 4, 6, and 8) pressing the [EXEC] key executes the program, producing the result almost immediately. Thus we find that:

1. $\sqrt{4^3}$ = 8
2. $\sqrt{3^3}$ = 5.1961
3. $\sqrt{1.234^3}$ = 1.3708

Program SSP-2: Average of Three Numbers

Step Number	Instruction	Comments
1	enter	Prepares for addition
2	var	Halts program to permit keying in of second number
3	+	Sums first two values
4	var	Halts program to permit third value to be keyed in
5	+	
6	'	
7	3	Enter constant 3
8	'	
9	÷	Divides sum by 3, giving result

Calculating the Average of Three Numbers. In the previous problem a single number was keyed in as data before the program was executed. In this program where we wish to calculate the average of three numbers, we must make provision for the keying in of a second and third number. Execution of a program may be interrupted for the keying in of an additional data item (variable) by inserting the instruction [Var] in the appropriate place. Once these three values to be averaged are resident within the calculator, their sum must be divided by the constant '3'. In order to include a constant number in program, it must be preceded and followed by a quote sign, as indicated above the [•/EE/__] key.

Notice in Program SSP-2 that the [Var] instruction is inserted in steps 2 and 4 to halt execution of the program to allow for the entering of additional data. Also, each time a constant is included in a program it must be sandwiched between two quotes.

Schematic SSP-2

S	1	2	3	4	5	6
K	B/E	⎡key in steps	C/CE	1	EXEC	2
		of Program				
D	0.	⎣ SSP-2 ⎦	0.0000	1	1.0000	2.
C				1st		
				value		

S	7	8	9	10	11	12
K	EXEC	3	EXEC	1.2	EXEC	3.4
D	3.0000	3.	2.0000	1.2	1.2000	3.4
C	partial	3rd	average of 1, 2,	1st		2nd
	sum	value	and 3	value		value

S	13	14	15	
K	EXEC	7.9	EXEC	. . . etc.
D	4.6000	7.9	4.1666	
C	partial	3rd	average of 1.2,	
	sum	value	3.4, and 7.9	

In running the program after new data has been entered, execution is restarted by pressing the [EXEC] key.

It is hoped that this brief explanation of programming mode will suffice to inspire the reader to try his hand at writing his own programs to solve the multitude of repetitive problems that occur in daily life.

CHAPTER FOUR
THE HEWLETT-PACKARD PROGRAMMABLE POCKET CALCULATORS

Features Common To All the Hewlett-Packard Models

Hewlett-Packard, a leading manufacturer of computers, has made a distinct mark in the market for sophisticated calculators. In Chaps. 4–10 we shall describe in detail the various Hewlett-Packard programmable pocket calculators: the HP-65, HP-55, HP-25, HP-25C, HP-19C, HP-29C, HP-33E, and HP-67. Each model has a rechargeable battery and operates in Reverse Polish Notation. In conjunction with this mode of logic, each has a four-register stack that enables the user to evaluate complex expressions without having to write down intermediate results. Furthermore, the stack automatically saves and retrieves these intermediate results when needed.

The Four-Register Stack

The reader might well wonder how the calculator is able to keep track of intermediate results and bring them into operation at precisely the right time. The stack is composed of four registers called x, y, z, and t, respectively. An understanding of the way in which the stack works is important for writing efficient programs. The x register is none other then the display register. Here is a diagram of the four-register stack, which operates identically on each of the Hewlett-Packard models.

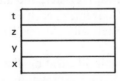

When the calculator is switched on, each of the registers contains a zero.* If now the number 2 is keyed in, it appears in the display, or as it is

---

*The continuous memory HP-25C, HP-19C, and HP-29C calculators retain the contents of the stack registers from the time the machine was last switched off.

also called, the x register. In order to multiply the number 2 by say 3, the 2 must be entered by means of the key marked [ENTER↑]. This has the effect of *copying* the 2 into the adjacent y register. Therefore, the stack registers will now have changed from

t	
z	
y	
x	2

to

t	
z	
y	2
x	2

Keying in the 3 will remove the 2 from the x register, replacing it with the number 3, as shown in the following diagram.

t	
z	
y	2
x	3

The effect of following this with the pressing of the [×] key will multiply the contents of the y register by the contents of the x register. This result will *automatically* go into the x register, to the display, making it unnecessary to have an equals key. Of course, the result appearing in the x register will replace its previous contents, and the y register becomes zero again.

Each time a calculation is followed by the keying in of a new number the stack "lifts." That is to say, what is in the x register is automatically transferred to the y, what is in the y register goes to the z, the contents of the z register go to the t (for top) register, and anything in there "pops out" of the machine and is lost. Conversely, each time a two-number operation is performed, the stack automatically "drops" down to its adjacent lower register.

Here is another example illustrating the operation of the stack in evaluating a slightly more complex expression.

Evaluate $(3 + 11.2) \times (6.7 - 21.2)$

1. The number 3 is keyed in.

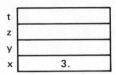

2. The [ENTER↑] button is now pressed.

```
t
z
y        3.
x        3.
```

3. The number 11.2 is keyed in.

```
t
z
y        3.
x       11.2
```

4. The [+] key is pressed.

```
t
z
y
x       14.2
```

Since the x register (the display) now contains the result (14.2) of a previous arithmetic operation of addition, keying in the next number, 6.7, will automatically "push up" the 14.2 currently in the x register into the y register, replacing the contents of the x register with the number 6.7, as illustrated below.

5. The number 6.7 is keyed in.

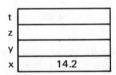

6. The [ENTER↑] key is now pressed again.

Previously we noted that this operation has the effect of copying the contents of the x register into the y register. However, the y register already contains a number, namely 14.2. This number 14.2 is automatically pushed up to register z in the following fashion.

t	
z	14.2
y	6.7
x	6.7

7. The number 21.2 is next keyed in.

t	
z	14.2
y	6.7
x	21.2

8. When the [-] key is pressed, the contents of the x register is subtracted from the contents of the y register, and the result is placed in the x register. In this case, 21.2 is subtracted from 6.7, placing -14.50 in the display. The value in the z register, 14.2, is pushed down into the y register, and the stack now looks as follows:

t	
z	
y	14.20
x	-14.50

9. Finally, pressing the [×] key performs the required multiplication of the two parenthesized expressions. Internally the contents of the x and y registers are multiplied together, sending the result of -205.90 to the x register.

t	
z	
y	
x	-205.90

The next example, shown on p. 43, is presented to thoroughly familiarize the reader with the operation of the stack.

To the reader who is being exposed to the concept of the stack for the first time, it might appear that we have gone to great lengths merely to calculate an expression that we could have done quite easily with a far less sophisticated calculator. Be that as it may, it should be pointed out that by means of the stack it was not necessary to write down a single intermediate answer, which would have been necessary using ordinary four-function calculators.

One of the most frequent sources of error is created when either copying down or reentering intermediate results, to say nothing of the fact that this additional chore can be quite time consuming.

Evaluate $(78.97 \times 38.6)/[(57.2 \times 81.6) - (33.7 + 22.1)]$

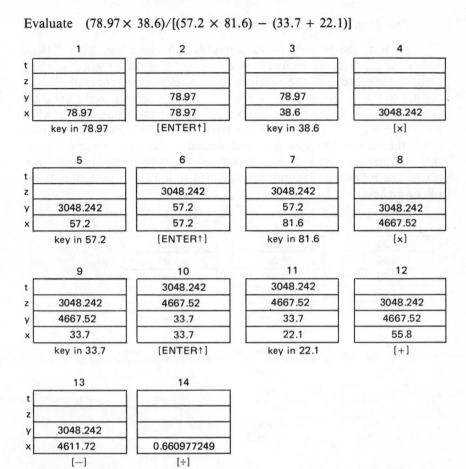

The reader will surely agree that a thorough understanding of the operation of the stack is critical in solving virtually any problem with such a calculator.

The x Interchange y Key

If during the course of calculation it is required to exchange the contents of the x register with that of the y register, the key marked [x ≥ y] is used. This is often useful in situations where one wishes to operate on the value in the y register without destroying the value in the x register, as illustrated below.

t	4.00	[x ≥ y] key	t	4.00
z	3.00	is now	z	3.00
y	2.00	pressed	y	1.00
x	1.00		x	2.00

The Roll Down Key

Each of the Hewlett-Packard models provides a key labeled [R↓], which has the effect of transferring the contents of the t register to the z register, the contents of the z register to the y register, the contents of the y register to the x register, and the contents of the x register to the t register simultaneously. This circular roll keeps each of the values intact while permitting access to any value in the stack. If the [R↓] key is pressed four times, the stack will have been rotated around so that all of the values are in their original registers in the stack, with no effective change having taken place. The following diagrams are intended to illustrate the action of the roll down key:

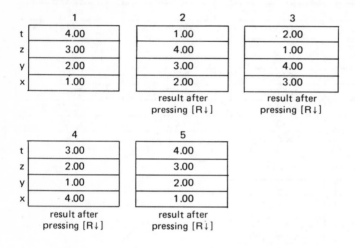

The Roll Up Key

Unlike the HP-55 and HP-25, the HP-65 and HP-67 also come equipped with a *roll up* button ([R↑]), which operates in precisely the reverse manner as the roll down key. Whenever the [R↑] key is pressed the stack is lifted, and the contents of the t register are moved to the x register.

The Clear x Key

In order to clear the display, the [CLx] key is pressed. It is pointed out that pressing this key in no way affects any of the memory registers or the other three stack registers (y, z, and t) so that any values that these registers contain are left intact.

Entering a Number in Scientific Notation

In normal operation of the calculator, whenever the result of a calculation becomes either so small or so large that it cannot be represented in the conventional manner in the display, it will be automatically displayed in scientific notation.

It is possible, however, to actually enter a number in scientific notation, if this is desired. This is done by first keying in the mantissa portion and entering the exponent by pressing the [EEX] button immediately before keying in the exponent itself. Incidentally, the exponent is always a positive or negative integer ranging from –99 to + 99.

If the exponent is negative, the [CHS] key must be pressed to change the sign of the exponent and is pressed immediately following the [EEX] key. The following examples will help to clarify this concept:

Number	Keystrokes
3.2×10^5	[3] [.] [2] [EEX] [5]
15.68×10^{13}	[1] [5] [.] [6] [8] [EEX] [1] [3]
-12.2×10^3	[1] [2] [.] [2] [CHS] [EEX] [3]
20.5×10^{-9}	[2] [0] [.] [5] [EEX] [CHS] [9]
-15.3×10^{-12}	[1] [5] [.] [3] [CHS] [EEX] [CHS] [1] [2]

Examples

In the examples that follow, two decimal place accuracy is assumed. Should a greater accuracy be required, the keys [f] [FIX]* followed by a digit from 0 to 9 will have the effect of fixing the number of decimal places to whatever digit was pressed. The display is rounded to that specified number of digits.

In all of the examples in this section, it is assumed that the calculator is in RUN mode, and a decimal place setting of f FIX 2 is used unless specified otherwise. These examples may be keyed in on most of the Hewlett-Packard programmable models precisely as shown. On the older Hewlett-Packard models, namely the HP-55 and HP-65, certain functions are preceded by different prefix keys.

Example 1: Evaluate $(5 \times 6.1) + 78^2$

S	1	2	3	4
K	5	ENTER↑	6.1	X
D	5.	5.00	6.1	30.50

S	5	6	7	8
K	78	g	x^2	+
D	78.	78.	6084.00	6114.50

---

*The [FIX] key is equivalent to the [DSP] key on the HP-67.

The LAST x Key

Whenever a calculation is effected using the x register, its contents before the calculation are automatically stored in a special register known as the *last x register*. The Hewlett-Packard calculators are deliberately engineered this way to permit the user to access this value for subsequent calculation if necessary. It can often save superfluous keystrokes in calculating a particular expression. For example, to compute

$$1/x + x + x^2$$

for any value of x, one need key in the value once and once only. The sequence of steps is:

Key in value [g] [1/x] [f] [LAST x] [+] [f] [LAST x] [g] [x²] [+]

The Hewlett-Packard Addressable Data Registers

The Hewlett-Packard programmable calculators each have a number of memory registers that may be used for the storing of data or intermediate results. The number of registers differs from one model to another, and on the HP-38E the user has the option of deciding for himself how many memory registers he wishes to allocate.

To store a number in the display into any register one merely presses the key labeled [STO] (for STOre) followed by the appropriate digit key. Whatever value is in the display is automatically *copied* into the designated register, replacing any previous contents of that register. The value in the display remains intact. For example, if the value 28.5 is currently in the display, the key sequence [STO] [3] will place a copy of this value into memory register 3, replacing any previous contents of this register.

To recall to the display a number previously stored in a memory register, one presses the recall key [RCL] followed by the apopropriate digit key. Whatever value is currently residing in the particular memory register is recalled to the display, automatically lifting the stack. The value in the memory register remains unaltered as the result of a recall operation.

Register Arithmetic on the Hewlett-Packard Programmable Models

Up till now all arithmetic operations have been effected by means of the x and y registers. For many situations this is perfectly convenient, but at other times it is necessary to operate arithmetically on the contents of the data registers. Naturally, one is always free to recall the contents of any particular register to the display, carry out whatever arithmetic is necessary, and store the result back in the register by means of the [STO] key. One of the nice features of the Hewlett-Packard models is that it enables the user to avoid having to recall the contents of a register into the display, in the manner described previously, in order to operate upon them. Instead, one is at liberty to operate *directly* on the contents of any one of the memory registers. For example, to add 7 to the contents of register 2 one simply keys in the sequence

$$7 \, [STO] \, [+] \, 2$$

In a similar fashion, the arithmetic operations of subtraction, multiplication, and division may be effected on any of the memory registers, as shown in the following examples.

Sequence	Comments
58.7 [STO] [−] 0	Subtracts 58.7 from memory register 0
3.67 [STO] [×] 1	Multiplies memory register 1 by 3.67
15 [STO] [÷] 7	Divides register 7 by 15

It is pointed out that in each case the result of the arithmetic operation replaces the previous contents of the particular memory register.

Example 2:   Evaluate $1.78325/(8.623 + \sqrt{98.7})$ to five decimal places of accuracy.

S	1	2	3	4	5	6
K	f	FIX	5	1.78325	ENTER↑	8.623
D	0.00	0.00	0.00000	1.78325	1.78325	8.623

S	7	8	9	10	11	12
K	ENTER↑	98.7	f	$\sqrt{x}$	+	÷
D	8.62300	98.7	98.7	9.93479	18.55779	0.09609

Example 3:   Evaluate $\log(2.64) - \pi^2/\sin(28.7°)$

S	1	2	3	4	5	6
K	2.64	f	log	g	π	g
D	2.64	2.64	0.42	0.42	3.14	3.14

S	7	8	9	10	11	12
K	x^2	−	28.7	f	sin	÷
D	9.87	−9.45	28.7	28.7	0.48	−19.67

In Example 4 that follows, which is an exercise in calculating numbers expressed in scientific notation, it will be noticed that if the result of a calculation goes beyond the calculator's ability to display the number in fixed decimal mode, that result is automatically converted to scientific notation.

Example 4:   Evaluate $(28.97 \times 10^{10} \times 2.96 \times 10^{-15})/(-4.24 \times 10^{12})$

S	1	2	3	4	5
K	28.97	EEX	10	ENTER↑	2.96
D	28.97	28.97 00	28.97 10	2.8970000 11	2.96

S	6	7	8	9	10
K	EEX	CHS	15	X	4.24
D	2.96 00	2.96 −00	2.96 −15	8.5751200 −04	4.24

S	11	12	13	14
K	CHS	EEX	12	÷
D	−4.24	−4.24 00	−4.24 12	−2.0224340−16

Example 5:   Evaluate $\ln(1.789^5) + \tan(3.45 \text{ radians})$

S	1	2	3	4	5	6	7
K	1.789	ENTER↑	5	f	y^x	f	ln
D	1.789	1.79	5.	5.	18.33	18.33	2.91

S	8	9	10	11	12	13
K	3.45	g	RAD	f	tan	+
D	3.45	3.45	3.45	3.45	0.32	3.23

There are two points in Example 5 that should be made. The first is that since the angle 3.45 is expressed in radians, the calculator must be switched to radian mode by pressing the blue prefix key labeled [g] followed by [RAD], which is the lower case [EEX] key. This is necessary since as soon as the calculator is switched on, it is automatically set to degree mode. Once it has been switched to radian mode, however, it remains in this mode until either it is changed by the user or the calculator is turned off. (Even the continuous memory models HP-25C, HP-19C, and HP-29C do not remember the trigonometric mode setting when the machine is switched off.)

The second point concerns the accuracy with which the calculation is done. Despite the fact that the calculator displays numbers to two decimal places, rounded, it nevertheless operates on the full accuracy of the number that is contained internally.

Example 6:   Illustration of the INT and FRAC functions

S	1	2	3	4	5	6
K	45.67	f	INT	122.8	g	FRAC
D	45.67	45.67	45.00	122.8	122.8	0.80

The purpose of the [INT] key is to truncate the integer portion of a number. The integer portion (the number without its fractional portion) replaces the original number in the display.

Conversely, the key labeled [FRAC] separates off the fractional portion of a displayed number that replaces the original number in the display. Generally, these two functions are used to greatest advantage in programming mode.

Example 7: Convert the point (3, 7) from rectangular to polar coordinates.

S	1	2	3	4	5	6
K	7	ENTER↑	3	g	→P	x ⩒ y
D	7.	7.00	3.	3.	7.62	66.80

Provision for conversion from and to polar and rectangular coordinates is made on most Hewlett-Packard programmable models. To convert a point expressed in rectangular coordinates of the form (x, y) to its equivalent point in the polar coordinate system (r, θ), one merely keys in the y-coordinate, presses the [ENTER↑] key to send it to the y register, and keys in the x-coordinate of the point so that it resides in the x register. Once this has been accomplished, pressing the [g] prefix key, followed by the [→P] key, calculates the position of the point in the polar system. The magnitude r appears in the x register (the display), while the value of θ is placed in the y register and can be accessed either by rolling down the stack once by the [R↓] key or by pressing the [x⩒y] key, as was illustrated in Example 7. Thus we find that the point (3, 7) is equivalent to (7.62, 66.80°) in the polar coordinate system.

Example 8: Convert the point (7.62, 66.8°) from polar to rectangular coordinates.

S	1	2	3	4	5	6
K	66.8	ENTER↑	7.62	f	→R	x ⩒ y
D	66.8	66.80	7.62	7.62	3.00	7.00

When converting from polar to rectangular coordinates, the value of θ must be keyed in first so that it will subsequently be placed in the y register, followed by the [ENTER↑] key. Next the value of r is keyed in. Pressing [f] [→R] has the effect of converting the polar coordinates keyed in into their rectangular coordinate equivalents, placing the x value of the coordinate in the x register and the y value in the y register.

Upon inspection the reader will notice that in Example 8 we have simply checked the results of Example 7. What may be helpful to the reader to notice in both these conversions is that it is always the *second* coordinate that is keyed in *first*.

Example 9: Convert 6.78 hours to hours, minutes, and seconds.

S	1	2	3	4	5	6
K	f	FIX	4	6.78	f	→H.MS
D	0.00	0.00	0.0000	6.78	6.78	6.4648

Time expressed in hours and fractions of an hour can be converted to hours, minutes, and seconds by means of the key labeled [→H.MS]. The reason for the [FIX] [4] in steps 2 and 3 is that the result is displayed in the following format:

$$H.MMSS$$

where

H is the integer number of hours
MM is a two-digit number representing minutes
SS is a two-digit number representing seconds

Thus it is clear from the schematic in Example 9 that 6.78 hours is equivalent to 6 hours, 46 minutes, 48 seconds.

Conversely, we can convert a time period expressed in hours, minutes, and seconds into decimal hours. To accomplish this the keys [g] [→H] are used, as shown in the following example.

Example 10: Convert 103 hours, 2 minutes, 58 seconds into decimal hours.

S	1	2	3
K	103.0258	g	→H
D	103.0258	103.0258	103.05

A direct analogy can be drawn between the units hours, minutes, and seconds, which we have just discussed, and degrees, minutes, and seconds. Knowing how to convert from degrees, minutes, and seconds to decimal degrees assumes importance since trigonometric functions on the Hewlett-Packard models operate on angles expressed in decimal degrees only, rather than in degrees, minutes, and seconds.

This topic is discussed in greater detail in Chap. 7, where the HP-65 is described. It is pointed out that on the HP-65, the key equivalent to the [→H.MS] key of the other H.P. models is the [→D.MS] key.

We have now covered those features that are identical in most respects on each of the Hewlett-Packard programmable calculators. The remaining features will now be treated separately for each particular calculator.

CHAPTER FIVE
THE HEWLETT-PACKARD 25 AND 25C

The HP-25

In July 1975, some seven months after the release of the HP-55, Hewlett-Packard announced its lightweight, programmable HP-25. It has almost all of the calculating features of the nonprogrammable HP-45, all of the programming features of the HP-55, plus some novel features of its own. In addition, it has eight addressable storage registers referred to as R0–R7, and 72 built-in functions. An interesting feature on the HP-25 is that it permits engineering notation in which the exponent of a number in scientific notation may be expressed in selectable multiples of three. This feature will be discussed in detail shortly.

The HP-25 is only one of several programmable calculators in which the emphasis has been on compactness, portability, light weight, and considerable computational power. As a result, a great deal of effort has gone into its design. One of the techniques used to save weight and space is to make the keyboard multi-functional—that is, most of the keys have not just one function but rather two or even three. If the face-on function is required, that key is pressed and that is it. If the function required is that appearing immediately *above* the key in yellow, the yellow key marked [f] must precede it. If the function required is that appearing on the lower surface of the key in blue, the blue key marked [g] must precede it. The HP-25 therefore has three faces, as shown in Fig. 5-1.

The HP-25C

After using the HP-25 over a period of time, one soon comes to the conclusion that, as efficient a tool as it is, it could be further enhanced if, somehow or other, a way could be found to keep the memory alive even after the machine is switched off.

Hewlett-Packard's engineers obviously gave this idea serious consideration for in July 1976 they announced and released their model HP-25C, the C standing for "continuous memory." By means of some very new technology known as CMOS (complementary metal oxide semiconductor)*

---

*Ordinarily, calculator chips are made either of PMOS or NMOS circuit elements. PMOS is the abbreviation for "positive metal oxide semiconductor," while NMOS is "negative metal oxide semiconductor." CMOS is a combination of both.

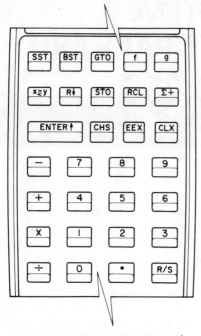

1. FACE VIEW (NO PREFIX REQUIRED)

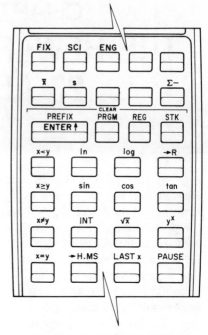

2. UPPER CASE (F PREFIX REQUIRED)

Fig. 5-1 Three faces of the HP-25

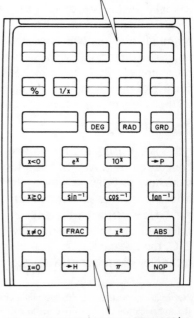

3. LOWER CASE (G PREFIX REQUIRED)

the calculator retains the information stored not only in the 49-step program memory but also in each of the eight addressable data registers and the last x register, *even when the calculator is switched off.* In addition, it is retained for a period of six weeks or even longer. The two CMOS chips in the HP-25C use only a trickle of current from the battery (1/80,000 of the normal operating power) and thus do not drain the battery too much. Even if it is necessary to change the battery pack, this may be done without fear of information loss because, with the calculator switched off, a small capacitor provides sufficient charge for the brief period of time required to install the fresh battery (5 seconds to 2 minutes).

In all other respects the HP-25C is identical to the HP-25, the earlier model that perhaps will become known as "discontinuous memory." In any event the continuous memory of the HP-25C is a most desirable innovation. It reduces considerably the need to repeatedly key in the program with all the inherent disadvantages such as the miskeying of instructions and battery drain, caused by the display being on. There is little question that continuous memory is a trend that is bound to catch on. In fact, rumor has it that Casio, a leading Japanese calculator manufacturer that so far has concentrated on low-cost nonprogrammable calculators, has now entered the field with their PRO-101 key programmable calculator. It is reputed to have batteries that keep the program alive for up to a year!

The HP-25C was released with a price tag of $200 at a time when the original HP-25 was reduced to $145. A picture of the HP-25C appears in Fig. 5-2.

Manual Operation of the HP-25 and HP-25C

In the discussion that follows, all references to the HP-25 apply equally to the HP-25C.

Example 1: Find the mean and standard deviation of the following five scores: 1.23, 2.63, 5.18, −2.16, 5.89.

S	1	2	3	4	5	6	7
K	1.23	Σ+	2.63	Σ+	5.18	Σ+	2.16
D	1.23	1.00	2.63	2.00	5.18	3.00	2.16

S	8	9	10	11	[oops! I meant 5.89, not 5.83]	12	13
K	CHS	Σ+	5.83	Σ+		5.83	f
D	−2.16	4.00	5.83	5.00		5.83	5.83

S	14	15	16	17	18	19	20
K	Σ−	5.89	Σ+	f	x̄	f	s
D	4.00	5.89	5.00	5.00	2.55	2.55	3.24

Fig. 5-2 HP-25C (*Courtesy* Hewlett-Packard Company)

If function keys were rated according to the amount of work they accomplish, the [Σ+] key would surely win hands down. It not only sums each successive data item when this key is pressed, but also

1. Places the accumulated sum in R7.
2. Adds the square of the number to the contents of storage register R6.
3. Multiplies the number by the contents of the y register, adding the product to storage register R5.
4. Adds the contents of the y register to the contents of R4.
5. Adds 1 to storage register R3, sending the total number in R3 into the display, without lifting the stack.

This information is given here even though it is not really necessary to know when solving the problem posed in Example 1. Later on, however, when we use the HP-25 in programming mode, we shall exploit this knowledge to good advantage.

Returning to the problem of finding the mean and standard deviation of the five scores in Example 1, each of the scores is keyed in separately, followed by the pressing of the [Σ +] key. After step 11, it was noticed that 5.83 was inadvertently keyed in in step 10, rather than the intended 5.89 (to err is human, after all). The situation is not hopeless, however, and can be rectified immediately. The incorrect inclusion of 5.83 can be subtracted by the [Σ -] key and the correct figure 5.89 added immediately afterwards.

The mean of the five scores is obtained by pressing [f] [x̄] and the standard deviation by pressing [f] [s].

Engineering Notation

With technology improving at the current phenomenal rate, engineers have found that there is a need, for example, to measure time, not only in milliseconds (thousandths of a second) but also in microseconds (millionths of a second) and even nanoseconds (billionths of a second) and yes picoseconds (trillionths of a second). These units of time, when expressed in scientific notation, follow a specific pattern:

$$1 \text{ millisecond} = 1 \times 10^{-3} \text{ seconds}$$
$$1 \text{ microsecond} = 1 \times 10^{-6} \text{ seconds}$$
$$1 \text{ nanosecond} = 1 \times 10^{-9} \text{ seconds}$$
$$1 \text{ picosecond} = 1 \times 10^{-12} \text{ seconds}$$

It will be noticed that each exponent is a multiple of three. The HP-25 is unique in that it was the first calculator in the world that provided the user with the option of displaying all numbers with exponents of 10 that are multiples of three.

Engineering notation is obtained by pressing [f] [ENG] followed by a number key from 0 to 5. This number key specifies the number of *additional* decimal digits that are to be displayed after the first three mantissa digits that are always present.

The following examples will help clarify this intriguing feature:

Number Keyed In	[SCI] 4	[ENG] 2
12345.	1.2345 04	12.345 03
.00078	7.8000 −04	780.00 −06
108.98×10^{11}	1.0898 13	10.898 12
3.29315×10^{-30}	3.2932 −30	3.2932 −30
10.6	1.0600 01	10.600 00

Programming the HP-25 and HP-25C

Programming the HP-25 is similar in many respects to programming a multi-million dollar computer. Whereas one has to sometimes resort to so-called higher level languages in order to solve a particular problem on a given computer, this is not the case with the HP-25. To write a *program*— that is, a sequence of instructions to solve a problem—on the HP-25, one writes the program using for the most part the keys that one would normally use to solve the problem manually, as if one were using a nonprogrammable calculator. The essence of the HP-25 is that each of these keyed entries may be stored in the machine's memory for subsequent execution and/or for unlimited repetitive execution. The HP-25 has 49 memory storage locations and has no provision for storing the program on a magnetic card.

The time has now arrived to come to grips with the concept of programming the HP-25. A little care and patience in reading what follows will be most rewarding.

First switch on the calculator and put it into PRGM position. (There is a PRGM/RUN switch just beneath the display.) The digits 00 appear in the extreme left-hand side of the display. This refers to a special memory location, called 00, which holds permanently an instruction that stops the machine from continuing an automatic sequence. This is often most desirable, as we shall see later on. However one may try, one cannot write any other information into this location. Location 00 is not included in the 49 locations of *program memory* that are available. These are labeled appropriately, 01 to 49. We are at liberty to write our program instructions into these 49 locations, beginning at the first location.

With the machine switched to program mode, press the [f] [PRGM] keys followed by the top left-hand key marked [SST] for single-step. This is what now appears in the display:

01   13   00

Pressing this [SST] key again will display:

02   13   00

Repeating this will display:

03   13   00

04   13   00

.

.

.

etc.

49   13   00

The two digits on the left refer to the memory locations 01 to 49. The number 13 appearing in each of these locations is a code that may be interpreted as "first row, third button" from the top of the calculator. What is the key in that position? A look at the keyboard will immediately show that it is the one marked [GTO], which stands for "go to." The number 00 at the extreme right indicates the transfer location of the "go to." In other words, every one of the 49 program memory locations is automatically filled with the instruction GTO 00 as soon as the calculator is switched on and put into program mode. But, as we stated earlier, a transfer to location 00 will halt the calculator when it is in RUN (automatic) mode. This is, of course, deliberate on the part of the designers, the philosophy being that each program instruction should *overwrite* the GTO 00. If a mistake is made in not keying in all the correct instructions, a GTO 00 will be encountered and the calculator will come to a halt because execution will have been passed to location 00, which contains a permanent halt instruction.

To familiarize the reader with the correspondence between individual keys and the manner in which they are stored internally, Table 5-1 is given. Some of the positions indicated with question marks have been deliberately omitted to enable the reader to acquire some practice for himself. The correct answers are given in the table footnote. Note that the digits 0 through 9 are coded as 00–09. Furthermore, the representation for 8, log, and 10^x, for example, all of which use the same key, is 08. This applies equally to the non-numeric, multiple function keys. Ambiguity is avoided by prefixing these keys where necessary with the appropriate shift key.

Table 5-1 Storing Keys on the HP–25/25C

	Key	Internal Code
1.	3	03
2.	ENTER↑	31
3.	f	?
4.	x < 0	41
5.	?	05
6.	FRAC	?
7.	?	73
8.	sin	04
9.	x̄	21
10.	8	?
11.	+	?
12.	y^x	03
13.	0	00

Answers: **3.** 14; **5.** [5]; **6.** 01; **7.** [·];
10. 08; **11.** 51

Without any further ado, we shall now proceed to write a program, albeit a rather elementary one. The purpose here is not to be profound, but rather to present the essential concepts involved. A little patience at this juncture will be amply rewarded later on.

Finding the Average of Two Numbers

We are often confronted with the problem of having to take the average, or to find the *arithmetic mean,* as it is often called. To find the average of two numbers hardly presents any difficulty to anyone, even without an ordinary pocket calculator, let alone a programmable model. What we propose to illustrate now is how to calculate the average manually and then by a program. Once that has been done we shall show how the *same* program may be used to calculate the average of an *infinite* number of pairs of values. To begin, we shall find the average of 1 and 8, our first pair of numbers.

Example 2

S	1	2	3	4	5	6
K	1	ENTER↑	8	+	2	÷
D	1.	1.00	8.	9.00	2.	4.50

The schematic in Example 2 is certainly easy to follow and probably requires no further explanation. Now, if we wanted to find the average of another pair of numbers we would merely repeat each of the six steps of the schematic, and the second result would appear in the display as before. Suppose, however, we had to find the average of *hundreds* of pairs of numbers. Would we have to repeat each of these six steps hundreds of times? With an ordinary calculator there would be no alternative, but with a programmable calculator the matter becomes incredibly easy to accomplish. The programmability of the HP-25 reduces this problem to one of merely keying in the appropriate numbers and little else. The program should, of course, display the result and permit the user to key in the next two numbers to be averaged.

Examine the schematic in Example 2 once again. After the first number (in this case 1) is keyed in, it is ENTERed. Now the second number, 8, is keyed in (step 3) and at step 6 the display gives the result. What we want to do is to write a program that will do this calculation for us automatically. Since the first number manually keyed in is ENTERed, so the first program instruction will be

[ENTER↑]

Since we wish to make the whole operation automatic, we must have provision for halting the calculator to enable us to key in the second of the two numbers. This is, in fact, provided by the RUN/STOP key, marked [R/S], located at the bottom right of the keyboard. The next instruction will therefore be

[R/S]

At this point the second number will be keyed in manually. Now both numbers reside in the calculator, the first in the y register and the second in the x register. To add them is quite simple; press the button for addition. The next instruction is therefore

[+]

The sum will now be sitting in the display, the x register, and it has to be divided by 2 to obtain the average. First we key in the 2.

[2]

In RPN the operator follows the two operands, so now we key in the operator for division:

[÷]

The result will now be in the display, and so long as the next instruction is a GTO 00, which halts the calculator in RUN mode, we will be able to view the result and proceed to average the next pair.

You might be surprised to know we have just written our first program.

Program HP-25-1: Average of Two Numbers

Step Number	Instruction	Comments
01	ENTER↑	Transfers first keyed in number from x register to y register
02	R/S	Stops automatic sequencing of calculator to allow the second number to be keyed in
03	+	Adds the two numbers
04	2	Keys in 2 for averaging
05	÷	Divides by 2 for average

We shall now illustrate the procedure for entering the program into the HP-25.

Keying in the Program

1. Switch to PRGM mode.
2. Press the [f] [PRGM] keys to clear the program memory.
3. Key in the five instructions as shown and described in Program HP-25-1.

Notice that with each instruction keyed in in program mode, the display automatically shows both the location counter and the operation code of the instruction stored in that location of the calculator's memory. Now to run the program.

Running the Program

1. Switch to RUN mode.
2. Press the [f] [PRGM] keys to set the program pointer to 00. This will execute the program from the beginning. It is very easy to forget this step. If it is forgotten, the instruction following the last one you keyed in (by default it will be a GTO 00) will be executed, and the calculator will come to an immediate halt. When these keys [f] [PRGM] are pressed in *program mode,* it has the sobering if not infuriating effect of clearing out the current program! So *always* write a program on a scrap of paper first for safety's sake, and be sure the calculator is in the correct mode.
3. Key in the first of the two numbers.
4. Press [R/S] to start the program.
5. Key in the second number.
6. Press [R/S] to restart the program.
7. The calculator will quickly come to a halt with the average of the two numbers in the display.
8. Repeat this sequence, 3 through 7, for each set of data. Here is a schematic using only the four pairs of sample data shown below:

1.0	2.0
12.34	56.78
83.9	−27.6
12.96	17.512

Schematic HP-25-1

S	1	2	3	4	5	6
K	switch	press	key in	switch	press	1
D	to PRGM mode	f PRGM	steps of Program HP-25-1	to RUN mode	f PRGM	1.

S	7	8	9	10	11	12
K	R/S	2	R/S	12.34	R/S	56.78
D	1.00	2.	1.50	12.34	12.34	56.78

S	13	14	15	16	17	18
K	R/S	83.9	R/S	27.6	CHS	R/S
D	34.56	83.9	83.9	27.6	−27.6	28.15

S	19	20	21	22
K	12.96	R/S	17.512	R/S
D	12.96	12.96	17.512	15.24

The four results are shown in steps 9, 13, 18, and 22. Notice that we can continue keying more data, but these four pairs will have illustrated the point sufficiently. It should also be noted that to key in a negative number into the display (as is the second number of the third pair) it is necessary to key in the positive number and to change its sign by pressing [CHS], the change sign key.

The strategy employed in solving our first problem is not the only one by any means. In fact, programming is a rather unique discipline in that it permits a rather great variety of strategies, each of which could be as good as the next one. This flexibility of operation is particularly pleasing to programmers who, as a general group, tend to be very individualistic and have strong preferences for their own particular approach. This might even account for its tremendous popularity.

As a matter of record, the ENTER↑ instruction may be omitted from Program HP-25-1 since, when the R/S instruction is encountered and the second value keyed in, the stack is *automatically* lifted. The reason it has been included is to keep it consistent with the manual method of solving the problem.

In the next program we shall be using the constant π, which is available on the HP-25 at the touch of a button; or more correctly, the touch of two buttons. It is located on the lower surface of the key with the decimal point on its face, and it must therefore be prefixed by the [g] button.

Computing the Circumference of a Circle

The next program we shall attempt is again one requiring very little knowledge of mathematics. It concerns the computation of the circumference of a circle, given its radius. From junior high school you will, no doubt, recall the formula:

$$C = 2\pi r$$

where

C = the circumference
π = the constant 3.14 (approx.)
r = the radius

We shall write a program that will permit the keying in of any value of r. After C is calculated, we shall *loop* around again to allow for the next value of r, and so on. Incidentally, it is precisely this feature of looping that makes programming such a powerful tool. It has been said, not without some propriety, that a program without a loop is like a summer without sunshine.

Here is the schematic for the manual version, using a *single* value of r. It is set equal to 10.98 in this case.

Example 3

S	1	2	3	4	5	6	7
K	10.98	ENTER↑	2	×	g	π	×
D	10.98	10.98	2.	21.96	21.96	3.14	68.99

Thus we find that for a radius of length 10.98 the circumference is computed to be 68.99. Again, once the procedure has been developed for calculating the value of C for a single value of r, it becomes an easy step to modify this procedure with a loop so that the program will solve an *infinite* number of cases. Here is such a program. The loop is effected by the GTO 00 in line 06 (by default), which transfers control to line 00 to allow for the next value of r to be keyed in.

Program HP-25-2: Circumference of a Circle

Step Number	Instruction	Comments
01	ENTER↑	Copies keyed in value of r to y register
02	2	Puts 2 into the x register
03	×	Puts 2r into x register
04	g π	Puts 2r into y register and π into x register
05	×	C = 2πr

To enter this five-line program into the calculator, we first clear any previous program by pressing [f] [PRGM] in program mode. The five instructions are then keyed in as before. If attention is given to the display while keying in Program HP-25-2, it will be of interest to note that after keying in step 04, in which the π function is accessed prefixed by [g], the display reads

04   15   73

This is an indication that the g (code 15) and π (code 73) keys are merged into a single instruction in the calculator's memory. It is for this reason that g and π are shown in a single step in Program HP-25-2. In general, *any* operation that requires multiple keys to execute that operation, are stored internally as a single merged instruction. Table 5-2 illustrates some of these merged instructions.

The schematic that follows shows the steps involved in calculating the circumference for four different values of r, but once again the program will solve for C for as many values of r as are keyed in. The data this time are 3, 2.5, 5.68, and 10.98.

Table **5-2** Merged Instructions on the HP-25

	Function	Keys Required		Merged Instruction Code	
1.	$\sqrt{x}$	f	$\sqrt{x}$	14	02
2.	10^x	g	10^x	15	08
3.	Fix the display to 5 decimal places	f	FIX 5	14 11	05
4.	Add the display to register 3	STO	+ 3	23 51	03
5.	Absolute value	g	ABS	15	03

Schematic HP-25-2

S	1	2	3	4	5
K	switch	press	key in steps	switch	press
D	to PRGM	f PRGM	of Program	to RUN	f PRGM
	mode		HP-25-2	mode	

S	6	7	8	9	10
K	3	R/S	2.5	R/S	5.68
D	3.	18.35	2.5	15.71	5.68
C	1st r	1st C	2nd r	2nd C	3rd r

S	11	12	13
K	R/S	10.98	R/S
D	35.69	10.98	68.99
C	3rd C	4th r	4th C

Finding the Volume of a Sphere

The volume of a sphere is given by the formula

$$V = (4/3)\pi r^3$$

Once again, before writing the program we shall devise a schematic to compute the value of V for a single value of r. Let the value of r be 12.34 inches.

Example 4

S	1	2	3	4	5	6
K	12.34	ENTER↑	3	f	y^x	4
D	12.34	12.34	3.	3.	1879.08	4.

S	7	8	9	10	11	12
K	X	3	÷	g	π	X
D	7516.32	3.	2505.44	2505.44	3.14	7871.08

Thus we find from Example 4 that the volume of a sphere whose radius measures 12.34 inches is equal to 7871.08 cubic inches.

A program can now be written easily, based on the schematic in Example 4. In fact, the identical keystrokes to those shown in this example can be used in our program to compute the volume of any number of spheres. The only difference is that where the schematic shows a specific value for r being keyed in, this step is omitted from the program. The reason for this is that the user must have the opportunity to key in his own value for r during the time of execution of the program. Of course, in order for him to do this, the program must be in a halted condition. Location 00 conveniently contains such a halt instruction.

Program HP-25-3: Volume of a Sphere

Step Number	Instruction	Comments
01	ENTER↑	Copies the value of r keyed in into the y register
02	3	Places 3 into display
03	f y^x	Computes r^3
04	4	Places 4 into display
05	X	$4r^3$
06	3	Places 3 into display
07	÷	$(4/3)r^3$
08	g π	Places value of π into display
09	X	Displays volume = $(4/3)\pi r^3$

The reader is reminded that before running the above program, with the calculator in RUN mode, the keys [f] [PRGM] should be pressed. This has the effect of resetting the location pointer to location 00 where the program begins execution.

Schematic HP-25-3

Calculate the volume of the sphere with radius =

(a) 12.34
(b) 3.61
(c) 2.175

S	1	2	3	4	5	6
K	switch	press	key in steps	switch	press	12.34
D	to PRGM mode	f PRGM	of Program HP-25-3	to RUN mode	f PRGM	12.34

S	7	8	9	10	11
K	R/S	3.61	R/S	2.175	R/S
D	7871.08	3.61	197.07	2.175	43.10

A Simple Counting Program

The purpose of the simple program that follows is not intended for its functional value so much as for an opportunity to introduce two important instructions.

The first of the two statements is the unconditional transfer GTO which, you will recall, means "go to." The GTO instruction is always associated with a two-digit number from 00 to 49. When executed, transfer is sent directly to that location in memory specified by this double digit number. Once control has been transferred, execution resumes from that location.

The second instruction has not been discussed before. It permits the user to insert a pause into the program. The purpose of this PAUSE instruction is to enable intermediate results to be displayed for one second intervals. A succession of PAUSE instructions may be inserted in a program, and this will have the effect of extending the period in which the intermediate result is displayed.

Use of these two instructions is made in the program that follows. The program will cause the display to be repeatedly incremented by one, beginning with whatever number is in the display. Each time the number is incremented, the program pauses to display that number before continuing the process. A close scrutiny of the program will confirm that an infinite loop is set up, one which is halted either by pressing the [R/S] key or by switching the machine off. If it is halted by use of the [R/S] key, a second pressing of this key will continue execution of the program from where it left off.

Program HP-25-4: Counting Program

Step Number	Instruction	Comments
01	f FIX 0	Displays integers only
02	1	Places 1 in display
03	+	Adds 1 to y register
04	f PAUSE	Displays x register for one second
05	GTO 02	Loops to location 02

Schematic HP-25-4

	1	2	3	4	5	6
S						
K	switch	press	key in steps	switch	press	CL x
D	to PRGM mode	f PRGM	of Program HP-25-4	to RUN mode	f PRGM	0.

	7	8	9	10	...etc.
S	R/S				
K					
D	1.	2.	3.	4.	

If the stack is clear and the program is initiated by pressing the [R/S] key, counting begins from zero. If counting is required from any other number, that number must be keyed in before executing the program.

Making Decisions on the HP-25

So far we have shown four programs in which each instruction was executed sequentially, starting with the first instruction in location 01 and going to the last. Upon reaching the end of each of the first three programs, the GTO 00 instruction, which by default occupies each unused memory location, returned us to location 00 where the built-in halt stopped the loop. This enabled us to view the result in the display and to start the cycle over again with new data, using the [R/S] key to restart the operation.

The GTO instruction is regarded as an *unconditional transfer* of control. It could be a GTO 23, which would send control to location 23 of the program, or it might be GTO 01, which would transfer control to location 01, and so on. In each case transfer of control is made with "no questions asked."

On occasion, however, we want to transfer control only when a given situation has transpired. For example, transfer of control might become necessary only if the contents of register x became equal to that of register y, or if the contents of the x register became less than zero, that is, negative. Transfer in these cases would be made only if some predetermined condition or other were met.

On the HP-25 there are eight such *conditional transfers.* They are:

$$x < y \qquad x < 0$$
$$x \geqslant y \qquad x \geqslant 0$$
$$x \neq y \qquad x \neq 0$$
$$x = y \qquad x = 0$$

The tests comparing the x and y registers are "upper case" and are therefore prefixed by the [f] key, while those comparing the x register with zero are "lower case" and are prefixed by the [g] button. The manner in which each of these eight tests works is as follows: If the test proves to be *true,* execution of the program continues sequentially in the ordinary way. However, if the test turns out to be *false,* the instruction following the test is skipped. This may be represented diagrammatically as shown on p. 67.

If the test in location 20 is true, control is transferred normally to the next instruction (at location 21). If the test is false, location 21 is skipped and execution is resumed from location 22.

If the reader has difficulty remembering which of the two sequences apply to a given situation, the following helpful hint is suggested: Think for a moment how you would react if told a *false* statement by someone whom you trust. Wouldn't your heart *skip* a beat?

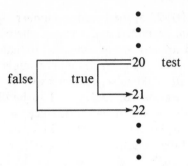

It is up to the programmer to select the specific test he wants and to decide what to do logically depending upon the outcome of the test.

On occasions it may be necessary to test whether the fractional part of a number is equal to zero. The fractional part of a number may be isolated and sent to the display by using the [FRAC] function prefixed by [g]. This is done in the next program, which tests whether a keyed in number is odd or even.

Determining Whether a Number Is Odd or Even

One of the problems to be considered concerns the manner in which the calculator makes its conclusions known to us. After all, a calculator cannot talk—not even a programmable calculator—at least, not yet. In the program that follows, it was decided quite arbitrarily to display the digit 1 if the number keyed in was odd and the digit 2 if it was even. The logic behind the program is quite straightforward, as the flowchart in Fig. 5-3 confirms.

Program HP-25-5: Is a Number Odd or Even?

Step Number	Instruction	Comments
01	f FIX 0	Displays only integers
02	ENTER↑	Copies keyed in value to y register
03	2	Puts 2 into the x register
04	÷	
05	g FRAC	Extracts fractional portion of x register
06	g x = 0	Is the fractional portion zero?
07	GTO 10	Yes; then original number is even; go to location 10
08	1	No; then original number is odd; send 1 to display
09	GTO 00	Halts program to permit display of result and option of keying in another number
10	2	Puts 2 into display, indicating original number is even. The default GTO 00 in location 11 halts the program, permitting the display of result and the option of re-running the program

68   Programmable Pocket Calculators

According to Program HP-25-5, the keyed in number is first divided by 2 and the fractional portion examined to determine whether or not it is equal to zero. If it is, control is transferred to statement 10 that displays a 2, indicating that the number is even. If the fractional portion is not equal to zero, making the test in location 06 false, statement 07 is skipped and control is passed instead to location 08, causing a 1 to be displayed, indicating that the original number keyed in was odd. Since the integer result in either case is a 1 or a 2, the display is initially set to FIX 0 by the program, which eliminates the display of the superfluous trailing .00.

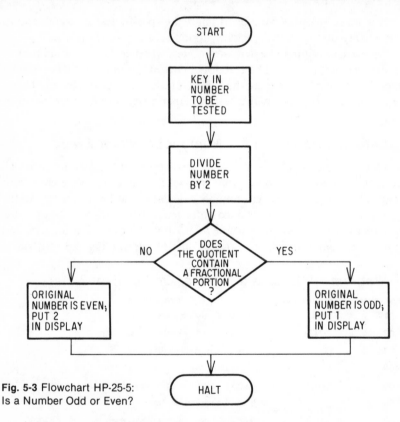

Fig. 5-3 Flowchart HP-25-5: Is a Number Odd or Even?

Schematic HP-25-5: Testing Odd-Even Program

S	1	2	3	4	5	6	7
K	switch to PRGM mode	press f PRGM	key in steps of Program HP-25-5	switch to RUN mode	press f PRGM	5	R/S
D						5.	1.

S	8	9	10	11	12	13
K	1666	R/S	424	R/S	55	R/S
D	1666.	2.	424.	2.	55.	1.

Halving a Number Problem

The program that follows has little mathematical merit but is intended as an exercise in the use of the conditional jump, the PAUSE instruction, and the x interchange y key. The idea behind the program is to key in any positive number. The calculator will repeatedly divide this number by 2, displaying the result each time until it becomes less than 1. At that point, the calculator halts with the final result in the display. The flowchart is shown in Fig. 5-4, followed directly by the program.

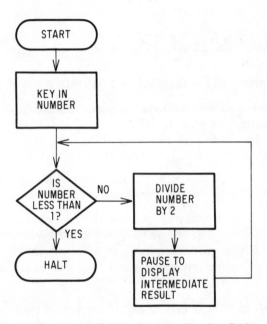

Fig. 5-4 Flowchart HP-25-6: Halving a Number Problem

Program HP-25-6: Halving a Number Problem

Step Number	Instruction	Comments
01	ENTER↑	Copies keyed in number into y register
02	1	Replaces display with 1
03	x ⇄ y	Interchanges x and y registers, placing 1 in y register and keyed in number in x register
04	f x < y	Is number in display less than 1?
05	GTO 00	Yes; halt program, displaying result
06	2	No; sends 2 to display, lifting stack
07	÷	Divides number by 2
08	f PAUSE	Pauses to display intermediate result
09	GTO 04	Continues processing

For those readers who do not have an HP-25 available, the following schematic is given to enable them to visualize the manner in which the display changes with each pass through the loop. Those numbers surrounded by dashes indicate that the number is displayed automatically for a period of about a second.

S	1	2	3	4	5
K	f	FIX	4	25	R/S
D	0.00	0.00	0.0000	25.	⌐ 12.5000 ⌐

S	6	7	8	9	10
K					
D	⌐ 6.2500 ⌐	⌐ 3.1250 ⌐	⌐ 1.5625 ⌐	⌐ 0.7813 ⌐	0.7813

Calculating the Factorial of a Number

Since the HP-25 does not have a factorial function in its repertoire, we shall shortly write a program to calculate this function. The factorial of a number n is the product of all the positive integers from 1 to n. For example, factorial 5 (written 5!) is defined in the following way:

$$5! = 5 \times 4 \times 3 \times 2 \times 1 = 120$$

In mathematics, 0! is defined to be 1.

There are a great many approaches one can adopt in calculating the factorial of a number. The one we have selected involves the use of storage register 1 in which the partial product is stored. Program HP-25-7 serves as an illustration of register arithmetic, which we discussed in Chap. 4.

Program HP-25-7: Factorial of a Number

Step Number	Instruction	Comments
01	f FIX 0	
02	ENTER↑	Copies keyed in value for n into y register
03	1	
04	STO 1	Initializes R1 to 1
05	f x ⩾ y	Tests to see if counter is greater than or equal to n
06	GTO 11	If it is, then go to statement 11
07	1	If not, then add 1 to counter
08	+	
09	STO × 1	Multiplies counter by R1, storing new result in R1
10	GTO 05	Go through loop again
11	RCL 1	Recalls final result to display; GTO 00 in location 12 halts program

The program also utilizes the storage capacity of the stack itself in which the value of n is retained in register y, while the number contained in register x is repeatedly incremented until it reaches the value of n in register y. With each pass through the loop this incremented value is multiplied by and replaces the contents of memory register 1, which contains the partial product of the factorial and is ultimately brought to the x register to display the final result. Since the logic to this program is somewhat more complex than that of previous programs in this chapter, the flowchart in Fig. 5-5 should prove to be helpful.

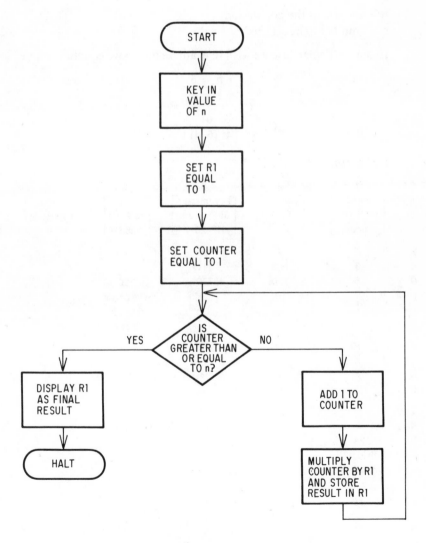

Fig. 5-5 Flowchart HP-25-7: Factorial of a Number

The computation of factorials is usually required in the field of probability when one has to calculate combinations and permutations. As an illustration of a particular problem in combinatorial mathematics, let us assume that six people are available to fill four positions on a committee. How many different ways can four people be selected from these six?

This problem is generally stated mathematically as:

$$_nC_r \; = \; \frac{n!}{r!\,(n-r)\,!}$$

where

     n = the size of the population
     r = number to be selected

In our particular case we wish to evaluate the above equation where

$$n = 6$$
$$r = 4$$

$$_6C_4 \; = \; \frac{6!}{4!\,(6-4)\,!} \; = \; \frac{6!}{4!2!}$$

Schematic HP-25-7

S	1	2	3	4	5
K	switch	press	key in steps	switch	press
D	to PRGM	f PRGM	of Program	to RUN	f PRGM
	mode		HP–25–7	mode	
S	6	7	8	9	
K	6.	R/S	STO	2	
D	6	720.	720.	720.	
C		6!		save partial	
				result in	
				register 2	
S	10	11	12	13	
K	4	R/S	STO	÷	
D	4.	24.	24.	24.	
C		4!			
S	14	15	16	17	
K	2	2	R/S	STO	
D	24.	2.	2.	2.	
C	divides 6!		2!		
	in register				
	1 by 4!				
S	18	19	20	21	
K	÷	2	RCL	2	
D	2.	2.	2.	15.	
C		divides register		$_6C_4 = 6!/4!2!$	
		1 by 2!			

According to this schematic, 6! is calculated by keying in 6 and pressing the [R/S] key. The result of 720 is then stored in register 2, care being taken not to use any of the registers employed by the program. Factorial 4 is then calculated and is divided into the contents of register 2. The result is subsequently divided by 2! to obtain the final solution. Thus we see that there are 15 ways to form a committee of four from six possible candidates.

The Newton-Raphson Iteration Technique

We are about to describe a scheme for computing the square root of a number. Why resort to any such scheme, one might ask, if the HP-25 has a preprogrammed square root function? Indeed, this is a valid question, but the fact of the matter is that this technique is extremely powerful and has applications in many other situations.

The technique is named after Sir Isaac Newton and a British contemporary of his named Raphson. In order to find the square root of a number by means of the Newton-Raphson scheme, one makes an arbitrary initial guess at the square root. This initial guess is repeatedly refined by the scheme until the square root is obtained.

New guess = (1/2) [(original number/old guess) + old guess]

Each time a new guess is calculated from the formula, it is substituted into the formula as the old guess for the next iteration. This process is repeated until the new guess approximates the square root to the desired accuracy.

To take a typical example, let us suppose we want to find the square root of 123. Let our first guess be 1, even though this is not a particularly intelligent guess. Despite this fact, it will shortly be seen that we can approximate the square root of 123 to any degree of accuracy we desire.

New guess = (1/2) [(original number/old guess) + old guess]
New guess = (1/2) [(123/1) + 1] = 62
New guess = (1/2) [(123/62) + 62] = 31.99193549
New guess = (1/2) [(123/31.99193549) + 31.99193549] = 17.91832721
New guess = (1/2) [(123/17.91832721) + 17.91832721] = 12.39140364
New guess = (1/2) [(123/12.39140364) + 12.39140364] = 11.15881995
New guess = (1/2) [(123/11.15881995) + 11.15881995] = 11.09074543

•
•
•

etc.

The question arises: When do we stop this process? We are obviously very close to the true square root. There are many criteria by which one may decide to stop the process. The one which we have chosen in the program that follows is to stop iterating when the absolute difference between the square of the new guess and the original number is less than say, 0.00001, a number usually referred to as epsilon (ϵ). Mathematically speaking, processing is stopped when:

$$\left|(\text{New guess})^2 - \text{original number}\right| < \epsilon$$

The strategy of the program is outlined in the flowchart shown in Fig. 5-6.

Program HP-25-8: The Newton-Raphson Technique

Step Number	Instruction	Comments
01	f FIX 9	Sets the display to 9 decimal places
02	STO 2	Stores the original keyed in number in register 2
03	1	Initializes old guess to 1
04	STO 3	
05	.	
06	0	
07	0	
08	0	Sets $\epsilon = 0.00001$
09	0	
10	1	
11	STO 1	
12	RCL 2	Recalls original number to display
13	RCL 3	Recalls old guess to display, pushing original number into y register
14	÷	original number/old guess
15	RCL 3	Old guess
16	+	(original number/old guess) + old guess
17	2	
18	÷	New guess = (1/2) [(original number/old guess) + old guess]
19	STO 3	Stores new guess as old guess for next iteration
20	g x²	(new guess)²
21	RCL 2	Original number
22	−	(new guess)² – original number
23	g ABS	|(new guess)² – original number|
24	RCL 1	ϵ
25	f x < y	Is |(new guess)² – original number| ≥ ϵ?
26	GTO 12	Yes; reiterate
27	RCL 3	No; then recall final answer to display
28	R/S	And halt to display result
29	GTO 02	Process next number

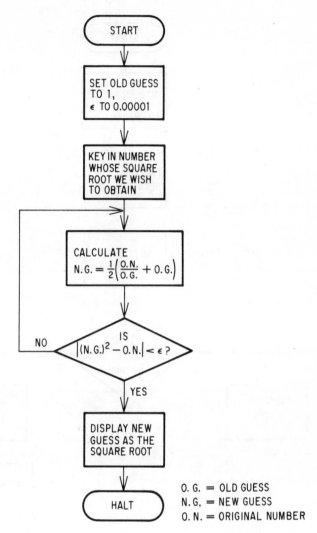

Fig. 5-6 Flowchart HP-25-8: The Newton-Raphson Technique

Schematic HP-25-8

S	1	2	3	4	5	6
K	⎡ switch ⎤	⎡ press ⎤	⎡key in steps⎤	⎡ switch ⎤	⎡ press ⎤	2
D	to PRGM	⎣f PRGM⎦	of Program	to RUN	⎣f PRGM⎦	2.
	⎣ mode ⎦		HP–25–8 ⎦	⎣ mode ⎦		

S	7	8	9	10	11
K	R/S	25	R/S	123	R/S
D	1.414215687	25.	5.000000000	123.	11.09053651
C	$\sqrt{2}$		$\sqrt{25}$		$\sqrt{123}$

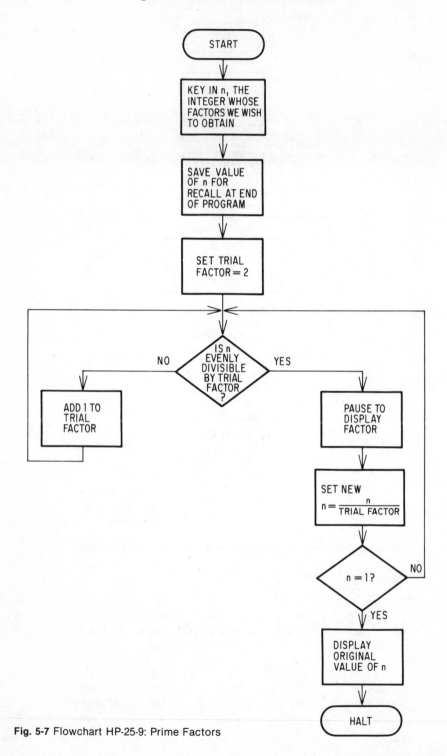

Fig. 5-7 Flowchart HP-25-9: Prime Factors

Prime Factors

The prime factors of a positive integer are defined to be that sequence of prime numbers which, when multiplied together, equals the original number. For example, the prime factors of 10 are 2 and 5 since $2 \times 5 = 10$, and both 2 and 5 are prime numbers.

Program HP-25-9 permits the user to key in any positive integer greater than 1. The number keyed in is tested to see whether the number 2 is one of its factors. If it is, division by two takes place and the process is repeated again. If, on the other hand, the number is not exactly divisible by two, a test is made to see whether three (2 plus 1) is a factor. This process is continued until all the prime factors are found. If any are found, they are displayed for a period of one second. When either no factors or no further factors are found, the original number is returned to the display. This is a particularly good strategy because it permits the user to rerun the program with the same original number by simply pressing [R/S].

Program HP-25-9: Prime Factors

Step Number	Instruction	Comments
01	f FIX 0	
02	STO 2	Saves value of n for recall at end of program
03	STO 0	
04	2	Sets trial factor to 2
05	STO 1	
06	RCL 0	Recalls current value of n to display
07	RCL 1	Recalls current value of trial factor to display, pushing value of n into y register
08	÷	Divides n by trial factor
09	ENTER↑	Copies quotient into y register
10	g FRAC	
11	g x = 0	Is n evenly divisible by trial factor?
12	GTO 16	Yes; go to 16
13	1	No; add 1 to trial factor and try division again
14	STO +1	
15	GTO 06	
16	RCL 1	Pauses to display factor
17	f PAUSE	
18	R↓	Rolls down the stack, placing quotient from z register into display
19	R↓	
20	STO 0	Stores quotient as new value for n
21	1	Are we done?
22	f x ≠ y	
23	GTO 06	No; then continue processing at step 6
24	RCL 2	Yes; then recall original value of n to display and stop program

The strategy outlined in Fig. 5-7 (see p. 76) suffers from a serious deficiency in design. Although the strategy employed in solving this problem is much simpler to program, it results in a much longer execution time; depending upon the situation, this may be a fair trade-off. Nevertheless, one of the major criticisms that may be levied at this strategy is the fact that although any even number greater than 2 cannot be a prime factor, the program tests for them anyway. It is left to the reader to devise his own scheme for improving Program HP-25-9.

Schematic HP-25-9

S	1	2	3	4	5
K	switch	press	key in steps	switch	press
D	to PRGM	f PRGM	of Program	to RUN	f PRGM
	mode		HP-25-9	mode	

S	6	7	8	9	10
K	100	R/S			
D	100.	2.	2.	5.	5.
C		1st prime	2nd prime	3rd prime	4th prime
		factor	factor	factor	factor

S	11	12	13	
K		41	R/S	...etc.
D	100.	41.	41.	
C	original		41 is	
	number		prime	

Pythagorean Triplets

Probably the most famous theorem learned in geometry is the Pythagorean theorem. It states that, given any right triangle, the square of the length of the hypotenuse is equal to the sum of the squares of the lengths of the other two sides (see Fig. 5-8). Stated mathematically,

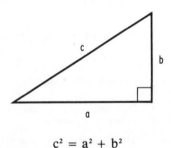

Fig. 5-8

$$c^2 = a^2 + b^2$$

Most of us will remember the familiar triplet 3, 4, and 5, which are the sides of a right triangle since

$$5^2 = 3^2 + 4^2$$

The question arises: Given any integer, representing one of the legs of a right triangle, is it possible to find two integers which, together with the first, form a Pythagorean triplet? The answer to this question is in the affirmative. If the given leg is an *odd* integer, the other leg and the hypotenuse can be computed by setting that integer to $2n + 1$ and solving for n. Once n has been found, the other leg is calculated by evaluating the expression $2n^2 + 2n$, while the hypotenuse is given by this last number with one added to it. For example, let us say the leg of a triangle is of length 5.

$$2n + 1 = 5$$
$$n = 2$$

with n equal to 2,

$$2n^2 + 2n = 12$$

while

$$2n^2 + 2n + 1 = 13$$

Thus we find that 5, 12, and 13 form a Pythagorean triplet.

But what if the leg of the triangle is an even integer? For this case that number is set equal to 4n from which the value of n is calculated. This value of n is then substituted into the expression $4n^2 - 1$ to give the other leg and into $4n^2 + 1$ for the hypotenuse.

For example, if one leg is equal to 8, we solve the linear equation:

$$4n = 8$$
$$n = 2$$

The expressions $4n^2 - 1$ and $4n^2 + 1$ are then evaluated for $n = 2$, and thus we find that 8, 15, and 17 represent a Pythagorean triplet.

A flowchart illustrating the strategy employed by this program is shown in Fig. 5-9.

Program HP-25-10: Pythagorean Triplets

Step Number	Instruction	Comments
01	f FIX 0	
02	STO 1	Save value of keyed in leg
03	2	
04	÷	Is this value even?
05	g FRAC	(Is it evenly divisible by 2?)
06	g x = 0	
07	GTO 23	Yes; then go to 23
08	RCL 1	No; solve for n in expression, leg $= 2n + 1$
09	1	
10	−	$2n = $ leg $- 1$

Program HP-25-10 (cont'd)

Step Number	Instruction	Comments
11	ENTER↑	Save value of 2n in stack
12	ENTER↑	
13	2	
14	÷	$n = (leg - 1)/2$
15	g x²	n^2
16	2	
17	X	$2n^2$
18	+	$2n^2 + 2n$
19	f PAUSE	Pauses to display value of other leg
20	1	
21	+	Hypotenuse $= 2n^2 + 2n + 1$
22	GTO 00	Transfers control to location 00 to halt program and display value of hypotenuse
23	RCL 1	Leg is even solve for n in expression, $leg = 4n$
24	4	
25	÷	$n = leg/4$
26	g x²	n^2
27	4	
28	X	$4n^2$
29	1	
30	—	$4n^2 - 1$
31	f PAUSE	Pauses to display value of other leg
32	2	
33	+	Hypotenuse $= 4n^2 + 1 = (4n^2 - 1) + 2$

Schematic HP-25-10

	1	2	3	4	5
S					
K	switch	press	key in steps	switch	press
D	to PRGM	f PRGM	of Program	to RUN	f PRGM
	mode		HP-25-10	mode	

	6	7	8	9	10
S					
K	3	R/S		5	R/S
D	3.	4.	5.	5.	12.
C	known	other	hypotenuse	known	other
	leg	leg		leg	leg

	11	12	13	14
S				
K		8	R/S	
D	13.	8.	15.	17.
C	hypotenuse	known	other	hypotenuse
		leg	leg	

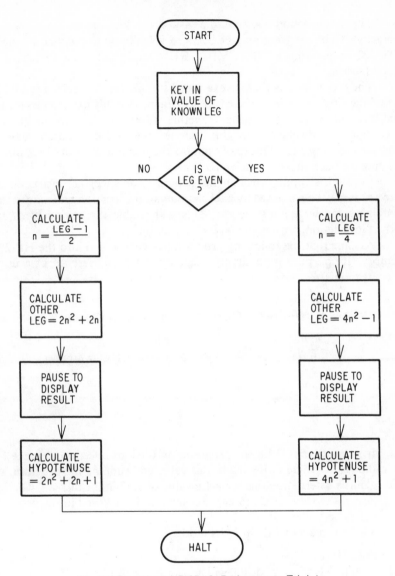

Fig. 5-9 Flowchart HP-25-10: Pythagorean Triplets

Debugging and Editing Programs on the HP-25 and HP-25C

What a Utopian world it would be if after once having written a program it were not necessary to modify it or to debug it. The HP-25 provides the programmer with some effective debugging tools.

Once a program has been keyed into the memory of the HP-25, the program should be executed using data whose answers are already known. If the answers do not correspond, the program is in need of debugging.

The first question that should be asked is: "Was the program keyed in correctly?" The program may be checked visually by first either keying in GTO 00 or pressing [f] [PRGM] in RUN mode and then switching to PRGM mode.

The program may then be examined step-by-step from location 00 by use of the single step key labeled [SST]. Each time this key is pressed, the next location number in sequence, together with the code of the instruction it contains, is displayed. In this manner the entire program may be examined for accuracy. One may examine the previous memory location by pressing the back step key labeled [BST].

If, when stepping through the program, an incorrect instruction is detected it may be corrected by backstepping to the location *previous* to that containing the wrong instruction. This will enable the keying in of the correct instruction, erasing the faulty instruction.

Assume that the following program has been keyed into the HP-25's memory. Its purpose is to simply calculate the circumference of a circle given its radius.

Program HP-25-11: Circumference of a Circle

Step Number	Instruction	Comments
01	ENTER↑	Copies value of r keyed in into the y register
02	2	
03	X	2r
04	g π	
05	X	2πr

In order to check out the program, an obvious selection to make for the radius is the value 1. Keying in this value and running the program, we find to our consternation that we get a value of 1.57 in the display, whereas we expected the value of 2π (6.28). Perhaps we have keyed in the program incorrectly. Let's check it.

With the machine still in RUN mode,

1. Press [f] [PRGM].
2. Switch to PRGM mode (00 will appear in the display).
3. Press [SST] to single-step the program.
4. The display reads

$$01 \qquad 31$$

This corresponds to the ENTER↑ instruction in step 1.
5. Press [SST] again to display the contents of location 2.

$$02 \qquad 02$$

This checks out.

6. Press [SST] again. Display now reads
03   71
The key that corresponds to the code 71 is the [÷] key rather than the multiplication key as intended. Alas, we have found a bug!

7. Press [BST] to get in position for entering correct instruction. Display now reads
02   02

8. Press the [×] key. The display now reads
03   61
an indication that the faulty instruction has been replaced by the correct instruction.

9. Switch to RUN mode and try the test data again. This time the correct answer is obtained. It seems the program is now debugged.

In general, it is a good practice to check out the whole of the program even beyond the point where a bug has been detected. For further ideas, the reader is respectfully referred to the techniques suggested in Chap. 1.

CHAPTER SIX
THE HP-55 PROGRAMMABLE SCIENTIFIC POCKET CALCULATOR

In December 1974, a year after Hewlett-Packard released their 100-step HP-65 programmable calculator, it introduced—almost as an encore—the 49-step programmable HP-55 at a retail price of $395.

The HP-55 differs functionally in several important respects from the HP-65, which it greatly resembles in external appearance. It does not have the ability to record a keyed-in program onto a magnetic card, so that once a program is resident in the HP-55's memory, switching the machine off causes the program to be lost. However, if the keystrokes are recorded on paper, for example, they can then be rekeyed in on a subsequent occasion.

The HP-55 has no fewer than 86 keyboard commands, more than on most other scientific calculators. Included in its functions is a most useful factorial key. Unlike the 9 memory registers of its "big brother," the HP-65, the HP-55 has 20 addressable data storage registers that greatly alleviate the need to write down intermediate results. With 10 of these registers, register arithmetic is possible. Another important and unique feature of the HP-55 is that it has a built-in timer, enabling the user to actually time up to 10 laboratory experiments, or tests.

Statistical and trigonometric and mathematical functions are present, two conditional branch instructions, an unconditional branch instruction, and two-way conversions between U.S. and metric units of measurement.

Many of the keys of the HP-55 are multi-purpose. The store key [STO], for example, has printed above it $\bar{x}$ (in yellow) and s (in blue). This key therefore is used for storing data into a register, for calculating the mean and the standard deviation. If the storing function is required, the key is pressed followed by a digit 1 through 20. If, however, it is the mean that is needed, the pressing of the key must be preceded by the yellow shift key labeled [f]. If it is the standard deviation that is required, the blue shift key labeled [g] must be pressed first. This system is used for all of the multi-functional keys on the HP-55.

The HP-55 has a rechargeable battery, which when fully charged gives about 5 hours of continuous operation. The adapter/recharger that is supplied free with the calculator can be plugged into an ac wall outlet using either a 115 or 230 volt supply. The calculator weighs 9 ounces (255 grams) and measures 5.8 by 3.2 inches by 0.7 to 1.3 inches. In metric measurement this is 14.7 by 8.1 centimeters by 1.8 to 3.3 centimeters.

A picture of the HP-55 is shown in Fig. 6-1.

Manual Operation of the HP-55

With the top right-hand switch in RUN mode, the HP-55 can be used manually. In order to familiarize the reader with the wide variety of functions available, we shall solve some elementary mathematical problems in which most of the available functions will be used.

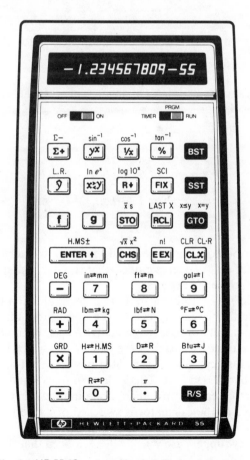

Fig. 6-1 HP-55 (*Courtesy* Hewlett-Packard Company)

Example 1: Evaluate $[(1.23 \times 3.21)/12.3]^2$

S	1	2	3	4	5	6	7	8
K	1.23	ENTER↑	3.21	×	12.3	÷	g	x^2
D	1.23	1.23	3.21	3.95	12.3	0.32	0.32	0.10

Example 2: Evaluate $\sqrt{[\ln (3.45) + e^{2.7}]/[\cos (12.38°) - \sin (10.5°)]}$

S	1	2	3	4	5	6
K	3.45	f	ln	2.7	g	e^x
D	3.45	3.45	1.24	2.7	2.7	14.88

S	7	8	9	10	11	12
K	+	12.38	f	cos	10.5	f
D	16.12	12.38	12.38	0.98	10.5	10.5

S	13	14	15	16	17
K	sin	—	÷	f	$\sqrt{x}$
D	0.18	0.79	20.29	20.29	4.50

Example 3: Evaluate $\sin^{-1} (5^4/6!)$ as an angle expressed in radians.

S	1	2	3	4	5	6
K	5	ENTER↑	4	y^x	6	f
D	5.	5.00	4.	625.00	6.	6.

S	7	8	9	10	11	12
K	n!	÷	f	RAD	g	$\sin^{-1}$
D	720.00	0.87	0.87	0.87	0.87	1.05

In common with the practice of all the Hewlett-Packard calculators, the HP-55 "wakes up" in degree mode—that is, all trigonometric functions treat angles as expressed in degrees.

In Example 3, the problem states that the evaluation is to be carried out with the resulting angle expressed in radians rather than degrees. It is necessary for the calculator user to manually change the mode from degrees to radians. This is done by means of the [RAD] key, which is the upper case function of the plus key. Since it is printed in yellow, it follows that the [f] prefix key must be pressed first. This is done in steps 9 and 10, from which point the calculator remains in radian mode until either the mode is subsequently changed or the calculator is switched off. In order to obtain the arc sine of the parenthesized expression, the [g] prefix key has to be pressed before the sin⁻¹ key (upper case y^x). It will be noticed that the –1 part of the sin⁻¹ label is printed in blue as an indication that the correct prefix is the blue [g] key.

Example 4:   Evaluate antilog $(6.98)/(-58.67 \times 10^7)$ expressing the result to five rounded decimal places.

S	1	2	3	4	5
K	6.98	g	10^x	58.67	CHS
D	6.98	6.98	9549925.87	58.67	−58.67

S	6	7	8	9	10
K	EEX	7	÷	·FIX	5
D	−58.67 00	−58.67 07	−0.02	−0.02	−0.01628

The antilog of a number x is ten raised to that power x (10^x). Since the problem uses a negative number (-58.67×10^7) the change sign key ([CHS]) is pressed after the mantissa portion is keyed in. To enter the exponent of this number that is expressed in scientific notation, the [EEX] (enter exponent) key must be pressed before keying in the exponent (7).

The problem states that the result is to be expressed to five decimal places. To accomplish this the key marked [FIX] is pressed followed by the digit 5, which specifies the number of rounded decimal places required. In general, pressing the [FIX] key followed by a digit key from 0 to 9 has the effect of automatically rounding any displayed numbers on the HP-55 to the specified number of decimal digits (in this case 5). This setting remains in effect until either the machine is switched off or it is subsequently changed. It will be noticed that whenever the calculator is switched on, the display defaults to a setting of two decimal places rounded. Furthermore, it is pointed out that regardless of the number of decimal places displayed, the full accuracy of the number is nevertheless retained internally in the calculator.

Example 5:   Evaluate $1/\pi^5$

S	1	2	3	4	5
K	f	π	5	y^x	1/x
D	0.00	3.14	5.	306.02	3.2677636-03

Pressing the key labeled [π], preceded by its appropriate [f] prefix key, has the effect of placing the approximation for π of 3.14 into the display (3.141592654 if [FIX] 9 is pressed). In step 5 the reciprocal is computed and the answer 3.2677636×10^{-3} is displayed. Since the answer is too small to be displayed in the normal FIX 2 setting of the machine, the answer is automatically converted to scientific notation.

Example 6: Evaluate $(15.6789 \times 10^{-12}) + (13.728 \times 10^{-12})/(63.915 \times 10^{3})$ and express the result to 3 rounded decimal places.

S	1	2	3	4	5
K	15.6789	EEX	CHS	12	ENTER↑
D	15.6789	15.6789 00	15.6789–00	15.6789–12	1.5678900–11

S	6	7	8	9	10
K	13.728	EEX	CHS	12	+
D	13.728	13.728 00	13.728–00	13.728–12	2.9406900–11

S	11	12	13	14	15
K	63.915	EEX	3	÷	f
D	63.915	63.915 00	63.915 03	4.6009387–16	4.6009387–16

S	16	17
K	SCI	3
D	4.6009387–16	4.601–16

The Data Storage Registers

Besides the last x register, and the x, y, z, and t stack registers, the HP-55 has 20 data storage registers referred to as R0 through R9 and R.0 through R.9. To store the displayed number 3 in register R7 the keys

[STO] 7

are pressed. This number may subsequently be recalled by pressing:

[RCL] 7

To store the displayed number 4 into register R.9, for example, the key sequence

[STO] [.] 9

is pressed. Later on the value stored in register R.9 may be recalled by pressing:

[RCL] [.] 9

Whenever a number is stored in a particular register, it replaces whatever number was residing there previously and leaves the contents of the display unchanged. Conversely, whenever a number is recalled from a particular register, the register contents are copied into the display, pushing the stack up.

Registers R0 through R9 and the stack may be cleared by pressing

[f] [CLR]

while to clear registers R.0 through R.9 and the stack the sequence

[g] [CL.R]

is pressed.

The Digital Timer

Although most electronic calculators possess a timer within their circuitry, the HP-55 is the only advanced calculator that has added a tiny quartz crystal to provide an accurate time base. As a result, this machine features an amazing precision timer with a range of 100 hours.

The Owner's Handbook that comes free with the calculator introduces this timing facility in a most intriguing way. Before spelling out in detail the list of other features that the calculator offers, the manual invites the reader to switch the unit on and to set the switch in the upper right-hand corner to TIMER. The timer is started by pressing the key [R/S]. Once the timer has been activated, the reader is encouraged to learn about the joys of using the HP-55 and is told to again press [R/S] when the complete passage is read. If this is done the reader, without being aware of it, has calculated his reading speed, which is displayed after pressing some specified arithmetic keys.

Whereas the calculator displays 0.00 when switched on in RUN mode, in TIMER mode it displays what, at first, seems to be a strange format:

0.00.00   00

This is the format for displaying time measured in hours, minutes, seconds, and hundredths of a second. Any time between 00 and 100 hours may be clocked. While the timer is "ticking" the hundredths-of-a-second digits increment at breathtaking speed.

If during a practical laboratory experiment, for example, it is necessary to time the period for say three events to reach their conclusion, the exact times may be recorded on the HP-55 merely by pressing any three different number keys 0 through 9. This has the effect of storing the elapsed time in the corresponding data storage registers 0 through 9 without having to press the [STO] key. The calculator is engineered this way to facilitate the clocking of the time as precisely as is humanly possible. The HP-55 behaves very much like a stopwatch in this respect, with the difference being that up to 10 simultaneously occurring events may be timed.

One does not have to necessarily commence timing from 0.00.00 00. Should it be necessary to start from some predetermined time, this starting time should be keyed into the display with the calculator switched to RUN mode, according to the following format:

HH.MMSShh

Thus, for example, to key in 12 hours, 34 minutes, 56.12 seconds one keys in:

$$12.345612$$

Switching back to TIMER mode this becomes:

$$12.34.56\ 12$$

The timer may then be activated from this starting point in the usual fashion by pressing the [R/S] key. It is worth noting that once the timer has been activated, switching to either RUN mode or PRGM mode will not affect the timer. If the [R/S] key is pressed when the timer is running in RUN mode, the timer will stop and the time currently in the display will automatically be converted to the format described above.

It will be noticed that when switching from TIMER to RUN mode the display will automatically be set to six decimal places. Advantage may be taken of this HH.MMSShh format in RUN mode for adding or subtracting two different times, or for that matter, angles expressed in degrees, minutes, seconds, and hundredths of a second. To add two such values the [H.MS +] key is pressed prefixed by [f]. In the examples that follow, it is assumed that the display has been preset to six decimal places.

Example 7:   Add 1 hour, 2 minutes, 3.45 seconds to 43 hours, 39 minutes, 12.53 seconds.

S	1	2	3	4	5	6
K	⌈switch⌉	1.020345	ENTER↑	43.391253	f	H.MS+
D	to RUN	1.020345	1.020345	43.391253	43.391253	44.411598
	⌊ mode ⌋					

The sum is calculated to be 44 hours, 41 minutes, 15.98 seconds.

Example 8:   Subtract 29° 13′ 58″ from 56° 12′ 52.4″

S	1	2	3	4	5	6
K	⌈switch⌉	56.12524	ENTER↑	29.1358	g	H.MS—
D	to RUN	56.12524	56.12524	29.1358	29.1358	26.585440
	⌊ mode ⌋					

Thus we find that $56°12′52.4″ - 29°13′58″ = 26°58′54.4″$

Frequently, time is expressed in hours and fractions of an hour. On the HP-55 one may readily convert such readings to the equivalent representation in hours, minutes, and seconds by using the key marked [▸H.MS], prefixed by the blue shift key [g]. Conversely, time expressed in hours, minutes, and seconds may be converted to its decimal equivalent by means of the [H◂] key, preceded by the gold shift key [f]. Two simple illustrations of this follow.

Example 9:   Convert 5.72 hours to its equivalent representation in hours, minutes, and seconds.

S	*1*	*2*	*3*
K	5.72	g	→H.MS
D	5.72	5.72	5.431200

It is clear from the above that 5.72 hours is equivalent to 5 hours, 43 minutes, 12 seconds.

Example 10:   Convert 15 hours, 27 minutes to its equivalent decimal representation.

S	*1*	*2*	*3*
K	15.27	f	H←
D	15.27	15.27	15.450000

Thus we find that 15 hours, 27 minutes is equivalent to 15.45 hours.

Statistics

The "key" to the range of statistics available at the press of the button on the HP-55 is the [Σ+] key. It operates on numbers in both the x register and the y register automatically. The number of entries keyed in — that is, the last value of n — is stored in register R.0. Some very useful totals are accumulated in registers R.1 through R.5, according to the following list:

Register	Data	Description
R.0	n	Number of entries
R.1	Σx	Summation of x values
R.2	Σx^2	Summation of x^2 values
R.3	Σy	Summation of y values
R.4	Σy^2	Summation of y^2 values
R.5	Σxy	Summation of xy values

From the above it is clear that

1. It is advisable to clear registers R.0 through R.5 before accumulating.
2. Values of x and y may be handled simultaneously. If only x values are required, clearing the y register initially will be sufficient.

To calculate the mean and standard deviation of both the x and y values, each y value is keyed in and ENTERed. Then the x value is keyed in and the key [Σ+] pressed. There is no limit to the number of pairs of data that can be keyed in. Once all the data has been entered, the mean of the x's is found by the key sequence:

$$[f]\ [\bar{x}]$$

To find the mean of the y's one must first bring it from the y register where it is stored to the x register. The [x⇄y] key will exchange the contents of these two registers and will display the mean of the y values.

In a similar fashion, the standard deviation of the x values is displayed by pressing

[g] [s]

and since the standard deviation of the y values is in the y register, the x interchange y key [x⇄y] is pressed to display the result.

Linear Regression

In business those with managerial responsibilities often have the task of having to estimate future trends such as production volume, costs, personnel, and so on. One of the statistical tools that is available to assist one in such predictions is that of linear regression, sometimes referred to as trend analysis.

After keying in any two or more data points using the accumulation key [Σ+], the linear regression may be found directly (via the least-squares method) by pressing the key labeled [L.R.]. Furthermore, other data points on the curve may be calculated by using the key marked [ŷ].

English/Metric Conversion

Most of the world operates on the metric system. The United States is one of the few countries that still functions on the English system of measurement. By all accounts this situation will not continue indefinitely because the United States is committed to convert some day to the metric system. We see evidence of this trend everyday, even in the supermarket where groceries are packaged and their weights stated in both the English and the metric measures.

With an eye to this inevitable changeover, the HP-55 comes replete with several conversions, namely:

Key Number	English		Metric
3	Btu	⇄	J
4	lbm	⇄	Kg
5	lbf	⇄	Newtons
6	°F	⇄	°C
7	in	⇄	mm
8	ft	⇄	m
9	gal	⇄	l

These conversions are located on the keys [3] through [9]. To convert from left to right (English to metric) the prefix key [g] is pressed, and to convert from right to left (metric to English) the prefix key [f] must be used. Here are some simple conversion examples:

1. Convert 1,250 Btu's to joules.

   1250 [g] [Btu→J] : 1,318,819.82 joules

2. Convert a mass of 509 kilograms to pounds.

   509 [f] [lbm←kg] : 1,122.15 pounds

3. Convert a force of 123.45 Newtons to pounds.

   123.45 [f] [lbf←N] : 27.75 pounds

4. Convert 36 inches to millimeters.

   36 [g] [in→mm] : 914.40 millimeters

5. Convert 98.4°F to its equivalent Celsius temperature (centigrade).

   98.4 [g] [°F→°C] : 36.89°C

6. Convert 4,023 meters to feet.

   4023 [f] [ft←m] : 13,198.82 feet

7. Convert 26 liters to U.S. gallons.

   26 [f] [gal←l] : 6.87 gallons

Programming the HP-55

Using a programmable pocket calculator without exploiting its programmability is like living in poverty while having a bank account containing millions of dollars. Even though the HP-55 may be used effectively in the nonprogrammable mode, an appreciation of its uniqueness and power cannot be realized until it is used in its programming mode. Without further ado then we shall go ahead and write our first program.

The Radius of a Circle Problem

The formula relating the area of a circle to its radius is familiar to most people from their high school days. Just in case you have forgotten, the formula is

$$\text{Area} = \pi r^2$$

where

      r = the radius of the circle
      π = the constant pi ≈ 3.14159265

It is implicit in this relationship that if one knows the area of a circle, one can calculate the radius since, by simple algebra,

$$r = \sqrt{\text{Area}/\pi}$$

The problem we propose to solve now is to calculate r, given the area of a circle.

To calculate the value of r for a single value of the area, say, 58.97 square units, we would, of course, do this manually in the following manner.

Example 11:   Evaluate $r = \sqrt{\text{Area}/\pi}$

S	1	2	3	4	5	6
K	58.97	f	π	$\div$	f	$\sqrt{x}$
D	58.97	58.97	3.14	18.77	18.77	4.33

The reader might, with good reason, question why the area of 58.97 is not ENTERed before pressing the [f] [π] keys. The reason for this is that each time the [π] key is pressed the stack is automatically raised, thereby obviating the need to ENTER the number 58.97.

Referring again to the schematic in Example 11, it is clear that on the assumption that the value of the area is already in the display, steps 2 through 6 would have to be repeated *in exactly the same order* for every new value of the area. These steps, therefore, will constitute the body of the program that will be retained inside the calculator for as long as is necessary.

Program HP-55-1: Computing the Radius of a Circle Given Its Area

Instruction	Comments
f π	Enters approximation for pi into display, lifting the stack
$\div$	Area/π
f $\sqrt{x}$	$\sqrt{\text{Area}/\pi}$

These steps are now keyed into the calculator with the top right-hand switch in the middle position, PRGM, which stands for programming mode.

After keying in Program HP-55-1 (see step 3 in Schematic HP-55-1) the calculator is switched to RUN mode preparatory to running the program. In order to execute the program from its beginning, it is necessary to press [GTO] [0] [0]. After this is done the first data item may be keyed in. The program is then executed by pressing the Run/Stop key marked [R/S]. Almost immediately after this key is pressed, the first solution of 4.33 is automatically calculated by the program and displayed. Subsequent solutions may be calculated simply by keying in the value of the area and pressing [R/S].

It will be noticed that it is not necessary to reset the program to its beginning for these subsequent cases. You might indeed wonder why this is so. The answer to this question lies in the clever engineering with which the HP-55 is constructed.

Schematic HP-55-1

S	1	2	3	4
K	⎡ switch ⎤	⎡ slide ⎤	⎡key in steps⎤	⎡ slide ⎤
D	⎣on HP-55⎦	TIMER/PRGM/RUN	of Program	TIMER/PRGM/RUN
		⎣ switch to PRGM ⎦	⎣ HP-55-1 ⎦	⎣ switch to RUN ⎦

S	5	6	7	8	9
K	GTO	0	0	58.97	R/S
D	0.00	0.00	0.00	58.97	4.33
C		resets program pointer		1st area	1st
		to beginning of program		value	radius

S	10	11	12	13	
K	100	R/S	314	R/S	. . . etc.
D	100.	5.64	314.	10.00	
C	2nd area	2nd	3rd area	3rd radius	
	value	radius	value		

Program Memory

As you will recall, the HP-55 has 49 program memory steps, which are referred to as 01 through 49. Actually, it has another step known as location 00. However, this location is not available to the programmer for storing instructions. It actually contains a permanent halt instruction. Directly related to this feature is the fact that when the HP-55 is switched on, each of the locations 01–49 is automatically filled with a GTO 00 instruction. When the program instructions are keyed in, they overwrite these GTO 00 instructions. The location following the last keyed in instruction will therefore be, by default, GTO 00 (as will the remaining locations through 49). This is particularly convenient from a programming point of view since advantage may be taken of this GTO 00 instruction. It serves the dual purpose of automatically branching to location 00 to halt execution of the program and secondly to automatically recycle the program to its beginning for subsequent execution of the program using different data.

It will be realized by the reader that within Program HP-55-1, which has just been described, we have actually set up a loop, a feature which is intrinsic to all computer programming. In this program the loop is effected by means of the GTO instruction.

Permutations Problem

Students of probability will recall the frequency with which they had to calculate permutations. For those without any experience in this interesting subject, suffice it to say that given n objects, the number of ways these may be arranged r at a time is obtained by the formula

$$P_{n,r} = \frac{n!}{(n-r)!}$$

In order to explain what is implied by this formula, we can take a simple example. Suppose we have six index cards on each of which is written one of the first six letters of the alphabet. Now our task is to select from these six cards, say, any two cards. Here are the various possibilities:

AB	AC	AD	AE	AF
BA	BC	BD	BE	BF
CA	CB	CD	CE	CF
DA	DB	DC	DE	DF
EA	EB	EC	ED	EF
FA	FB	FC	FD	FE

You will notice that whenever dealing with permutations the order is important so that a selection of AB is different from a selection of BA. If you count up the above selections, you will find that it comes to exactly 30. This figure is arrived at mathematically by substituting 6 for the value of n and 2 for the value of r in the formula:

$$P_{n,r} = \frac{n!}{(n-r)!}$$

where n = 6
      r = 2

$$P_{n,r} = \frac{6!}{(6-2)!}$$

$$= \frac{6 \times 5 \times 4 \times 3 \times 2 \times 1}{4 \times 3 \times 2 \times 1}$$

$$= 6 \times 5$$

$$= 30$$

Example 12

S	1	2	3	4	5
K	6	f	x!	f	LAST x
D	6.	6.	720.00	720.00	6.00

S	6	7	8	9	10
K	2	—	f	x!	÷
D	2.	4.00	4.00	24.00	30.00

Advantage is taken of the LAST x register in which the value of n is still stored. Using this feature obviates the need to key in the value of n a second time for the computation of (n – r)!.

As you are probably aware, the steps indicated in the schematic in Example 12 form the essence of the program by which one can calculate the number of permutations, for any value of n and r, simply by keying in the value of n (maximum value of n on the HP-55 is 69) and the value of r of one's choosing.

Obviously the programmer must make provision for the keying in of these two data items at the appropriate time. The value of n may be keyed in at the beginning of each problem, which was done in a similar fashion with the various area values of Program HP-55-1. Advantage may be taken of the [R/S] key which, when used as an instruction in a program, stops its execution, permitting both for the reading of the display and for the keying in of any additional data as appropriate. Execution of the program may then by resumed by pressing the [R/S] key in RUN mode.

Here, then, is a program to compute $P_{n,r}$.

Program HP-55-2: Permutation

Instruction	Comments
f x!	Calculates n!
f LAST x	Recalls value of n from LAST x register to display, automatically lifting the stack
R/S	Halts program execution, permitting value of r to be keyed in
—	n − r
f x!	(n − r)!
÷	$P_{n,r} = n!/(n-r)!$

Just in case the reader has observed that there is no instruction following the division to loop back to the beginning of the program, he is respectfully reminded that, if the calculator was switched on prior to keying in this program, by default, a GTO 00 would be the next instruction.

When keying in Program HP-55-2, the reader's attention is drawn to the display which, when the calculator is switched to program mode, shows the program line number and the keycode corresponding to each instruction. It will be noticed that, in general, each separate keystroke occupies its own location in memory.

Here is what the display shows as each program instruction is keyed in.

	Display	
Keystroke	Line No.	Keycode
Switch to PRGM mode	00.	00
f	01.	31
x!	02.	43
f	03.	31
LAST x	04.	34
R/S	05.	84
—	06.	51
f	07.	31
x!	08.	43
÷	09.	81

Schematic HP-55-2

S	1	2	3	4	5	6	7
K	switch	switch to	key in steps	switch	GTO	0	0
D	on	PRGM	of Program	to RUN	0.00	0.00	0.00
	HP–55	mode	HP–55–2	mode			
C						reset program to beginning	

S	8	9	10	11	12
K	6	R/S	2	R/S	10
D	6.	6.00	2.	30.00	10.
C	n = 6	R/S initiates program execution	r = 2	R/S resumes program execution. Program halts showing $P_{6,2} = 30$	n = 10

S	13	14	15	
K	R/S	3	R/S	. . . etc.
D	10.00	3.	720.00	
C		r = 3	$P_{10,3} = 720$	

From the table on p. 98 it is clear that a prefix (in this case the f prefix) occupies a separate location in the HP-55's memory, as indeed does each of the remaining instructions.

Confining our attention for the moment to the keycode for the [f] prefix key, we notice that its code is 31. This is actually a matrix code that refers specifically to the [f] key. As you will readily observe, the [f] key is located in the third row down, first key in from the left of the keyboard. In a similar fashion, the factorial key, which has a keycode of 43, is to be found at the intersection of the fourth row, third column. Of course, the same keycode also indicates the enter exponent key [EEX]. Ambiguity is avoided, however, by the prefix — if one precedes it or not. An ability to read these keycodes and to relate them to the specific instructions of a program can be most helpful, particularly in the editing and debugging stages. In the remaining programs illustrating the use of the HP-55, we shall list the keystrokes according to the way they are stored in memory.

Pearson's Correlation Coefficient Problem

When we were discussing the manual operation of the HP-55, we saw how easy it was to find the mean and standard deviation of one or two sets of scores by using the [Σ+], [$\bar{x}$], and [s] keys. You may also recall that the [Σ+] key affects several different registers that store $n, \Sigma x, \Sigma y, \Sigma xy, \Sigma x^2$, and Σy^2. This proves to be of particular value to the statistician who would like to calculate the correlation coefficient between two sets of scores. This coefficient may vary in value from –1 to +1 where a correlation of –1 indicates a direct inverse correlation and a correlation of +1 a direct correlation. A coefficient of zero indicates that, according to the data, no correlation exists between the two variables. A formula used for the computation of this coefficient sometimes called Pearson's Correlation Coefficient is:

$$r_{x,y} = (n\Sigma xy - \Sigma x \Sigma y)/\sqrt{[n\Sigma x^2 - (\Sigma x)^2]\,[n\Sigma y^2 - (\Sigma y)^2]}$$

Even though this formula might look somewhat intimidating at first glance, a close scrutiny of it will reveal the fact that all of the summations indicated are calculated automatically by the [Σ+] key.

By way of recapitulation, the effect of pressing the [Σ+] key is:

n is accumulated in register R.0
Σx is accumulated in register R.1
Σx^2 is accumulated in register R.2
Σy is accumulated in register R.3
Σy^2 is accumulated in register R.4
Σxy is accumulated in register R.5

In view of the fact that so many accumulations are done automatically, the amount of work left to be done by the programmer becomes minimal.

Program HP-55-3: Pearson's Correlation Coefficient

Location	Instruction	Comments
01	RCL	
02	•	Recalls n from R.0 to display
03	0	
04	RCL	
05	•	Recalls Σxy to display, pushing value of n
06	5	from the x register into the y register
07	X	$n\Sigma xy$
08	RCL	
09	•	Σx
10	1	
11	RCL	
12	•	Σy
13	3	
14	X	$\Sigma x\Sigma y$
15	—	$n\Sigma xy - \Sigma x\Sigma y$
16	RCL	
17	•	n
18	0	
19	RCL	
20	•	Σx^2
21	2	
22	X	$n\Sigma x^2$
23	RCL	
24	•	Σx
25	1	
26	g	
27	x^2	$(\Sigma x)^2$
28	—	$n\Sigma x^2 - (\Sigma x)^2$
29	RCL	
30	•	n
31	0	
32	RCL	
33	•	Σy^2
34	3	
35	X	$n\Sigma y^2$

Program HP-55-3 (cont'd)

Location	Instruction	Comments
36	RCL ⎫	
37	. ⎬	Σy
38	3 ⎭	
39	g	
40	x^2	$(\Sigma y)^2$
41	−	$n\Sigma y^2 - (\Sigma y)^2$
42	×	$[n\Sigma x^2 - (\Sigma x)^2]\,[n\Sigma y^2 - (\Sigma y)^2]$
43	f	
44	$\sqrt{x}$	$\sqrt{[n\Sigma x^2 - (\Sigma x)^2]\,[n\Sigma y^2 - (\Sigma y)^2]}$
45	÷	$r_{x,y} = (n\Sigma xy - \Sigma x \Sigma y)/$

$$\sqrt{[n\Sigma x^2 - (\Sigma x)^2]\,[n\Sigma y^2 - (\Sigma y)^2]}$$

This program assumes that each x_i and y_i is keyed in using the [Σ+] key prior to running the program. The program comes to a halt with the value of the correlation coefficient in the display.

One of the most commonly talked about correlations is that of height and weight since, in general, the taller a person is the more he weighs, and one would expect a positive and relatively high correlation between these two variables. On a commercial level, one would expect that the sale of soda would increase during the hot summer months and decrease in the colder months. Regardless of the two variables that are under investigation, the procedure adopted in keying in the corresponding data items will now be explained.

Suppose we have the following list of data for which we would like to determine a correlation coefficient. Even though the number of pairs of data should never, for statistical reasons, be less than 30, we shall confine ourselves to five pairs merely to illustrate the principles involved.

Data Pair	x	y
1.	23	31
2.	13	12
3.	22	15
4.	29	33
5.	48	51

Assuming all of the registers are clear, which would be the case if the machine were just switched on, the first y value, 31, is keyed in and ENTERed. Now the corresponding x value, 23, is keyed in and the [Σ+] key pressed. The same procedure is followed for keying in the remaining four pairs of data. After each pressing of the [Σ+] key—that is, after each pair has been keyed in—the current value of n is automatically displayed.

Schematic HP-55-3

S	1	2	3	4	5
K	⎡ switch ⎤	⎡ switch ⎤	⎡key in steps⎤	⎡ switch ⎤	GTO
D	on	to PRGM	of Program	to RUN	0.00
	⎣HP–55–3⎦	mode ⎦	HP–55–3 ⎦	mode ⎦	

S	6	7	8	9	10
K	0	0	31	ENTER↑	23
D	0.00	0.00	31.	31.00	23.
C			y_1		x_1

S	11	12	13	14	15
K	Σ+	12	ENTER↑	13	Σ+
D	1.00	12.	12.00	13.	2.00
C	1st	y_2		x_2	2nd
	data				data
	pair				pair

S	16	17	18	19	20
K	15	ENTER↑	22	Σ+	33
D	15.	15.00	22.	3.00	33.
C	y_3		x_3	3rd	y_4
				data	
				pair	

S	21	22	23	24	25
K	ENTER↑	29	Σ+	51	ENTER↑
D	33.00	29.	4.00	51.	51.00
C		x_4	4th	y_5	
			data		
			pair		

S	26	27	28		
K	48	Σ+	R/S		
D	48.	5.00	.94		
C	x_5		correlation		
			coefficient		

The calculated correlation of 0.94 is, of course, an extremely high correlation. If a new set of data is to be correlated, care should be taken to clear R.0 through R.5 before keying in the new data. The key sequence

$$[g] \ [CL.R]$$

automatically clears storage registers R.0 through R.9 and the stack in one fell swoop.

The Sum of the Reciprocals Problem

Suppose we wanted to write a program to calculate the sum of the series

$$S = (1/1) + (1/2) + (1/3) + \ldots + (1/n)$$

for any value of n. We notice that in this sequence the successive denominators consist of the consecutive integers 1 through n. A loop can be set up where a counter, initially set equal to one, is incremented by one, at which point its reciprocal is calculated and accumulated. The loop should be terminated after the counter has reached the value of n. When it reaches n its reciprocal must be calculated and added to the accumulated sum.

Since the logic to this program is a little more difficult to follow than the previous program, we are presenting a flowchart that might make for easier understanding of the program, as shown in Fig. 6-2.

As is clear from the flowchart in Fig. 6-2, it is necessary to make a decision based on whether the value of the counter is equal to n. The HP-55 provides the user with the ability for making such decisions directly in a program. This is done by means of one of the two conditional branch instructions located above the [GTO] key. The f $x \leqslant y$ instructions pose the question: Are the contents of the x register less than or equal to the contents of the y register? Similarly, the g $x = y$ instruction compares the contents of the x register and the y register for equality. In either case if the result of the test is false—that is, the specific condition is *not* met—then the next location in memory immediately following the test instruction is automatically skipped. If, on the other hand, the test condition *is* met—that is, the result of the test is true—then execution proceeds in the normal manner with the next instruction in program memory.

As an example of the "less than or equal to" test instruction, let us consider the following sequence of instructions:

Location	Instruction
.	.
.	.
.	.
22	f
23	x $\leqslant$ y
24	1/x
25	y^x
.	.
.	.
.	.

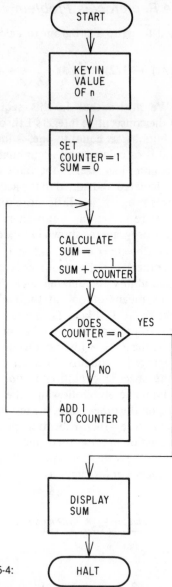

Fig. 6-2 Flowchart HP-55-4:
Sum of the Reciprocals

Let us assume that the x register contains the value 5.0 and the y register contains the value 1.6. Upon execution of the sequence of instructions (shown in the table on p. 103), the conditional test instruction f x < y is first encountered. Since the test proves false—that is, the contents of the x register is not less than or equal to that of the y register, the instruction in location 24 that takes the reciprocal of the value in the display is automatically skipped, and execution resumes at location 25, where $(1.6)^5$ is calculated.

For those situations where an unconditional transfer is required from one point in a program to another, the GTO instruction may be used. For example, the instruction GTO 43 will transfer control to location 43 in memory. Execution of the program will continue in the normal way with the instruction contained in location 43. Naturally, only the numbers 00 through 49 may be specified in a GTO instruction. A "go to" to location 9 must be written as

$$GTO\ 09$$

and similarly for all the locations less than 10.

Having covered all the necessary information required for the solution of this problem, we present the following program to calculate the sum of the reciprocals of the first n integers.

Program HP-55-4: Sum of the Reciprocals

Location	Instruction	Comments
01	STO	Stores keyed in value of n into register 1
02	1	
03	1	
04	STO	Initializes counter in register 2 to one
05	2	
06	0	
07	STO	Initializes sum in register 3 to zero
08	3	
09	RCL	Recalls counter to display
10	2	
11	1/x	1/counter
12	STO	
13	+	Adds 1/counter to sum in register 3
14	3	
15	RCL	Recalls counter to display
16	2	
17	RCL	Recalls n to display, pushing value of counter
18	1	from x register into y register
19	g	
20	x = y	Does the counter equal n?
21	GTO 27	Yes; then go to location 27

Program HP-55-4 (cont'd)

Location	Instruction	Comments
22	1	
23	STO	No; add 1 to counter in register 2
24	+	
25	2	
26	GTO 09	And loop back to location 09
27	RCL	Recalls sum to display; GTO 00 instruction
28	3	in location 29 halts program execution

Schematic HP-55-4

S	1	2	3	4	5	6
K	switch	switch	key in steps	switch	GTO	0
D	on	to PRGM	of Program	to RUN	0.00	0.00
	HP–55	mode	HP–55–4	mode		

S	7	8	9	10	11	12
K	0	5	R/S	2	R/S	100
D	0.00	5.	2.28	2.	1.50	100.
C		$n = 5$	$(1/1) + (1/2)$ $+ (1/3) + (1/4)$ $+ (1/5)$	$n = 2$	$(1/1) + (1/2)$	$n = 100$

S	13	14	15	
K	R/S	FIX	9	. . . etc.
D	5.19	5.19	5.187377520	
C	$\sum_{i=1}^{100} 1/i$			

Debugging and Editing Programs on the HP-55

The programmer is yet to be born who writes anything but a nontrivial program without making a mistake of one kind or another. One should not be too sensitive about creating errors, since this seems to be intrinsic to programming. It does not necessarily mean that a program containing errors is completely useless. Oftentimes all that is necessary is a slight modification to the program to make it work properly. As much patience is required as are programming skills. The HP-55 comes equipped with several features to help you to both debug and edit your programs quickly and efficiently. These features are:

1. The ability to display the instruction stored in any particular location in program memory.
2. The ability to replace any instruction in memory by another one.
3. The ability to single step in a forward or backward direction through a program using the [SST] or [BST] keys.

Advantage of the single step key may be taken in both program and run modes. In program mode pressing the [SST] key has the effect of automatically displaying the *next* location number in memory along with its corresponding instruction keycode.

Successive presses of the [SST] key enable the programmer to examine each instruction step by step.

In RUN mode, the [SST] key may be used to trace through the execution of a program. A single pressing of this key has the effect of *executing* the next location in line in program memory. Thus one can trace through a program by successively pressing the [SST] key.

CHAPTER SEVEN
THE PROGRAMMABLE HEWLETT-PACKARD 65

The HP-65 programmable pocket calculator, manufactured by Hewlett-Packard, represented a major technological breakthrough with its release in 1973. The miniaturization that made possible such a small, personal computer was a direct spin-off of Space Age technology.

The development of the HP-65 took no less than two years of concentrated effort and exploited the resourcefulness of Hewlett-Packard's engineers and technicians to the fullest. According to Hewlett-Packard, the model HP-65 was developed to satisfy the demand for easily used, personal computing power in portable form. It resembles the standard computer in two important respects: (1) it can operate on a stored program and (2) it is able to jump to different parts of the program, depending upon the results of decisions incorporated in the program.

Besides the standard arithmetic, scientific, and engineering functions, the HP-65 is fully programmable with a 100-step memory, has nine addressable registers, and has the ability to read and store programs from and to small magnetic cards.

This 11-ounce wonder has 51 preprogrammed functions, which are accessed directly on the keyboard.

A picture of the HP-65 is shown in Fig. 7-1.

Manual Operation of the HP-65

The user must remember that the HP-65, as with all the other Hewlett-Packard calculators, operates in Reverse Polish Notation (RPN). Therefore, we should not be surprised by the absence of the equals key and the presence of the key marked [ENTER↑]. In order to conserve space, some of the keys have a triple function. To operate a blue-colored function shown on the lower surface of the button, one would first press the blue key labeled [g]. To access the function indicated in gold above a key, the gold shift key labeled [f] is first pressed.

For those who would like to review our discussion of Reverse Polish Notation and the operation of the four-register stack, we would respectively refer you to Chaps. 2 and 4. Meanwhile, we will evaluate some simple expressions in manual mode before describing the manner in which programs are written and recorded.

Fig. 7-1 HP-65 (*Courtesy* Hewlett-Packard Company)

Example 1: Evaluate $[(3.2 \times 7)/(28 - 6.3)] + \sqrt{3.87}$

S	1	2	3	4	5	6
K	3.2	ENTER↑	7	×	28	ENTER↑
D	3.2	3.20	7.	22.40	28.	28.00

S	7	8	9	10	11	12
K	6.3	−	÷	3.87	f	$\sqrt{x}$
D	6.3	21.70	1.03	3.87	3.87	1.97

S	13
K	+
D	3.00

Example 2:　Evaluate $[(\sin 23.4°/\cos 14.97°) + \log 123]^2$

S	1	2	3	4	5	6
K	23.4	f	sin	14.97	f	cos
D	23.4	23.40	0.40	14.97	14.97	0.97

S	7	8	9	10	11	12
K	÷	123	f	log	+	f^{-1}
D	0.41	123.	123.00	2.09	2.50	2.50

S	13
K	$\sqrt{x}$
D	6.26

When the HP-65 is switched on, it is automatically set to degree mode. However, if the user finds this fact difficult to remember, he is at liberty to convert the calculator to degree mode by pressing the buttons marked [g] [DEG] before commencing. Once the expression within the brackets is calculated, it is squared by means of the keys labeled [f⁻¹] and [√x]. The gold key marked [f⁻¹] has the effect of calculating the *inverse* of those functions printed in gold above many of the keys.

Thus to find the inverse sine, one would press the [f⁻¹] followed by the sin key (the digit 4 key), and similarly for the other functions.

Polar Coordinates

Example 3:　Convert the rectangular coordinates (2, 3) into polar coordinates.

S	1	2	3	4
K	3	ENTER↑	2	f
D	3.	3.00	2.	2.00

S	5	6	7
K	R → P	g	x ≷ y
D	3.61	3.61	56.31

There are various points that have to be clarified in Example 3. For one, the rule for keying in rectangular coordinates is to ENTER the y-coordinate first, followed by the x-coordinate. Secondly, the gold [R→P] key effects the conversion from the two coordinates just keyed in to their polar coordinates. The value of r is sent to the display while the value of 0 resides in the y register. Once the value of r is noted, the [x ≷ y] key is pressed, which sends the value of θ to the display. Thus we find that the point whose rectangular coordinates are (2, 3) translates into the point (3.61, 56.31°) in the polar coordinate system.

Example 4:   Convert (4, 50°) into rectangular coordinates.

S	*1*	*2*	*3*	*4*
K	50	ENTER↑	4	f⁻¹
D	50	50.00	4.	4.00

S	*5*	*6*	*7*
K	R → P	g	x ≥ y
D	2.57	2.57	3.06

In the above example where we are converting from polar to rectangular coordinates, the value of θ is ENTERed first, followed by the value of r. This time, since we want to go in the *reverse* direction indicated by the [R→P] key (rectangular to polar) the inverse button [f⁻¹] must be pressed first. This places the x-coordinate in the display and the y-coordinate, which is in the y register, is accessed by pressing the [x≥y] key.

From Example 4 it is clear that (4, 50°) is equivalent to (2.57, 3.06) when expressed in rectangular coordinates.

Angle Conversions

Ordinarily, an angle may be expressed in degrees, minutes, and seconds, or alternatively, in degrees and decimal fractions of a degree. For example, 35°30′ is equivalent to 35.5°. One may convert from one form to the other quite readily on the HP-65, as shown in the following examples.

Example 5:   Convert 29.2° to degrees, minutes, and seconds.

S	*1*	*2*	*3*	*4*	*5*	*6*
K	DSP	.	4	29.2	f	→ D.MS
D	0.00	0.00	0.0000	29.2	29.2000	29.1200

The angle 29.2° is found to be equivalent to 29°12′.

The reader will probably have noticed that every time the calculator is switched on, the display is automatically set to two decimal places. Frequently, this is very useful, especially when we are not interested in superfluous decimal digits. There are occasions, however, where it is necessary to override this automatic, rounded two-decimal place setting. When dealing with degrees, minutes, and seconds, it is essential to extend the accuracy of the display to four decimal places because an angle expressed in degrees, minutes, and seconds is displayed as follows on the HP-65:

$$D.MS$$

where
     D = the unit degrees
     M = a two-digit number representing the minutes
     S = a two-digit number representing the seconds

For example:

D.MS Representation	Equivalent
12.3456	12° 34′56″
5.4800	5° 48′0″
13.0012	13° 0′12″
0.0010	0° 0′10″

The key that affects the way numbers are displayed on the HP-65 is labeled [DSP]. If this key is pressed, followed by a digit from 0 to 9, it will have the effect of displaying numbers in scientific notation, with the mantissa rounded to the designated number of decimal places—not that this is required in this instance. If the [DSP] key is pressed and is followed by the pressing of the [·] key, and then any digit from 0 to 9, the display will be fixed with the designated number of decimal places. Such a setting will remain in force until either it is changed in the same way described above or the calculator is switched off.

Example 6: Convert 23°46′2″ to decimal degrees. (Assume that the display is still fixed at four decimal digits.)

S	1	2	3
K	23.4602	f^{-1}	→ D.MS
D	23.4602	23.4602	23.7672

From this schematic, it is clear that 23°46′2″ (notice that 2 seconds *must* be keyed in as the two-digit number 02) is equivalent to 23.7672°.

To add degrees, minutes, and seconds the [D.MS +] key is used in the following manner.

Example 7: Evaluate 29°13′48″ + 22°48′17″ − 18°3″

S	1	2	3	4	5	6
K	DSP	·	4	29.1348	ENTER↑	22.4817
D	0.00	0.00	0.0000	29.1348	29.1348	22.4817

S	7	8	9	10	11
K	f	D.MS+	18.0003	f^{-1}	D.MS+
D	22.4817	52.0205	18.0003	18.0003	34.0202

Notice in Example 7 that the display is first set to four decimal places. The first angle is entered followed by the second angle. These angles are added by pressing the prefix key [f] followed by the [D.MS +] key, which gives the result of 52°2′5″. From this value, 18°3″ is to be subtracted. Notice how this last angle is keyed in—18.0003. The inverse prefix key [f^{-1}] is pressed, followed by the [D.MS +] key, which carries out the required subtraction and displays the final result of 34°2′2″.

Since there is a natural correspondence between degrees, minutes, and seconds in angular measure and hours, minutes, and seconds in time measure, the [→D.MS] and [D.MS +] keys also can be used with the latter form of measure.

Example 8:   Evaluate sin⁻¹ [1/(ln 12.34 − cos 31°)] as an angle expressed in degrees, minutes, and seconds.

S	1	2	3	4	5	6
K	DSP	•	4	12.34	f	LN
D	0.00	0.00	0.0000	12.34	12.3400	2.5128

S	7	8	9	10	11	12
K	31	f	cos	—	g	1/x
D	31.	31.0000	0.8572	1.6557	1.6557	0.6040

S	13	14	15	16
K	f⁻¹	sin	f	→ D.MS
D	0.6040	37.1556	37.1556	37.0920

The HP-65 provides the user with the option of performing operations on angles expressed in radians or grads, in addition to degrees. It is pointed out that when the calculator is switched on it "defaults" to degree mode. Thus any angle either keyed in or sent to the display is expressed in degrees. If it is desired to work with angles expressed in either radians or grads, pressing either the [RAD] or [GRD] key will treat all subsequent angles in the appropriate unit of measure. This will remain in effect until either the mode is changed manually or the machine is switched off.

Example 9:   Evaluate cos⁻¹ [π·² − (0.8)⁴] as an angle expressed in radians, rounded to two decimal places.

S	1	2	3	4	5	6	7	8
K	g	RAD	g	π	.2	g	yˣ	.8
D	0.00	0.00	0.00	3.14	.2	0.20	1.26	.8

S	9	10	11	12	13	14	15
K	ENTER↑	4	g	yˣ	—	f⁻¹	cos
D	0.80	4.	4.00	0.41	0.85	0.85	0.56

The calculator is set to radian mode at the outset, after which the expression in brackets is calculated. The constant π is raised to the power 0.2 by means of the [yˣ] key, and 0.8 is raised to the power 4 by the same method. After the subtraction is done, the arc cosine is obtained by following the [f⁻¹] inverse key with the [cos] key. Thus we arrive at the answer of 0.56 radians.

Factorial

The factorial of a positive integer n is the product of the consecutive integers from 1 to n. For example, the factorial of 5, written 5!, is

$$1 \times 2 \times 3 \times 4 \times 5 = 120$$

The factorial of any positive integer to 69 may be computed directly on the HP-65 by keying in the specific number and pressing the key marked [n!], which must be preceded by the shift key [g]. By definition, the factorial of zero is one, and this is indeed what the calculator returns. Any attempt to compute the factorial of a number other than a positive integer, less than or equal to 69, will cause a flashing zero to appear in the display.

The factorial function finds its greatest use in the area of mathematics known as statistics, which includes probability, permutations, and combinations.

Separation of a Decimal Number to Its Integer and Fractional Parts

It is sometimes useful to separate a decimal number that appears in the display into its integer portion and its fractional portion. (In programming mode this can be of extreme importance.) Both of these operations are possible on the HP-65, using the key labeled [INT].

If it is the integer portion that is required, pressing the [f] shift key followed by the [INT] key replaces the number in the display by the integer portion of the original number, retaining the sign of that number. In a similar way, preceding the pressing of the [INT] button by the [f⁻¹] shift key replaces the number in the display by its fractional portion, once again retaining the sign of the original number.

Example 10:   Illustration of INT function

S	1	2	3	4	5	6
K	123.4567	f	INT	424.55	f⁻¹	INT
D	123.4567	123.4567	123.	424.55	424.55	0.55

In Example 10 we have truncated the original number 123.4567, leaving 123. in the display. With the new number (424.55) keyed in, pressing the inverse INT function keys replaces this number in the display by the fractional portion 0.55.

The Absolute Value Function

To compute the absolute value of a number in the display, one merely presses the [ABS] key, preceded by the [g] shift key. This has the effect of replacing the original number in the display by the absolute value of that number (the number without its negative sign, if it had one).

Example 11:   Illustration of absolute value

S	1	2	3	4	5	6	7
K	5	CHS	g	ABS	22.9	g	ABS
D	5.	—5.	—5.00	5.00	22.9	22.9	22.90

Octal to Decimal Conversion

Although we customarily express numbers in base 10, numbers can in fact be expressed in any base. In computer science, it is often necessary to express numbers in base 8, which is known as the octal number system. The HP-65 permits the user to convert a decimal integer in the display into its octal number representation and, conversely, to convert an integer in the display expressed in octal notation into its base 10 equivalent. As in previous examples, the appropriate shift key has to be used before the [→OCT] key is pressed.

Example 12:

1. Convert 124_{10} into its base 8 (octal) equivalent.
2. Convert 7732_8 into its base 10 (decimal) equivalent.

S	1	2	3	4	5	6	7	8	9
K	DSP	.	0	124	f	→ OCT	7732	f^{-1}	→ OCT
D	0.00	0.00	0.	124.	124.	174.	7732.	7732.	4058.

The LaST x Key

Immediately following any calculation, the previous contents of the x register are automatically saved in a register known as the *last x* register. The contents of this register is accessed by pressing the key labeled [LST x], which on the HP-65 is the lower case [0] key. In other words, it must be accessed by prefixing the [LST x] key with the blue [g] key. This feature could be valuable when one is confronted by the following situation. If, during the course of a long calculation, the wrong operation was performed, the situation may be corrected without having to restart the entire calculation, as illustrated in the following simplified example. In this example, the intention was to calculate 103 × 5. To our consternation, however, we find that we have inadvertently calculated 103 ÷ 5. After all, none of us is perfect. The situation may be corrected in the following way.

	Keystrokes	Display	Explanation
1.	103 [ENTER↑] 5 [÷]	20.60	Oops! I meant [x] not [÷].
2.	[g] [LST x]	5.00	Retrieves the last x register value
3.	[x]	103.00	Reverses the wrong division
4.	[g] [LST x]	5.00	Retrieves last number
5.	[x]	515.00	Correct result sent to display

It is pointed out that the last x feature can be of great utilitarian value in many different situations. For example, in the sequence

[f] [INT]
[g] [LST x]
[f⁻¹] [INT]

a number in the display can be separated into its integer and fractional portions not only in the minimum number of steps but also without having to key in the original number again.

The HP-65's Nine Addressable Memory Registers

By this time, having worked through several elementary arithmetic type problems, the reader will have become somewhat familiar with the operation of the four-register stack. The stack, it will be clear, acts as a special type of storage facility, saving and retrieving intermediate results as needed. Sometimes it is more convenient to save the result of a calculation in special registers from which they may subsequently be recalled when needed. The HP-65 has nine such memory registers, referred to as R1 through R9, each of which is addressable. Once a number has been stored in any one of these registers, it remains there until it is either replaced or the machine is switched off. Even when it is recalled to the display, a copy of it is still retained in the memory register. These registers are typically used to accumulate sums, to store constants or intermediate results, or to act as counters.

To store a number from the display into a register, say R4, one presses the key [STO] followed by the number 4. This has the effect of *copying* the value in the display into memory register 4, leaving the display unaltered. To recall to the display a number previously stored in a memory register, say R7, one presses the key labeled [RCL], which is followed by the appropriate register number—in this case 7. This has the effect of transferring a copy of that memory register into the display, leaving the value in the register intact.

An important secondary effect of pressing the [RCL] key is that when the recalled number is transferred to the x register, all previous contents of the stack are pushed up.

Register Arithmetic on the HP-65

Normal arithmetic operations on the HP-65 involve the x and y stack registers, the result of the operation being placed in the x register for display purposes. However, frequently it is desired to perform arithmetic operations on the contents of one of the nine memory registers. Of course, this can be done indirectly by recalling the contents of the register to the display, performing the required operation, and storing the result back into the register. However, this rather circuitous route may be circumvented by taking advantage of a particularly useful feature of the HP-65, by means of which the four standard arithmetic operations may be performed directly on any of the nine memory registers.

For example, to add 1 to the contents of register 3, one merely keys in the sequence

$$1 \ [STO] \ [+] \ 3$$

Here are some further examples of direct register arithmetic:

Sequence	Comments
3 [STO] [÷] 8	Divides contents of memory register 8 by 3
1.6 [STO] [−] 2	Subtracts 1.6 from memory register 2
66 [STO] [×] 5	Multiplies memory register 5 by 66

In each case the result of the arithmetic operation replaces the previous contents of the particular memory register.

This concludes our discussion on how to operate the HP-65 in manual mode. The reason why we have not as yet described all of the keys in the HP-65 is because many of them are concerned only with operation of the calculator in program mode. So without further ado, we shall proceed to the section on programming the HP-65.

Programming the HP-65

When writing a program for the HP-65, one must realize that the only tools that are available are the functions found on the keyboard and one's own ingenuity. There is virtually no limit to the variety and intricacy of programs that can be written.

The wide selection of function keys on the HP-65, combined with the branching and testing features that are also available, have the combined effect of making possible highly sophisticated programs. It is not difficult to write programs that will cause the calculator to compute for many hours on end. The major restriction of which the user of an HP-65 must be aware is that no program may be longer than 100 steps. This is not to suggest that only trivial programs can be written. On the contrary, programs of considerable complexity may be written within this limitation.

Computation of x^3 Problem

For our first illustration we will write a program that computes a simple function that is not found on the HP-65's keyboard. This program will compute x^3, for any keyed in value of x. This is admittedly a rather simplistic problem, but our major concern at the moment is to learn how to write a program for the HP-65 rather than to solve some profound mathematical problem.

How would we solve this problem manually on the HP-65? One way would be to resort to the following sequence of instructions:

1. Key number into display
2. [ENTER↑]
3. [ENTER↑]
4. [x]
5. [x]

The above sequence of instructions is fine for calculating the function x^3 for a single value of x. If we had a whole series of numbers whose cubes we wished to obtain, it would be necessary ordinarily to execute these four instructions (2 through 5) repeatedly for each value of x. However, these steps may be incorporated into a program, which will relieve the user of the chore of having to physically execute these instructions manually for each value of x.

In essence, here is the body of the program to accomplish our task:

ENTER↑

ENTER↑

x

x

In order to use these instructions as a working program, they must be "sandwiched" between two instructions that identify the sequence as a function.

The first assigns a name to the function. There are five possible labels (names) that we may select: A, B, C, D, or E. Let us arbitrarily select A. The instruction LBL A when inserted before the above sequence serves as a means of identifying this function program.

A function program must always conclude with an RTN instruction, which acts as a terminator to the program, halting program execution and returning control to the keyboard.

Here then is the complete program to compute the value of x^3 for an unlimited series of values of x.

Program HP-65-1: Computation of x^3

Step Number	Instruction	Comments
01	LBL A	Assign the label A to the function
02	ENTER↑	Copies value in display into y register
03	ENTER↑	Value of x is now in x, y, and z registers
04	x	Calculates x^2
05	x	Calculates x^3
06	RTN	Stops program, returning control to the keyboard

Keying the Function into Memory

1. On the top right-hand corner of the unit is a switch labeled W/PRGM-RUN. Set this switch to W/PRGM.
2. Press the [f] [PRGM] keys to clear the memory.
3. Press the following keys *in the order shown.* This enters the program into the calculator's memory.

[LBL] [A] [ENTER↑] [ENTER↑] [x] [x] [RTN]

No matter how careful we have been in devising a program, there is no guarantee that it accomplishes its purpose. Experience has shown that one of the most common characteristics of computer programming is the seeming inevitability of mistakes occurring in the program. These may be mistakes of logic, errors of keying in information, or whatever. The safest procedure is to check out the program thoroughly once it has been keyed in before relying on results. In order to do this for the above program, the following is suggested.

Running the Program

1. Switch W/PRGM-RUN to RUN.
2. Key in any value of x and press the label key [A]. The cube of the number should now appear automatically in the display. Some typical examples are shown in the following schematic.

Schematic HP-65-1

S	1	2	3	4	5
K	switch	key in steps	press	switch to	1
D	to	of Program	f PRGM	RUN mode	1.
	W/PRGM	HP–65–1			

S	6	7	8	9	10
K	A	3	A	2.5	A
D	1.00	3.	27.00	2.5	15.62

S	11	12	13
K	3.98	CHS	A
D	3.98	−3.98	−63.04

The astute reader might question why the program was written in the way shown rather than advantage being taken of the [y^x] key. The fact of the matter is that this second method would certainly work, but only for positive values of x. The reason for this is that the [y^x] key uses logarithms internally, and one cannot take the logarithm of a negative number. If this is nevertheless attempted, the display will flash on and off, indicating an invalid operation.

Thus we have written our first successful program on the HP-65. Wouldn't it be a good idea to save this program for all time? Here is the way to record the function on a magnetic strip.

1. Select a blank magnetic card, several of which are supplied with the calculator. A picture of a magnetic card is shown in Fig. 7-2.
2. Switch the calculator to W/PRGM.
3. Pass magnetic card through the calculator slot provided, as shown in Fig. 7-3.

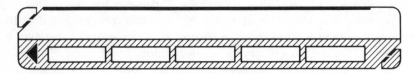

Fig. 7-2 Magnetic card

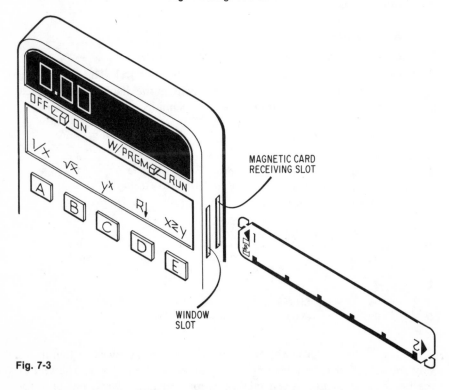

MAGNETIC CARD
RECEIVING SLOT

WINDOW
SLOT

Fig. 7-3

The action of inserting the card through the receiving slot initiates a tiny electric motor in the calculator that drives the card through the calculator to the other side from where it emerges a second or two later. The program will now have been automatically written on the blank magnetic card.

Since the intention is to preserve this program for posterity, it may be protected from subsequent erasure by clipping off the upper left-hand corner of the card. Once this corner is clipped, passing the card through the calculator subsequently in W/PRGM mode will prevent the card from being overwritten. A special internal device detects the clipped corner, thus disabling the writing mechanism.

Running a Recorded Program

Once a program is recorded on a magnetic card, it is a good idea to manually write the name or purpose of the program for future reference. This may be done in the space provided along the top edge of the card. The five rectangular boxes on the lower half of the card are intended to record the role played by each individual function. In our particular case where we have used just one function labeled A, we might write the following, as shown in Fig. 7-4.

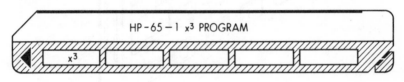

HP-65-1 x^3 PROGRAM

Fig. 7-4

Let us suppose that at some time later we want to run this same program again in order to calculate the cubes of another series of values. In order to do so the following procedure should be followed:

1. Set W/PRGM-RUN switch to RUN.
2. Slide the magnetic card through the receiving slot until it is engaged by the motor and exits the slot. The program will now have been copied (read) from the card into the calculator's memory.
3. Place card in window slot for identification purposes, as shown in Fig. 7-5.

Since the program is now stored in the calculator's memory, it may be run as described on page 119 under the heading "Running the Program."

Area of a Circle Problem

The area of a circle is defined as

$$\text{Area} = \pi \, r^2$$

where r = the radius of the circle. To calculate the area of a circle manually for any specific radius, say 5.29, the following sequence of keystrokes may be used.

Example 13

S	1	2	3	4	5	6
K	5.29	ENTER↑	x	g	π	x
D	5.29	5.29	27.98	27.98	3.14	87.91

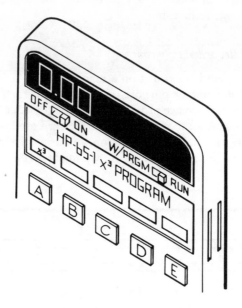

Fig. 7-5

In order to convert Example 13 into an acceptable program on the HP-65, we have to once again assign a label name to our function and terminate the program with an RTN instruction. Here is the complete program to calculate the area of a circle for as many values of r as are needed. This time we have arbitrarily selected B as the label name for our function.

Program HP-65-2: Area of a Circle

Step Number	Instruction	Comments
01	LBL B	Assigns the label name B to the function
02	ENTER↑	Copies keyed in value of r into y register
03	X	Calculates r^2
04	g π	Places value for π into display, pushing value of r^2 into y register
05	X	Calculates πr^2
06	RTN	Logical end of program

By way of a reminder, before keying in this program the reader should clear the calculator's memory by pressing [f] [PRGM] with the machine in W/PRGM mode.

While keying in the program steps, it might be of interest to the user to notice what transpires in the display each time an instruction is keyed in. For the benefit of the reader who does not have a calculator, we append below the correspondence between the keys and the display code.

	Key	Display
1.	LBL	23
2.	B	12
3.	ENTER↑	41
4.	X	71
5.	g	35
6.	π	02
7.	X	71
8.	RTN	24

It will be noticed that when the [LBL] key is pressed the number 23 appears in the display. This display code of 23 signifies that the key marked [LBL] is located in the second row down from the top of the calculator, third key along. Similarly the key B has a corresponding display code of 12, indicating first row, second key. In a like fashion, all of the keys have a corresponding numeric display that unambiguously specifies its location on the keyboard.

It will be noticed that the numeric display for π is 02. The reason for this is that each of the numeric keys (0 through 9) has as its display code that corresponding digit (preceded by a zero). The π function has the display code of 02 because it is one of the two functions associated with the digit 2 key. Ambiguity is avoided because it is preceded by the appropriate prefix key.

It should be borne in mind that each separate display code listed above occupies a sequential location in the calculator's 100 program step memory. Thus it is clear that the above program occupies 8 of the 100 locations.

Use of these display codes will be made later on when we discuss means of locating and correcting an error in a program.

Schematic HP-65-2

S	1	2	3	4	5	6
K	⌜ switch ⌝	⌜ key in steps ⌝	⌜ press ⌝	⌜ switch ⌝	3	B
D	to	of Program	⌊ f PRGM ⌋	to RUN	3.	28.27
	⌊ W/PRGM ⌋	HP-65-2 ⌋		mode ⌋		

S	7	8	9	10	11	12
K	4.63	B	22.69	B	5.29	B
D	4.63	67.35	22.69	1617.41	5.29	27.98

Running the Area of a Circle Program

After the program has been keyed in, the calculator is switched to RUN mode. Schematic HP-65-2 on the previous page illustrates the program in RUN mode using three different values of r.

Volume of a Cylinder Problem

It is time to expand our geometric horizons somewhat to find the volume of a cylinder given its radius and height. According to the formula, the volume of a cylinder whose radius is r and whose height is h is

$$\text{Volume} = \pi r^2 h$$

In RUN mode using the values 5.29 and 6.1 for r and h, respectively, the volume may be calculated according to the following schematic.

Example 14

S	1	2	3	4
K	5.29	ENTER↑	×	g
D	5.29	5.29	27.98	27.98

S	5	6	7	8
K	π	×	6.1	×
D	3.14	87.91	6.1	536.28

In many respects this schematic is quite similar to that shown in Schematic HP-65-2 (manual mode). In fact, steps 1 through 6 are identical. This is deliberate since our purpose in this program is to illustrate the point that, unlike the previous program, *two* input data items are required rather than one. In manual mode this presents no problem whatever, since the two data items are keyed in when necessary. However, when translating this schematic directly into a program we have to make provision somehow for the keying in of the *second* data item during program execution. This difficulty has not arisen previously because the *first* data item was keyed in *before* the program was executed. This situation is handled by including the program step Run/Stop obtained by pressing the black key labeled [R/S] in the bottom right-hand corner of the keyboard.

Without further ado, here is the program to calculate the volume of a cylinder, and this time we have arbitrarily selected C as our label.

Program HP-65-3: Volume of a Cylinder

Step Number	Instruction	Comments
01	LBL	Names the function C
02	C	
03	ENTER↑	Copies value of r in x register to y register
04	×	Calculates r²

Program HP-65-3 (cont'd)

Step Number	Instruction	Comments
05	g	Activates the lower case functions
06	π	Puts 3.14 in display, pushing r^2 up into y register
07	X	πr^2
08	R/S	Halts the calculator to allow the user to key in the value for h
09	X	$\pi r^2 h$
10	RTN	

Running the Volume of a Cylinder Program

According to Program HP-65-3, the R/S instruction is encountered in step 8. This has the effect of halting the calculator's automatic sequential processing. The user now has the opportunity to key in the second data item—the value of h. Execution of the program is then reinitiated by pressing this *same* key—namely the [R/S] key. It is for this reason that this key is appropriately called the Run/Stop key.

Schematic HP-65-3

S	1	2	3	4	5
K	switch	key in steps	press	switch to	2.93
D	to	of Program	f PRGM	RUN mode	2.93
	W/PRGM	HP–65–3			
C					1st value for r

S	6	7	8	9	10
K	C	1.3	R/S	5.29	C
D	26.97	1.3	35.06	5.29	87.91
C		1st value for h	1st volume	2nd value for r	

S	11	12
K	6.1	R/S
D	6.1	536.28
C	2nd value for h	2nd volume

Counting Problem Using Unconditional Branching

In programming one usually exploits the fact that instructions are executed in sequence. For many types of problems this proves to be quite satisfactory, but for a great many other problems it is imperative that provision be made for transfer to an instruction other than the next one in sequence.

Transfer from one point of a program to another may be effected by means of an unconditional transfer. The instruction that provides this ability—that is, to transfer unconditionally to another point in a program—is the GoTO instruction, which is accessed by the key labeled [GTO].

Naturally, if execution is to be transferred to another point of the program, that point of the program must be supplied with a "handle," so to speak, to link up with the go to. This handle, as we described it, takes the form of a label. Labels may be specified by following the [LBL] key with any digit 0 through 9.

This information is needed in order to understand the following program. It does nothing other than repeatedly add one to the display, halting the calculator with each increment. In other words we are converting the calculator into a counter. Each time the Run/Stop key is pressed, the loop is executed once again. The purpose of the R/S instruction is not to permit the entry of further data but rather to allow for the number in the display to be observed.

Program HP-65-4: Counting

Step Number	Instruction	Comments
01	LBL	Names the function A
02	A	
03	DSP	Fixes the display at no decimal places, i.e., integers only
04	.	
05	0	
06	CL x	Clears the display
07	LBL	Defines the beginning of the loop
08	1	
09	1	Places increment in display
10	+	Adds x and y registers
11	R/S	Halts program to display latest count
12	GTO 1	Unconditionally transfers control to beginning of loop
13	RTN	Program terminator

If this program is not understood at first reading, the flowchart shown in Fig. 7-6 may help the reader to follow the flow of control and the logic of the program.

Here is a corresponding schematic showing how the display is incremented with each press of the Run/Stop key.

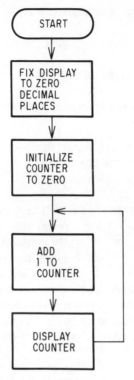

Fig. 7-6 Flowchart HP-65-4: Counting

Schematic HP-65-4

S	1	2	3	4	5
K	switch	key in steps	press	switch	A
D	to	of Program	f PRGM	to RUN	1.
	W/PRGM	HP–65–4		mode	

S	6	7	8	
K	R/S	R/S	R/S	. . . etc.
D	2.	3.	4.	

Conditional Branching

We have already seen how one can change the sequential manner in which a program is executed by resorting to the GTO instruction. The GTO instruction is the way in which unconditional jumps are performed—that is, with "no questions asked."

However, the HP-65 does, in fact, provide the means of making a jump when indeed a question has been asked. The following are the kinds of questions that can be asked:

1. Is the value contained in register x equal to that contained in register y?
2. Is the value contained in register x not equal to that contained in register y?
3. Is the value contained in register x greater than that contained in register y?
4. Is the value contained in register x less than or equal to that contained in register y?

Each of these four logical tests operates in a similar way. The test for equality, for example, is made by including the instruction:

$$x = y$$

This is found on the lower case [DSP] key. Since it is lower case, it is of course prefixed by the [g] key. When this instruction is included in a program, a test is made comparing the contents of the x register with that of the y register. If they are equal—that is, the test is true—execution is transferred to the next instruction in sequence in the ordinary way. However, if the test proves false—that is, the contents of the x register do not equal that of the y register—the next *two* memory locations are skipped and control is sent immediately to the instruction contained in the third memory location in sequence. Diagrammatically, here is what happens:

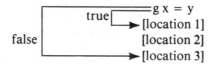

If the test is true, execution continues with the instruction in location 1. Otherwise, control is transferred directly to location 3.

Perfect Square Problem

The next program is offered not so much for its mathematical ingenuity—although it does have some mathematical interest—but rather to illustrate the branching instruction described above. Despite the fact that this program contains only a single branching instruction, it is pointed out that a very sophisticated logical network may be devised by placing a series of these decision-making instructions at appropriate points in a program.

The perfect square program poses the question: Is the number in the display a perfect square? In other words, is its square root an integer? The number 9 is a perfect square since its square root is 3, an integer. Similarly, 144 is a perfect square since squaring the integer 12 gives 144. The number 57, however, is not a perfect square since its square root is 7.55.

The strategy employed follows from the nature of the problem; that is to say, the square root is taken of the number in the display, and the result is tested to detemine whether or not it is an integer. If it is, a 1 is displayed indicating that the original number is a perfect square. If, on the other hand, the number is not a perfect square, a zero is displayed.

This strategy is demonstrated in the flowchart shown in Fig. 7-7.

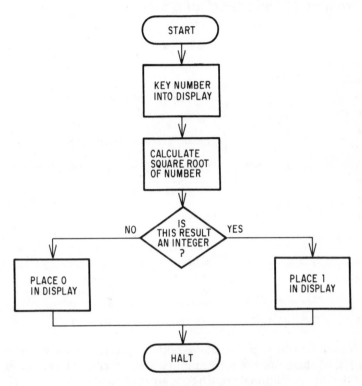

Fig. 7-7 Flowchart HP-65-5: Perfect Square

The manner that determines whether or not the square root of the displayed number is an integer perhaps requires some clarification. When the square root of the displayed number is calculated, it is automatically sent to the x register. Executing the ENTER↑ instruction has the effect of copying this value into the y register. The display is then replaced by the integer portion of the number. At this point the square root of the original number is contained in the y register and the integer portion of that same number is in the display. Now we are in a position to ask whether the contents of the x register is equal to that of the y register. If it is, control falls through to the next location that contains the constant "1." This number is placed in the display. The R/S instruction that follows halts execution of the program. The 1 in the display indicates that the original number keyed in was a perfect square.

On the other hand, if the test proves to be false, the two locations containing "1" and R/S, respectively, are skipped. The instruction that places a "0" in the display is now executed, and the program terminates by execution of the RTN instruction.

Program HP-65-5: Perfect Square

Step Number	Instruction	Comments
01	LBL	Names the function D
02	D	
03	DSP	
04	.	Displays only integers
05	0	
06	f	
07	√x	Calculates square root of number
08	ENTER↑	Copies value of square root into y register
09	f	
10	INT	Truncates display
11	g x = y	Does the contents of x register equal that of the y register?
12	1	Yes; then number is a perfect square; place 1 in display
13	R/S	Halts program to display result
14	0	No; then number is not a perfect square; place 0 in display
15	RTN	Halts program to display result

The reason why step 11 contains both the prefix and the test is because on the HP-65 these two are merged into a single memory location. In fact, each of the four conditional branch tests are merged with their [g] prefix key into a single instruction.*

Schematic HP-65-5

S	1	2	3	4	5
K	switch	key in steps	press	switch	9
D	to	of Program	f PRGM	to RUN	9.
	W/PRGM	HP-65-5		mode	
C					Is 9 a perfect square?

S	6	7	8	9	10
K	D	144	D	57	D
D	1.	144.	1.	57.	0.
C	yes	Is 144 a perfect square?	yes	Is 57 a perfect square?	no

---

*The other merged codes in the HP-65 are LST x, NOP, x≷y, R↓, R↑, STO 1 through 8, RCL 1 through 8, but not STO 9 and RCL 9.

Sum of the Integers from 1 to n

We have already encountered the four relational tests that provide the means for branching from one point of a program to another depending upon whether certain conditions are met or not. Each of these four tests compares the contents of the x register with that of the y. The HP-65 provides yet another means for branchng under specified conditions. It is called the DSZ instruction.

The Decrement and Skip on Zero Instruction (DSZ)

The reader will recall that on the HP-65 are nine (R1 through R9) addressable memory registers. One of these registers—specifically register 8—plays a unique role in conjunction with the DSZ instruction. This decrement and skip on zero instruction behaves in the following way: Whatever value is stored in R8 is decremented by one—that is, one is subtracted from it. If after subtracting one from register 8 its contents are reduced to zero, then the next two program locations are automatically skipped. If the resulting value in register 8 is not zero, execution proceeds to the next step in sequence.

The DSZ instruction is incorporated in the following program, which sums the integers from 1 to any integer n keyed into the calculator. It sums them by the so-called brute force method. The sum of the integers from 1 to 5 is 5 + 4 + 3 + 2 + 1 = 15, and that from 1 to 100 is 5050. The general logic of the program is illustrated in the flowchart shown in Fig. 7-8.

Immediately after the value of n is keyed in, a counter is initialized to that same value n, and a register that will eventually store the sum of the integers from 1 to n is also initially set to n. A loop commences with 1 being subtracted from the counter. This counter is then tested to see whether it is equal to zero. If it is not, then this value is added to the summation register and the loop is reinitiated. If it is equal to zero—meaning that the task has been completed—the value of the sum is displayed and the machine comes to a halt.

In effect, the sum is computed according to the mathematical expression

$$\text{Sum} = n + (n-1) + (n-2) + \ldots + 2 + 1$$

Program HP-65-6: Sum of the Integers from 1 to n

Step Number	Instruction	Comments
01	LBL	Names the program E
02	E	
03	STO 8	Initializes counter in register 8
04	STO 7	Initializes sum in register 7

Program HP-65-6 (cont'd)

Step Number	Instruction	Comments
05	DSP	
06	.	Displays only integers
07	0	
08	LBL	
09	1	Defines beginning of loop
10	g	Subtracts 1 from register 8 and then tests if
11	DSZ	register 8 is zero
12	GTO	
13	2	If counter is not zero, then go to label 2
14	RCL 7	Counter is zero then recall sum to display
15	R/S	Halts calculator
16	LBL	
17	2	Identifies transfer point
18	RCL 8	Recalls counter to display
19	STO	
20	+	Adds counter to sum in register 7
21	7	
22	GTO	
23	1	Reinitiates loop
24	RTN	End of program

The DSZ instruction that appears in step 11 of the program is really a dual role instruction. It not only subtracts 1 from register 8 but also makes a logical test for zero on register 8.

Schematic HP-65-6

S	1	2	3	4	5
K	switch	key in steps	press	switch	5
D	to	of Program	f PRGM	to RUN	5.
	W/PRGM	HP-65-6		mode	

S	6	7	8	9	10
K	E	50	E	100	E
D	15.	50.	1275.	100.	5050.

The reader is probably aware of the fact that there is a simple formula attributed to Gauss, which computes the sum of the integers from 1 to n directly:

$$Sum = n\,(n + 1)/2$$

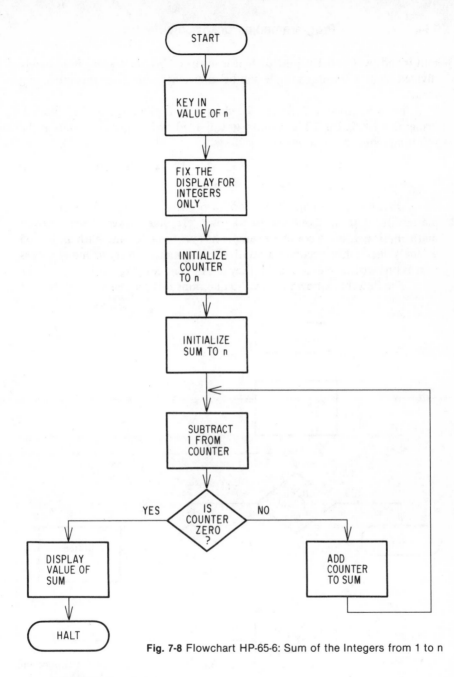

Fig. 7-8 Flowchart HP-65-6: Sum of the Integers from 1 to n

Ulam's Conjecture

The problem we are now about to describe is, we think, interesting for its own sake. It was formulated by Stanislav Ulam, who conjectured that all positive integer numbers when treated in a special way converge to 1. What is that special way? Simply that if the number is odd (or becomes odd) it is multiplied by 3 and 1 is added. If it is even (or becomes even) it is merely divided by 2. A simple example will be sufficient to illustrate this intriguing idea.

Let n be equal to 7. Since 7 is odd it is multiplied by 3 and 1 is added, bringing it to 22. But 22 is even, so it is divided by 2, and so on. Here is the resulting sequence of numbers:

$$7 \quad 22 \quad 11 \quad 34 \quad 17 \quad 52 \quad 26 \quad 13 \quad 40 \quad 20 \quad 10$$
$$5 \quad 16 \quad 8 \quad 4 \quad 2 \quad 1$$

Obviously, 7 reaches 1, but do all positive integers? The fact of the matter is that no one really knows. It has never been proved mathematically, but a counter example has yet to be found. With an HP-65 at one's disposal, it becomes a relatively easy matter to try as many values of n as one wishes to determine if they do, in fact, converge to 1.

The flowchart shown in Fig. 7-9 diagrams this process.

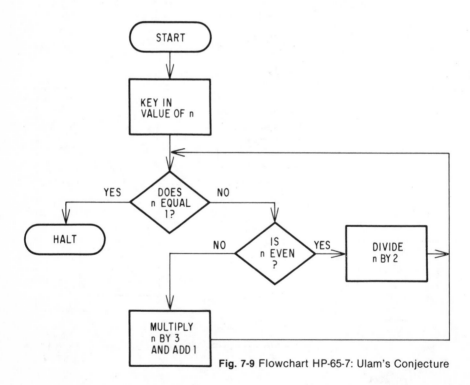

Fig. 7-9 Flowchart HP-65-7: Ulam's Conjecture

The program that follows for testing any value of n is heavily stack-oriented. This approach was taken merely to illustrate the manner in which the stack may be manipulated. There are two new features in the program, but we will discuss them after you have had a chance to study the program.

Program HP-65-7: Ulam's Conjecture

Step Number	Instruction	Comments
01	LBL	Names the function A
02	A	
03	ENTER↑	Copies keyed in value of n into y register
04	1	Tests if n is equal to 1
05	g x = y	
06	R/S	It is; stop the program
07	g NOP	Filler
08	g R↓	Rolls down stack, placing value of n in display
09	ENTER↑	Places copies of n in y and z registers
10	ENTER↑	
11	2	Calculates n/2
12	÷	
13	ENTER↑	Tests to see if n/2 is an integer—i.e., if n is even
14	f	
15	INT	
16	g x = y	
17	GTO	If it is, then loop back to beginning of program with n/2 in display as new value for n
18	A	
19	g R↓	Otherwise, n is odd so retrieve value of n residing in z register
20	g R↓	
21	3	Calculates 3n + 1
22	X	
23	1	
24	+	
25	GTO	Loops back to beginning of program with 3n + 1 in display as new value for n
26	A	
27	RTN	

The No OPeration Instruction

With the HP-65 in W/PRGM mode, pressing [f] [PRGM] has the effect of clearing the entire 100 program memory locations to the merged code 35 01, which is the g NOP code. No-OPs, as they are called, are useful as a filler in tests. Even though it might sound like a contradiction, the NOP instruction which does exactly nothing, nevertheless, often proves to be extremely useful. Suppose a logical test is made and we wish to halt the program if the result is true. If it is false, we wish to continue processing after skipping two locations. To halt the program, we need just the R/S instruction that occupies only one location in memory. Putting an NOP instruction in the next location fills out the second of the two instructions, both of which are skipped if the test is false.

The next point concerns the unconditional transfer to the beginning of the program. Since this particular program is headed LBL A, a GTO A instruction will send control to the first location of the program.

As we pointed out above, the program for Ulam's Conjecture makes heavy use of the HP-65's stack of registers.

In order to more closely follow precisely what transpires within these registers, the following stack schematic is offered. It shows the contents of each stack register after the instruction written below each stack diagram has been executed. Notice the correspondence beween the program itself and the stack schematic.

Stack Schematic HP-65-7

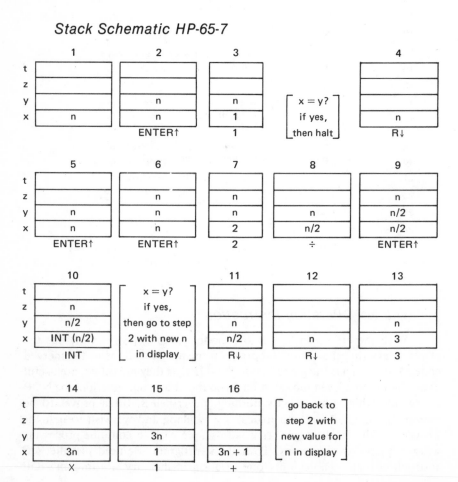

Schematic HP-65-7

S	1	2	3	4	5
K	⌈ switch ⌉	⌈key in steps⌉	⌈ press ⌉	⌈ switch ⌉	7
D	to	of Program	⌊f PRGM⌋	to RUN	7.
	⌊ W/PRGM ⌋	⌊ HP-65-7 ⌋		⌊ mode ⌋	
C					first case

S	6	7	8	
K	A	27	A	. . . etc.
D	1.00	27.	1.00	
C	converges to 1		converges to 1	

Setting and Testing Flags

We are all familiar with the railroad track switch, which sets the correct course for a train that can travel in one of two directions, as shown in Fig. 7-10. The switch is set ahead of time for one direction or the other. It cannot be in any other position.

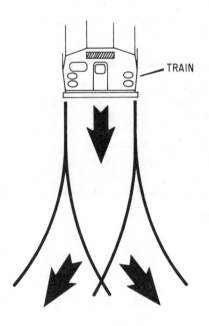

TRAIN

Fig. 7-10

The HP-65 provides yet another method for making decisions. It is done by means of flags, which work in a way analogous to the track switching illustration (see Fig. 7-10).

There are two flags that may be set "on" or "off" or, as many people prefer to regard it, "true" or "false." The instructions are Set Flag 1 represented by the [SF1] key and Set Flag 2 with its corresponding [SF2] key, each of which is prefixed by the [f] key. To set the flags off the [f⁻¹] key is used for both flags. When the calculator is first switched on, both flags are in the "off" position.

Since both these flags are either on or off, they may be treated as values to be tested within a program. The key marked [TF1] is used for testing the value of Flag 1, while the one marked [TF2] tests the value of Flag 2. In both cases these keys are prefixed by the [f] shift key. If the flag is false, two memory locations are immediately skipped. However, if the flag is true, then execution continues with the next instruction in sequence.

The analogy between these two logical tests and the relational tests already described is that both skip two memory locations if the test proves false and continues normally otherwise.

If the [f⁻¹] key (the inverse key) is used as a prefix to either the [TF1] or [TF2] key, two memory locations are automatically skipped if the flag is true.

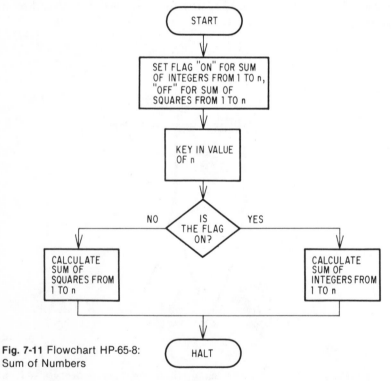

Fig. 7-11 Flowchart HP-65-8:
Sum of Numbers

Sum of Numbers Problem

To illustrate how a flag may be incorporated into a program, the following program was devised. It finds the sum of the integers 1 through n using the formula

$$\text{Sum} = n(n+1)/2$$

if Flag 1 is turned on. Otherwise, it computes the sum of the squares from 1 through n according to the formula

$$\text{Sum} = n(n + 1)(2n + 1)/6$$

The flowchart in Fig. 7-11 diagrams this program.

Program HP-65-8: Sum of Numbers

Step Number	Instruction	Comments
01	LBL	} Names the function A
02	A	
03	f	} Tests the value of Flag 1. If Flag 1 is on, then steps 5 and 6 are executed. Otherwise, control is transferred to step 7
04	TF1	
05	GTO	} Transfers to label 1 to compute sum of integers
06	1	
07	ENTER↑	
08	ENTER↑	
09	ENTER↑	n is now in x, y, z, and t registers
10	1	} $n + 1$ in x register
11	+	
12	x ⪌ y	Places $n + 1$ from x register into y register and n from y register into x register
13	2	
14	X	2n
15	1	
16	+	$2n + 1$
17	X	$(n + 1)(2n + 1)$
18	X	$n(n + 1)(2n + 1)$
19	6	
20	÷	Sum of squares $= n(n + 1)(2n + 1)/6$
21	R/S	Displays result
22	LBL	
23	1	Transfer point
24	ENTER↑	} Copies value of n into y and z registers
25	ENTER↑	
26	1	
27	+	$n + 1$
28	X	$n(n + 1)$
29	2	
30	÷	Sum $= n(n + 1)/2$
31	RTN	Ends program and displays result

Schematic HP-65-8

S	1	2	3	4	5
K	switch	key in steps	press	switch	DSP
D	to	of Program	f PRGM	to RUN	0.00
	W/PRGM	HP-65-8		mode	

S	6	7	8	9	10
K	.	0	f	SF1	50
D	0.00	0.	0.	0.	50.
C				turns Flag 1 "on"	

S	11	12	13	14	15
K	A	f^{-1}	SF1	10	A
D	1275.	1275.	1275.	10.	385.
C	sum of integers from 1 to 50		turns Flag 1 "off"		sum of the squares from 1 to 10

S	16	17
K	100	A
D	100.	338350.
C		sum of the squares from 1 to 100

Steps 5 through 7 in this schematic (DSP.0) were included to eliminate the superfluous zeros in the display, after the decimal point. This could have been included in the program, as we have indicated in other programs, but this is an option that is left open to the programmer.

Although Program HP-65-8 illustrates a rather trivial example of the use of a flag, it should be pointed out that in more complex situations flags may be turned on and off in several places within a program, considerably increasing the program's versatility.

Multi-Function Programming

In each of the HP-65 programs illustrated thus far, we confined ourselves to a single function. This does not necessarily have to be the case, however. In the program that follows, we shall illustrate four independent functions, each of which will be resident in the memory simultaneously. Whenever a particular function is needed, it will be accessed separately.

Compound Interest Problem

Compound interest is computed according to the following formula:

$$S = P(1 + r)^n$$

where

$S =$ the accumulated sum
$P =$ the initial principle invested
$r =$ the rate of interest per interest period
$n =$ the number of interest periods

For example, if we were to invest \$100 at 6% interest compounded quarterly for a period of two years, we could calculate the accrued sum by direct substitution into the formula.

$$S = 100 (1 + 0.015)^8$$

where

$100 =$ the principle amount
$0.015 = (6/100)/4 =$ rate of interest per interest period
$8 =$ the number of interest periods $= 2 \times 4$

The compound interest formula as stated above solves for S in terms of P, r, and n. With a little algebraic manipulation, we can solve for P, r, and n given the other three variables.

$$P = S/(1 + r)^n$$
$$r = (S/P)^{1/n} - 1$$
$$n = \ln (S/P)/\ln (1 + r)$$

To permit the user to solve for any of these four variables, each formula is programmed as a single function labeled A, B, C, and D, respectively.

An important question that now arises is the order in which the input data is to be keyed in. Obviously, it cannot be entered in a haphazard order, since it is unlikely that it will yield the correct result. The approach we have adopted is to key in the known variables in the order in which they appear, as stated in the formulas in accordance with the following table.

Formula	Label Name	Order of Input Variables		
$S = P(1 + r)^n$	A	P	r	n
$P = S/(1 + r)^n$	B	S	r	n
$r = (S/P)^{1/n} - 1$	C	S	P	n
$n = \ln (S/P)/\ln(1 + r)$	D	S	P	r

Once the required formula has been selected, the first input variable is keyed in and the appropriate label key pressed. The machine comes to a halt to enable the second variable to be keyed in. Pressing the [R/S] key permits the program to continue. Again the program comes to a halt so that the last variable may be keyed in. Within a few seconds of pressing the [R/S] key, the required solution appears in the display.

Program HP-65-9: Compound Interest

Step Number	Instruction	Comments
01	LBL	Names the function A
02	A	Solves for $S = P(1 + r)^n$
03	ENTER↑	Copies keyed in value of P into y register
04	R/S	Halts program to permit value of r to be keyed in
05	ENTER↑	
06	1	
07	+	$1 + r$
08	R/S	Halts program to permit value of n to be keyed in
09	g	
10	y^x	$(1 + r)^n$
11	x	$S = P(1 + r)^n$
12	RTN	Ends function A
13	LBL	Solves for $P = S/(1 + r)^n$
14	B	
15	ENTER↑	Copies keyed in values of S into y register
16	R/S	Halts program to permit value of r to be keyed in
17	ENTER↑	
18	1	
19	+	$1 + r$
20	R/S	Halts program to permit value of n to be keyed in
21	g	
22	y^x	$(1 + r)^n$
23	÷	$P = S/(1 + r)^n$
24	RTN	End function B
25	LBL	Solves for $r = (S/P)^{1/n} - 1$
26	C	
27	ENTER↑	Copies keyed in value of S into y register
28	R/S	Halts program to permit value of P to be keyed in
29	÷	S/P
30	R/S	Halts program to permit value of n to be keyed in
31	g	
32	1/x	$1/n$
33	g	
34	y^x	$(S/P)^{1/n}$

Program HP-65-9 (cont'd)

Step Number	Instruction	Comments
35	1	
36	—	$r = (S/P)^{1/n} - 1$
37	RTN	Ends function C
38	LBL	
39	D	Solves for $n = \ln(S/P)/\ln(1 + r)$
40	ENTER↑	Copies keyed in value of S into y register
41	R/S	Halts program to permit value of P to be keyed in
42	÷	S/P
43	f	
44	LN	$\ln(S/P)$
45	R/S	Halts program to permit value of r to be keyed in
46	ENTER↑	
47	1	
48	+	$1 + r$
49	f	
50	LN	$\ln(1 + r)$
51	÷	$n = \ln(S/P)/\ln(1 + r)$
52	RTN	Ends function D

Schematic HP-65-9

Solve each of the following:

1. P = 100; r = 0.015; n = 8; S = ? (See steps 1–10.)
2. S = 4,562; r = 0.024; n = 5; P = ? (See steps 11–16.)
3. S = 3,000; P = 1,560; n = 12; r = ? (See steps 17–22.)
4. S = 25,000; P = 12,500; r = 0.055; n = ? (See steps 23–28.)

S	1	2	3	4	5
K	⌈ switch ⌉	⌈key in steps⌉	⌈ press ⌉	⌈ switch ⌉	100
D	to	of Program	⌊f PRGM⌋	to RUN	100.
	⌊W/PRGM⌋	⌊ HP-65-9 ⌋		⌊ mode ⌋	
C					P

S	6	7	8	9	10
K	A	.015	R/S	8	R/S
D	100.00	0.015	1.02	8.	112.65
C		r		n	S

Schematic HP-65-9 (cont'd)

S	11	12	13	14	15
K	4562	B	.024	R/S	5
D	4562.	4562.00	0.024	1.02	5.
C	S		r		n

S	16	17	18	19	20
K	R/S	3000	C	1560	R/S
D	4051.87	3000.	3000.00	1560.	1.92
C	P	S		P	

S	21	22	23	24	25
K	12	R/S	25000	D	12500
D	12.	0.06	25000.	25000.00	12500.
C	n	r	S		P

S	26	27	28
K	R/S	.055	R/S
D	0.69	0.055	12.95
C		r	n

In view of the complexity of Program HP-65-9, it might be a good idea to record it on a magnetic card, as explained earlier, so that it may be run at any future time without having to key in the instructions again. It is suggested therefore that the magnetic card be documented, as shown in Fig. 7-12, in which the order of the input variables are indicated. Perhaps it would be a good idea to clip the corner of the card to prevent accidental erasure.

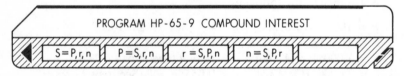

PROGRAM HP-65-9 COMPOUND INTEREST

S=P,r,n   P=S,r,n   r=S,P,n   n=S,P,r

Fig. 7-12

When this magnetic card is inserted in the window, each of the handwritten titles will appear above the appropriate function label key, conveniently reminding the user not only which label key has to be pressed for the given function but also the order in which the variables are to be keyed in.

Subroutines

The concept of subroutines is a very important one in computer programming and can be used to equal advantage on the HP-65. In order to provide insight into the power of subroutines, we shall pose a problem and solve it first in the ordinary way without resorting to their use. After a short discussion of the resulting program, we shall then rewrite it using the subroutine feature. The reader will then be in a position to compare the two programs and gain some appreciation of subroutines.

The Kilometer Conversion Problem

The day is surely approaching when all measurements in the United States will be specified in metric units. Until that day arrives, however, we have to contend with the fact that in Europe all distances, for example, are expressed in meters and kilometers, etc., whereas in the United States we customarily express distances in miles, yards, feet, and inches.

Here are the relationships between these units of measurement:

$$1 \text{ km} = 0.62137 \text{ mi}$$
$$1 \text{ mi} = 1{,}760 \text{ yd}$$
$$1 \text{ yd} = 3 \text{ ft}$$
$$1 \text{ ft} = 12 \text{ in}$$

Suppose now we are confronted with a distance expressed in kilometers. We would like to write a program that will convert this distance into its equivalent in American units. For example,

$$100 \text{ km} = 62 \text{ mi}, 241 \text{ yd}, 0 \text{ ft}, 4.32 \text{ in}$$

The manner in which the above conversion is performed is to multiply the specified number of kilometers by the constant 0.62137. This converts from kilometers to miles and *decimal fractions of a mile*. The integer portion of this number represents the integral number of miles. The fractional portion is then multiplied by the constant 1,760 to convert it to yards. Again, it is the integral portion of this number that represents the number of yards, and its fractional portion is then multiplied by the constant 3 to convert it to feet. For the last time, the integral portion is the number of feet, and multiplying its fractional portion by 12 converts it to inches. Here is the sequence of calculations:

1. $100 \times 0.62137 = 62.137$ [62 miles]
2. $0.137 \times 1{,}760 = 241.12$ [241 yards]
3. $0.12 \times 3 = 0.36$ [0 feet]
4. $0.36 \times 12 = 4.32$ [4.32 inches]

Program HP-65-10A: Kilometer Conversions

Step Number	Instruction	Comments
01	LBL	Names function A
02	A	
03	DSP	⎫
04	°	⎬ Display miles, yards, and feet as integers without trailing zeros
05	0	⎭

Program HP-65-10A (cont'd)

Step Number	Instruction	Comments
06	•	
07	6	
08	2	Places constant 0.62137 into display
09	1	
10	3	
11	7	
12	X	Converts kilometers to miles and fractions of a mile
13	ENTER↑	
14	f	
15	INT	Extracts integral number of miles
16	R/S	And stops to display result
17	—	Extracts fractional portion of number to be converted to yards
18	1	
19	7	Places constant 1760 into display
20	6	
21	0	
22	X	Converts to yards and fractions of a yard
23	ENTER↑	
24	f	
25	INT	Extracts integral number of yards
26	R/S	And stops to display result
27	—	Extracts fractional portion of number to be converted to feet
28	3	Places constant 3 into display
29	X	Converts to feet and fractions of a foot
30	ENTER↑	
31	f	
32	INT	Extracts integral number of feet
33	R/S	And stops to display results
34	—	Extracts fractional portion of number to be converted to inches
35	1	
36	2	Places constant 12 into display
37	X	
38	DSP	
39	•	Displays inches to two decimal places
40	2	
41	RTN	End of program

Schematic HP-65-10A: Kilometer Conversions

S	1	2	3	4	5
K	switch	key in steps	press	switch	100
D	to	of Program	f PRGM	to RUN	100
	W/PRGM	HP–65–10A		mode	
C					kilometers

S	6	7	8	9
K	A	R/S	R/S	R/S
D	62.	241.	0.	4.32
C	miles	yards	feet	inches

A careful perusal of this last program will reveal that the sequence of instructions

$$\times$$
$$\text{ENTER}\uparrow$$
$$\text{f}$$
$$\text{INT}$$
$$\text{R/S}$$
$$-$$

appears in precisely this order three separate times. They are in fact performing the same role during the execution of the program. The HP-65 permits one to include a sequence of instructions such as these six steps as a separate function called a subroutine, which may be invoked whenever it is needed. In doing so the program is shortened considerably. Subroutines lend themselves to greater efficiency, minimize the possibility of error, and improve the readability of a program.

Here then is the program rewritten with the inclusion of a subroutine.

Program HP-65-10B: Kilometer Conversions

Step Number	Instruction	Comments
01	LBL	
02	A	
03	DSP	
04	.	
05	0	
06	.	
07	6	
08	2	
09	1	
10	3	
11	7	
12	B	Invokes subroutine B

Program HP-65-10B (cont'd)

Step Number	Instruction	Comments
13	1	
14	7	
15	6	
16	0	
17	B	Invokes subroutine B
18	3	
19	B	Invokes subroutine B
20	12	
21	X	
22	DSP	
23	.	
24	2	
25	RTN	
26	LBL	Beginning of subroutine B
27	B	
28	X	
29	ENTER↑	
30	f	
31	INT	
32	R/S	
33	—	
34	RTN	End of subroutine B

As will be observed from this program, subroutine B is structured exactly like a regular function program. In this case it is located at the end of the program. In step 12, where subroutine B is first invoked, control is transferred directly to the subroutine. Once the subroutine has been executed, the RTN instruction returns control to step 13—the location immediately following that from which B was invoked. In step 17 subroutine B is again invoked as indeed it is in step 19, each time returning to steps 18 and 20 respectively. Steps 1 through 25 are sometimes spoken of as the "main routine." On the HP-65, only a main routine can "call" a subroutine. In other words, a subroutine cannot in turn invoke another subroutine.

There are various alternatives to the sequence of instructions for subroutine B indicated above. Not all of the alternatives, however, are equally efficient. Selecting a more efficient sequence of instructions (this generally means fewer instructions) is known as *optimization*. Oftentimes the optimizing of a program is a very subtle art and uses all of the expertise at the programmer's command. Subroutine B provides a good illustration of the concept of optimization. Initially, this routine was written:

LBL
B
×
ENTER↑
f
INT
R/S
x≥y
f⁻¹
INT
RTN

In this version of the subroutine, the whole of the number, including the decimal and fractional portion, was saved in the y register by ENTERing it. The INT function replaced this number in the display with its integral portion, and the R/S instruction stopped the calculator so that this value could be noted. In order to operate on the fractional portion of the number, the contents of the x register were interchanged with that of the y, and the fractional portion was extracted by use of the inverse INT function. However, the same role may be accomplished with fewer instructions by replacing the three consecutive instructions

x≥y
f⁻¹
INT

with a solitary minus instruction. The reason why this works is because the fractional portion may be obtained by a direct subtraction of the integral portion of the number in the display from the whole of the number in the y register.

Although the above example of optimization is a rather simple one, in situations where a subroutine or a loop is executed many times, the savings in program execution time can be considerable.

Debugging and Editing Programs on the HP-65

It often transpires that once a program has been keyed into the calculator further consideration of the problem being solved might necessitate some minor or even major modification to the program.

To make such modifications relatively easy, the HP-65 comes equipped with four editing features. One can:

1. Display the instruction stored in any particular location in program memory.
2. Delete an instruction and automatically adjust for it by using the [DEL] key.
3. Insert a new instruction between two instructions.
4. Single step in a forward direction through a program using the [SST] key.

Advantage of the single step key may be taken in both program and run modes. In programming mode, it enables the programmer to check the program step by step, thus allowing one to examine each individual instruction code to ascertain its correctness. It could easily happen that what one intended to key in does not coincide with what one actually keyed in.

In RUN mode, execution of the program may be traced step by step, thereby enabling the programmer to check intermediate results.

We have now covered all of the features of the HP-65, and few will deny that this portable computer-calculator represented a major technological triumph. Familiarity with each of its features is of paramount importance if the owner is to exploit the calculator to its fullest extent.

It is of interest to note that in midsummer 1975, the HP-65 was taken aloft by the American Apollo team for use as a backup for the on-board computers and to calculate two critical mid-course correction maneuvers just prior to the linkup of the U.S. Apollo and Russian Soyez spacecrafts. In the event that the on-board computer failed, the crew would have had to rely entirely upon the HP-65 since, at that stage of the mission the spacecraft would not have been in communication with any of the ground stations. The scientists at the National Aeronautics and Space Administration had written programs of up to 1,000 steps and recorded them on the magnetic cards (100 per card).

CHAPTER EIGHT
THE HEWLETT-PACKARD 67

In the summer of 1976 Hewlett-Packard announced the HP-67 programmable pocket calculator. This card programmable calculator surpassed all the company's previous models both in versatility and in programming power. Each of the 35 keys controls up to four separate operations, thereby making for a very compact function-laden instrument. Besides having magnetic cards on which programs may be permanently recorded, the HP-67 provides for 224 steps of program memory, 26 data storage registers, fully merged prefix and function keys, editing features for both correcting and modifying programs, unconditional and conditional branching facilities, three levels of subroutines, four flags, and indirect addressing. This incredible package, which weighs no more than 10 1/2 ounces, was released with a price tag of $450, including the ac adapter/recharger.

A picture of the HP-67 is shown in Fig. 8-1. Like its predecessors, it operates in Reverse Polish Notation via the standard four-register stack.

Manual Operation of the HP-67

When the HP-67 is switched on, it shows 0.00 in the display. It "wakes up," so to speak, in a rounded, two-decimal place format.

In line with the general tendency of Hewlett-Packard calculators to provide for additional functions within the same dimension, a third prefix key has been added. Not only is there an [f] and [g] prefix key, but for the first time we have yet another prefix key labeled [h]. One wonders whether eventually we can expect to see a [z] prefix key!

As usual, pressing a function key causes the calculator to perform that function directly on the number in the display. If the function is shown on the face of the key, no prefix key is required. To select the function printed in black on the slanted key face, the black prefix key [h] must be pressed first. If the required function is shown in gold below the function key, the gold prefix key [f] is pressed first. Similarly, the function printed in blue below a function key is accessed by first pressing the blue prefix key labeled [g]. Here are a few examples of functions that require prefixes:

$$\begin{array}{cc} g & x^2 \\ f & \sqrt{x} \end{array}$$

151

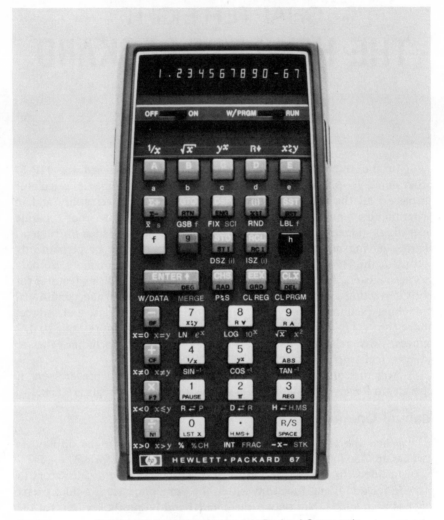

Fig. 8-1 HP-67 (*Courtesy* Hewlett-Packard Company)

In the latter case where the square root of the number in the display is calculated, one should *not* normally use the function shown above the key labeled [B] in the top row of the keyboard, since it is a so-called default function, about which we'll have more to say later on. Meanwhile it is recommended that you use the $\sqrt{x}$ function located below the digit 9 key. Lastly, here is a function requiring the black prefix key [h]:

$$h \qquad 1/x$$

What follows is a sequence of arithmetic expressions to familiarize the reader with the various arithmetic and prefix keys.

Example 1: Evaluate 2.1 + 3.2

S	1	2	3	4
K	2.1	ENTER↑	3.2	+
D	2.1	2.10	3.2	5.30

Example 2: Evaluate (9.87 × 3.23) − 6.9

S	1	2	3	4	5	6
K	9.87	ENTER↑	3.23	X	6.9	−
D	9.87	9.87	3.23	31.88	6.9	24.98

Example 3: Evaluate (2 + 3)/(4 − 5)

S	1	2	3	4	5
K	2	ENTER↑	3	+	4
D	2.	2.00	3.	5.00	4.

S	6	7	8	9
K	ENTER↑	5	−	÷
D	4.00	5.	−1.00	−5.00

Example 4: Evaluate −123.45 + (6.78)^2

S	1	2	3	4	5	6	7
K	123.45	CHS	ENTER↑	6.78	g	x^2	+
D	123.45	−123.45	−123.45	6.78	6.78	45.97	−77.48

Example 5: Evaluate [$\sqrt{191.2}$ + ln(17.26)]/cos (19.38°)

S	1	2	3	4	5	6
K	191.2	f	$\sqrt{x}$	17.26	f	ln
D	191.2	191.2	13.83	17.26	17.26	2.85

S	7	8	9	10	11
K	+	19.38	f	cos	÷
D	16.68	19.38	19.38	0.94	17.68

The HP-67 operates in degree mode as soon as it is switched on. Since the angle specified in the above problem is stated in degrees, it is not necessary to do anything special to the calculator. If it is necessary to operate on an angle expressed in radians or grads, the appropriate mode may be set by pressing either [h] [RAD] for radians, or [h] [GRD] for grads. Whichever mode is selected will be retained until either the calculator is switched off or is changed by the user.

Example 6: Evaluate sin^{-1}(.3876) as an angle expressed in radians.

S	1	2	3	4	5
K	h	RAD	.3876	g	sin^{-1}
D	0.00	0.00	0.3876	0.3876	0.40

Notice that on the HP-67 keyboard the –1, indicating the inverse of the function, is printed in blue. This means that the blue prefix key should be used. This applies to all of the trigonometric functions.

Time Conversions

Ordinarily, time is expressed in hours, minutes, and seconds. Sometimes, however, it is more convenient for computational purposes to express time in hours and decimal fractions of an hour. For example, 4 hours, 30 minutes may be expressed as 4.5 hours. On the HP-67 one may convert readily from one form to another, as shown in the following examples.

Example 7: Convert 29.24 hours to its equivalent measure in hours, minutes, and seconds.

S	1	2	3	4	5
K	DSP	4	29.24	g	←H.MS
D	0.00	0.0000	29.24	29.24	29.1424

The reader will no doubt have noticed that each time the calculator is switched on, the display is automatically set to two decimal places. This is often very convenient, but for those occasions where it is necessary to override this automatic, rounded, two-decimal-place setting, one may press [DSP] (for display) followed by a digit 0 through 9. The display will be fixed with the designated number of decimal places. Once this is done such a setting will remain in effect until it is changed in the same manner just described or the calculator is switched off.

When calculating with hours, minutes, and seconds it is essential to extend the setting of the display to four decimal places because hours, minutes, and seconds are displayed on the HP-67 as

$$H.MS$$

where

H = the unit number of hours
M = a two-digit number representing the minutes
S = a two-digit number representing the seconds

For example:

H.MS Representation	Equivalent
12.3456	12 hr, 34 min, 56 sec
5.4800	5 hr, 48 min, 0 sec
13.0012	13 hr, 0 min, 12 sec
0.0010	0 hr, 0 min, 10 sec

In Example 7, therefore, 29.24 hours is equivalent to 29 hours, 14 minutes, 24 seconds.

Numbers may be displayed on the HP-67 in three distinct modes: (1) fixed point notation, (2) scientific notation, and (3) engineering notation.

The normal operating mode of the HP-67 is fixed point. As mentioned previously, the automatic rounded two-decimal-place setting may be changed by pressing [DSP] followed by a digit 0 through 9.

If, during the course of computation in fixed point mode, a displayed intermediate result becomes either too small or large to be expressed in fixed point mode, such numbers will automatically be converted to scientific notation. One can, however, set the HP-67 to scientific notation mode at the outset by pressing [g] [SCI], in which case all subsequent results will be displayed in scientific notation. Once again, the decimal accuracy of the mantissa can be reset to any other desired setting by using the [DSP] key.

As with some other Hewlett-Packard models, engineering notation also is available. This permits numbers to be expressed with exponents of 10 that are multiples of three. (See Chap. 5 for more information.)

Regardless of the notation adopted or of the decimal setting of the display, the HP-67 always retains the full accuracy of the displayed number internally to 10 significant digits with a two-digit exponent. For those situations where it is required to eliminate trailing digits from a mantissa— that is, those digits that are not visible in the display—one may do so by pressing the [RND] key, prefixed by the gold [f] shift key.

Example 8:　　Illustration of the DSP and RND functions

S	1	2	3	4	5	6
K	18.7859	DSP	1	DSP	4	DSP
D	18.7859	18.7859	18.8	18.8	18.7859	18.7859

S	7	8	9	10	11
K	2	f	RND	DSP	4
D	18.79	18.79	18.79	18.79	18.7900

The purpose of this illustration is to reinforce the concept that even though a number with four decimal places such as 18.7859 appears as 18.8 when the calculator has been set to display one decimal place, nevertheless, the full accuracy of the number is retained within the machine. All that has happened is that in displaying the number it has been rounded in the conventional sense to the specified number of decimal places. However when using the RND function the number 18.79 becomes the *actual* number retained within the machine rather than the original 18.7859. It is for this reason that in the last two steps when [DSP] 4 is keyed in the number 18.7900 is displayed.

For those situations where it is required to extract the integer or fractional portions of a displayed number, recourse to the [f] [INT] keys for the integer portion or [g] [FRAC] for the fractional portion may be made. In both these cases, however, the display is replaced by the extracted portion.

Example 9:   Illustration of the INT and FRAC functions

S	1	2	3	4	5	6
K	7.1655	f	INT	424.55	g	FRAC
D	7.1655	7.1655	7.00	424.55	424.55	0.55

Percentages

The HP-67 has two different functions to assist one in calculations involving percentages. One is the common percentage key, permitting one to calculate the given percentage of a number. This is the key labeled [%], which is prefixed by the gold [f] shift key. The other function calculates percentage change, which is appropriately labeled [% ch], and is prefixed by the blue [g] shift key. Since both these percentage functions are two-number functions, both the x and the y registers have to be used. In terms of registers the [%] function calculates x% of y, while the [% ch] function calculates the percentage increase or decrease from y to x.

The Automatic Memory Stack

The HP-67 has the four-register stack common to all Hewlett-Packard models. As usual, they are called the x, y, z, and t registers. The contents of the x and y registers may be exchanged by using the [x ⋛ y] key, prefixed by the [h] key. There also is a roll up key, designated as [h] [R↑], and a roll down key [h] [R↓].

What is significantly different in the operation of the stack on the HP-67 is that provision is made to automatically review its contents. This is done by keying in [g] [STK]. It has the effect of displaying one register at a time: the t, z, y, and finally the x register contents again. Each register is displayed for about one-half of a second. In effect, the [g] [STK] acts exactly as four successive presses of [h] [R↑]. If for any reason, the automatic review is to be halted, pressing the [R/S] key or any other key will do the trick. So long as the key is depressed the contents of the stack register will remain "frozen" in the display. As soon as the key is released, the stack resumes its automatic motion.

The Data Storage Registers

The data storage registers on the HP-67 represent a shift from the customary design found on all the other models described so far. The stack contains the same four registers (x, y, z, and t) and there also is a last x register. But there are an additional 26 addressable data storage registers that are completely independent of the stack. These data storage registers may be used for storing and recalling data both in manual and programming mode. They fall into two categories: (1) primary registers and (2) protected secondary registers.

1. *Primary Registers.* There are 16 primary registers consisting of 10 registers called R0 through R9, 5 more R_A through R_E, and a single, special register called the I register.

To store the number 1.23 in R3, the following sequence of keys is used:

$$1.23 \; [STO] \; 3$$

To subsequently recall it, this sequence is used:

$$[RCL] \; 3$$

Similarly, to store 7.89 in register R_D and to recall it later, the following sequence of steps is used:

1. 7.89 [STO] D
2. [RCL] D

It should be remembered that whenever a number is recalled, a *copy* of the number is sent to the display, leaving the number in the register unaltered.

The role of the I register will become more apparent when we discuss programming mode. It may nevertheless be used in manual mode in much the same way as the other 15 primary registers, except that the keys [STI] (store in I) and RCI (recall I) are used. To store 3.45 in register I, key in the following:

$$3.45 \; [h] \; [STI]$$

To recall it subsequently, key in:

$$[h] \; [RCI]$$

2. *The Protected Secondary Storage Registers.* These 10 registers represent a distinct advance over the conventional method of register usage. They are intended to provide special protection from the possibility of inadvertently storing data into them (and thereby erasing any previous contents) and also from accessing these registers unintentionally. None of these registers are directly affected by either the STO or the RCL functions; it is in this sense that they are protected. In order to store information into a protected register, it would first have to be stored in a primary register and then exchanged with its corresponding protected, secondary register, using the [f] [P $\gtrless$ S] keys. The 10 protected registers are Rs0 through Rs9 (where s signifies secondary and is associated with the 10 unprotected, primary registers R0 through R9).

To store the number 7.89 in the protected secondary register Rs7, the following sequence is keyed in:

$$7.89 \text{ [STO] 7 [f] [P} \gtrless \text{S]}$$

The effect of the [P $\gtrless$ S] (primary exchange secondary) key is to exchange the contents of all the registers R0 through R9 with those of Rs0 through Rs9, with no other registers (and this includes the I register as well as R_A through R_E) being affected in the exchange process. The utilitarian value of such an exchange system will become more apparent when we reach the section on programming the HP-67, but this brief introduction will suffice for now.

Automatic Register Review

In order to observe the contents of, say, register 4, all you need do to recall it is to key in:

$$\text{[RCL] 4}$$

This brings a copy of the contents of primary register 4 to the x register—that is, the display. This is very convenient for viewing the contents of a single register. However, on the HP-67 you can review the contents of *all* the primary storage registers, with a single operation.

If you press [h] [REG], the contents of each of the primary storage registers are *automatically* displayed in succession, beginning with register R0 and continuing through register R9, followed by R_A through R_E and finally register I. But this is not all; the address identifying the register being displayed appears on the right-hand side of the display immediately prior to the register about to be displayed. The codes used are:

Register	Display Code
R0	0
R1	1
.	.
.	.
.	.
R9	9
R_A	20
R_B	21
R_C	22
R_D	23
R_E	24
I	25

If during the review of the registers you wish to stop the automatic sequencing for any reason, press the [R/S] key or any other key on the keyboard. If a function key is pressed, that function will *not* be executed.

To review the contents of the secondary storage registers, they would first have to be exchanged with the primary registers by means of the [f] [P ⪴ S] keys and then reviewed by pressing [h] [REG]. Of course, to return the original contents back to the protected registers the [f] [P ⪴ S] keys would have to be actuated once more.

Clearing Registers

Primary storage registers may be cleared individually by simply storing zero in them as required. However, for those situations when it is expeditious to clear all the primary storage registers to zero simultaneously, one may press [f] [CL REG], which clears all the primary storage registers at the same time. None of the stack registers nor the secondary storage registers are affected by this clearing function.

Once again, to operate on the secondary storage registers, they would first have to be exchanged into the primary registers by pressing [f] [P ⪴ S], after which they may be cleared together by pressing [f] [CL REG]. To clear the display, the [CLx] key is pressed.

Storage Register Arithmetic

To operate on a number stored in one of the primary storage registers you may merely recall it, perform whatever operation or function you need, and restore the result. On the HP-67, however, it is possible to operate arithmetically directly on the primary registers R0 through R9, but not on any of the other registers.

For example, the value in the display may be added to the contents of register R1 by keying the sequence:

$$[STO] [+] 1$$

Similarly,

$$[STO] [-] 2$$

will subtract the displayed value from the contents of register R2. In like manner multiplication and division may be effected with the keystroke sequence

$$[STO] [\times] 3$$

which multiplies the display by the contents of register R3, sending the result to R3, and finally

$$[STO] [\div] 4$$

which divides the contents of primary register R4 by the display, sending the quotient to R4 and leaving the display unaffected.

The LST x Function

Regardless of the calculation that has just been performed, the contents of the x register before the calculation was initiated is automatically stored in a special internal register known as the last x register. The contents of this last x register may be recalled to the display either for viewing or for calculation purposes simply by pressing the [LST x] key, prefixed by the black [h] shift key. The advantage of this register lies in the fact that if the last value of the x register is required, it may be accessed without having to key it in again.

Example 10: Evaluate $\sin(\pi/5) + \cos(\pi/5)$

S	1	2	3	4	5	6	7
K	h	RAD	h	π	5	÷	f
D	0.00	0.00	0.00	3.14	5.	0.63	0.63

S	8	9	10	11	12	13
K	sin	h	LST x	f	cos	+
D	0.59	0.59	0.63	0.63	0.81	1.40

By taking advantage of the last x register, it is not necessary to calculate $\pi/5$ twice or even to store it into one of the storage registers.

For those functions that have not been covered we would respectfully refer the reader to the HP-67 Owner's Handbook, in which all of the functions are described. In view of the fact that the HP-67 is so rich in features used in its programming mode, we proceed immediately with the section on how to program this personal computer.

Programming the HP-67

To the person who is unaware of the existence of programmable calculators, the HP-67 will appear as just another advanced scientific calculator. This, however, is far from the case. The HP-67 represents a marked advance over each of Hewlett-Packard's previous sophisticated models.

The HP-97 Interchangeable Software

Simultaneous with the release of the HP-67, Hewlett-Packard announced a compatible desk top model called the HP-97. The major difference between the HP-67 and the HP-97 besides physical size is that the HP-97 comes equipped with a printer. Although the HP-67 has no printer, programs may be written on the HP-67 and run on the HP-97 and vice versa. The printing functions available on the HP-97 are, for the sake of compatibility, also available on the HP-67. A program written for the HP-97 using these printer functions may be run on the HP-67 where, rather than the printer being affected, the relevant information is sent to the display. By the same token, all of the printing features of the HP-97 are available on the keyboard of the HP-67 to enable programs to be written on the HP-67 for subsequent running on the HP-97.

Evaluation of an Algebraic Expression

For our first example we shall evaluate the simple algebraic expression

$$y = x^2 - 2x + 3$$

for x equals 1.23. All this means is that 1.23 is substituted for x into this formula and the value of y calculated. The sequence of steps to do this on the HP-67 in RUN mode would be those shown in the following schematic.

Example 11:　Evaluate $y = (1.23)^2 - 2(1.23) + 3$

S	1	2	3	4	5
K	1.23	g	x^2	h	LST x
D	1.23	1.23	1.51	1.51	1.23

S	6	7	8	9	10
K	2	×	−	3	+
D	2.	2.46	−0.95	3	2.05

If we wanted to evaluate the above expression for many other values of x, it is quite obvious that we would have to repeat the *same* sequence of instructions for each value. Not only would this be time consuming and monotonous, but would also invite keystroke errors. The great advantage of having a programmable calculator is that one can easily avoid these problems. The sequence of instructions to be repeated for each value of x may be incorporated into a program, which may then be initiated for each desired value of x.

Here is the body of the program to evaluate $y = x^2 - 2x + 3$ for *any* value of x:

$$
\begin{array}{ll}
g & x^2 \\
h & \text{LST x} \\
2 & \\
\times & \\
- & \\
3 & \\
+ &
\end{array}
$$

In order to incorporate this sequence of steps into a program, all that is necessary is to select a label to put in front of the sequence and to append an h RTN to the end of it. Assuming we arbitrarily select A as the label name, here is the complete program.

Program HP-67-1:   Evaluation of $y = x^2 - 2x + 3$

Step Number	Instruction	Comments
001	f LBL A	Identifies the program
002	g x^2	Squares the value in the display
003	h LST x	Recalls the last contents of the x register into display
004	2	Enters 2 into display, lifting stack
005	x	2x
006	—	$x^2 - 2x$
007	3	
008	+	$y = x^2 - 2x + 3$
009	h RTN	Signals the end of the program

Schematic HP-67-1

S	1	2	3	4	5	6	7
K	switch to	press	key in steps	switch	1.23	A	.5
D	W/PRGM mode	f CL PRGM	of Program HP–67–1	to RUN mode	1.23	2.05	0.5

S	8	9	10	11	12	13
K	A	3.7	A	12.9	CHS	A
D	2.25	3.7	9.29	12.9	−12.9	195.21

Having established all of the program steps, we are now ready to illustrate the manner for entering the program into the HP-67.

Keying in the Program

1. Switch to W/PRGM mode.
2. Press the [f] [CL PRGM] keys to clear the program area.
3. Key in the 9 instructions, as shown in Program HP-67-1.

Notice that as you key in each of the instructions the display reveals some information that will not be very meaningful at this point. It is, nevertheless, very useful and shall be fully explained shortly.

Running the Program

1. Switch to RUN mode.
2. Key in the value of x to be substituted into the equation
$$y = x^2 - 2x + 3$$
3. Press the ley labeled [A]. The HP-67 will automatically search in its memory for the sequence of instructions headed by f LBL A. When this is found, execution of the program is initiated using the keyed in value in the display as the value of x. When the h RTN instruction is

encountered, program execution is terminated, and the program halts with the calculated value of y in the display.

4. Repeat steps 2 and 3 for each different value of x.

In Schematic HP-67-1 the corresponding values of y are calculated for values of x equal to 1.23, 0.5, 3.7, and –12.9.

Obviously, once the program has been keyed in, it may be reinitiated as often as is desired for any subsequent value of x. Each time merely pressing the key labeled [A] yields the correct result. This is not only a valuable time-saving device (since we do not have to key in the instruction each time) but is an extremely efficient and fast way to evaluate the expression, even if we have several hundred values of x to process. This leads us immediately to the idea of recording the program for future use or to pass on to another HP-67 or HP-97 user.

Recording a Program on the HP-67

1. Select a blank magnetic card, which is shown in Fig. 8-2.
2. Slide the top right switch from RUN to W/PRGM (Write/ PRoGraM).
3. Insert edge 1 of blank magnetic card into the lower slot on the top right side of the calculator, as shown in Fig. 8-3.
4. The card will be automatically engaged by the HP-67's card reader mechanism and will pass through to the left side of the calculator. The card will now contain the keyed in program.
5. For identification purposes, let us write a suitable title on the magnetic card. For example, perhaps the title "Evaluation of $y = x^2 - 2x + 3$" may be appropriate. To ensure that the program will not be subsequently overwritten, each HP-67 magnetic card may be protected by clipping off the corner at the top left of side 1. A diagram of the protected card is shown in Fig. 8-4.

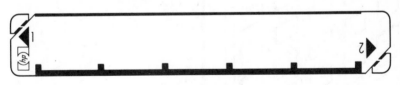

Fig. 8-2

Program HP-67-1 required nine memory locations only. In more complicated situations, of course, the programs will be considerably longer. Any program containing 112 or fewer instructions can conveniently fit on one side of a magnetic card. If, however, the program contains 113 or more instructions (maximum 224), the second side also will have to be written on. The user is alerted to this fact by the display that reads Crd, indicating that edge 2 of the card should be inserted. Similarly the second side of the card may be protected by clipping the edge 2 corner.

The reason for writing x → y is simply to remind the user that, according to this program, a value of x must be keyed in in order to yield the value of y. Its placement on the card will shortly be meaningful.

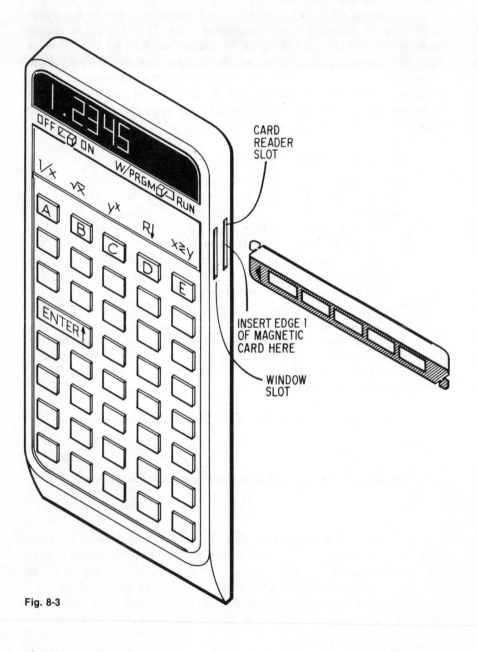

CARD
READER
SLOT

INSERT EDGE 1
OF MAGNETIC
CARD HERE

WINDOW
SLOT

Fig. 8-3

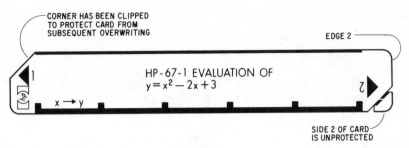

CORNER HAS BEEN CLIPPED
TO PROTECT CARD FROM
SUBSEQUENT OVERWRITING

EDGE 2

HP-67-1 EVALUATION OF
$y = x^2 - 2x + 3$

x → y

SIDE 2 OF CARD
IS UNPROTECTED

Fig. 8-4

Running a Prerecorded Program

The advantage of writing a program on a magnetic card is that, for all intents and purposes it will remain stored on that card forever. On some subsequent occasion we may want to run the program again. The question now arises: How does one load this prerecorded program into the calculator's memory? The following procedure is suggested:

1. Switch to RUN mode.
2. Insert edge 1 of the card into the card reader slot on the right-hand side of the HP-67.
3. The card will be sensed by the reading mechanism which, after engaging the card, ejects it out the left slot.
4. If the program written on the card contains more than 112 instructions, the HP-67 will automatically prompt the user to insert the second side of the card by displaying Crd.
5. The program written on the card will now have been read into the memory of the calculator. Insert the card into the HP-67's window slot. It will now rest conveniently above the function label keys A through E, as shown in Fig. 8-5. It should now be apparent why x → y was written in the leftmost position of the card. When the card is inserted in the window slot, this heading lines up directly above the key marked A. This reminds the user that, after he has keyed in his value of x, pressing the key labeled [A] will calculate and display the value of y.
6. Now that Program HP-67-1 is resident in the memory, it may be used in the ordinary way simply by keying in any value of x and pressing the key labeled [A].

Volume of a Right Cylinder

You will no doubt recall that the formula for calculating the volume of a right cylinder given its radius and height is:

$$\text{Volume} = \pi r^2 h$$

where

> r = the radius of the base
> h = the height of the cylinder

Suppose we know the volume of the cylinder as well as its radius. We could solve for h, the height of the cylinder, by a simple algebraic transformation:

$$h = \text{Volume}/(\pi r^2)$$

As we have pointed out before, writing a program that solves for many cases is not very different from the sequence of steps required to solve for a single case in manual mode.

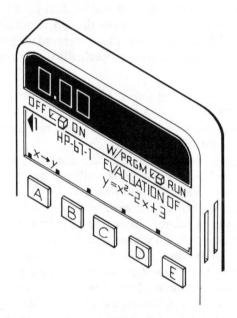

Fig. 8-5

Example 12: Find the perpendicular height of a right cylinder whose radius measures 10.3 cm and whose volume is 159.68 cm³.

S	1	2	3	4
K	159.68	h	π	10.3
D	159.68	159.68	3.14	10.3
C	Volume			r

S	5	6	7	8
K	g	x^2	X	÷
D	10.3	106.09	333.29	0.48
C		r^2	πr^2	$h = \text{Volume}/(\pi r^2)$

It is clear that the previous sequence of steps will be quite satisfactory for calculating the value of h for a single case. Advantage of a calculator's programmability, however, may be taken most effectively when we have not one but rather a whole series of similar cases where only the input data changes.

When transforming the sequence in Example 12 into a program, one must bear in mind that provision must be made for the keying in of two separate data items (the volume and the radius) rather than the single data item (the value of x) that was necessary in Program HP-67-1. In that program, the single input item was keyed in before execution of the program. A similar approach can be adopted here—at least for the first data item. But how will we arrange for the second data item to be keyed in? One answer to this question is to resort to the [R/S] key. The Run/Stop instruction may be inserted in the program at an appropriate point. When this instruction is encountered during execution of a program, the machine is halted, permitting the keying in of the second data item. Execution may then be resumed by pressing the [R/S] key from the keyboard in RUN mode.

As you will recall, a program on the HP-67 has a label instruction at its beginning and a return at its conclusion. Here is one possible program to solve the problem.

Program HP-67-2:   Volume, Radius, and Height of a Right Cylinder

Step Number	Instruction	Comments
001	f LBL B	Names the program B
002	h π	
003	R/S	Halts execution of the program, permitting the value of r to be keyed in
004	g x^2	r^2
005	X	πr^2
006	÷	$h = \text{Volume}/(\pi r^2)$
007	h RTN	Halts program

This seven line program may now be keyed into the memory of the calculator and executed for as many values of the volume and the radius as are necessary.

Schematic HP-67-2

S	1	2	3	4
K	switch to	press	key in steps	switch
D	W/PRGM	f CL PRGM	of Program	to RUN mode
	mode		HP-67-2	

Schematic HP-67-2 (cont'd)

S	5	6	7	8
K	159.68	B	10.3	R/S
D	159.68	3.14	10.3	0.48
C	Volume	program halts to permit value of r to be keyed in	r	Run/Stop key resumes program execution. Program halts with value of h in display.

S	9	10	11	12	
K	800	B	5.25	R/S	. . . etc.
D	800	3.14	5.25	9.24	
C	Volume		r	h	

It may be of interest to the reader who has access to an HP-67 to watch very carefully what happens in the display as instructions are keyed in in W/PRGM mode. Returning for a moment to Program HP-67-2, for example,

[f] [LBL][B]

occupies only one memory location, despite the fact that it required three keystrokes. This "merging" of instructions is a significant advance in the design of the calculator for it minimizes the space that the program occupies in memory. This technology reaches it zenith in the HP-67 where up to a maximum of three keystrokes are sometimes merged. Of course, some *single* instructions occupy a complete location such as CHS, ENTER ↑ , and the four basic arithmetic operations. Nevertheless, the savings of memory space made possible by merged instructions increases the capacity of a programmable calculator to a considerable degree. It is effectively extending the size of the memory.

Quite apart from this merged instruction feature is another equally interesting one. It concerns the manner in which the instructions appear in the display. The contents of the first instruction (f LBL B), for example, appear as:

001   31   25   12

The number on the left, 001, is the location number. As each location is filled, so the location number is automatically incremented by one. Next we have the number 31. This refers to the key located on the third row down, first column. What key is located there? None other than the [f] prefix key. Now for the number 25; this refers in a similar fashion to the key located in the second row down, fifth key in, [LBL], since it is prefixed by [f]. The last number 12 is the matrix code for the first row, second key in—the [B] key. The digits 0 through 9 are always shown as 00 through 09 in program mode.

In order to familiarize the reader with this concept of matrix codes—a feature that can be used to advantage when checking, debugging, or editing a program—we present Table 8-1, consisting of instructions with their corresponding matrix codes. The reader is invited to fill in those places indicated with a question mark.

Table 8-1 Matrix Codes

Function	Keys Required	Merged Instruction Code
1. Subtraction	—	51
2. Store the display in memory register 4	STO 4	33 04
3. Add the display to memory register A	STO + A	33 61 11
4. Take the square root of the value in the display	f √x	31 64
5. Change the sign of the number in the display	CHS	?
6. ?	?	34 63
7. Enter the digit 8 in the display	8	08
8. ?	DSP 9	?
9. ?	h RTN	35 22
10. 10^x	?	?
11. ?	STO ÷ 7	?
12. ?	?	00

How does one clear a program prior to keying in a new one? One way is to switch the calculator off and switch it on again. Another way is to press the keys

[f] [CL PRGM]

in program mode. Both of these methods have the effect of writing R/S instructions in each of the memory locations—all 224 of them. In fact, whenever a program is written each instruction *overwrites* an R/S instruction. You may wonder why this design was decided upon. It seems reasonable to suppose that by putting R/S instructions in every location the calculator would come to a halt in the event that "something in the program went awry." Of course, advantage can be taken of the fact that the instruction following the last keyed in program instruction is, by default, an R/S instruction.

Area of a Triangle Problem

Those of us for whom high school mathematics is a distant memory will probably not remember the formula to calculate the area of a triangle given the lengths of each of the three sides. It is called Heron's Formula and is usually written:

$$\text{Area} = \sqrt{s\,(s-a)\,(s-b)\,(s-c)}$$

where

a, b, c = the lengths of the three sides of the triangle

s = (a + b + c)/2 = one-half the perimeter of the triangle

A close scrutiny of this formula will reveal that the value s (half the sum of the three sides of the triangle) is referenced no fewer than four times. It would be a wise strategy, therefore, to calculate the value of s once and store it in a memory register. This value may then be subsequently recalled whenever it is required.

Since the input data to this problem are the values a, b, and c, provision must be made for keying in these values. As done in the previous programs, the first value, a, can be keyed in prior to program execution and use made of the R/S instruction to halt the calculator to permit the keying in of the remaining two values. As usual, the program must be suitably headed and terminated. Without further ado, here is the program.

Program HP-67-3: Area of a Triangle

Calculate the area of a triangle given three sides.

Step Number	Instruction	Comments
001	f LBL A	
002	STO 1	Stores the value of a in R1
003	R/S	Halts program execution to permit the value of b to be keyed in
004	STO 2	Stores b in R2
005	R/S	Halts program to permit c to be keyed in
006	STO 3	Stores c in R3
007	RCL 1	a
008	+	a + c
009	RCL 2	b
010	+	a + b + c
011	2	
012	÷	s = (a + b + c)/2
013	STO 4	Stores value of s in R4
014	RCL 1	Recalls a to display, pushing s into y register
015	−	(s − a)
016	RCL 4	s
017	X	s(s − a)
018	RCL 4	s

Program HP-67-3 (cont'd)

Step Number	Instruction	Comments
019	RCL 2	b
020	−	(s − b)
021	×	s(s − a) (s − b)
022	RCL 4	s
023	RCL 3	c
024	−	(s − c)
025	×	s(s − a) (s − b) (s − c)
026	f √x	Area = $\sqrt{s(s-a)(s-b)(s-c)}$
027	h RTN	

Schematic HP-67-3

Find the area of triangle ABC (see Fig. 8-6) where

1. a = 5; B = 4; c = 3
2. a = 10.1; b = 9.6; c = 13.8
3. a = 10; b = 15; c = 20

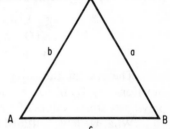

Fig. 8-6

S	1	2	3	4	5	6
K	switch to	press	key in steps	switch	5	A
D	W/PRGM	f CL PRGM	of Program	to RUN	5.	5.00
	mode		HP–67–3	mode		
C						a

S	7	8	9	10	11	12
K	4	R/S	3	R/S	10.1	A
D	4.	4.00	3.	6.00	10.1	10.10
C	b		c	area		a

S	13	14	15	16	17	18
K	9.6	R/S	13.8	R/S	10	A
D	9.6	9.60	13.8	48.47	10.	10.00
C	b		c	area		a

S	19	20	21	22
K	15	R/S	20	R/S
D	15.	15.00	20.	72.62
C	b		c	area

Modified Area of a Triangle Problem

If you followed Program HP-67-3, you will probably agree that the approach adopted was quite straightforward and no particular difficulties were encountered in keying in the input data. The HP-67 provides for even greater flexibility by permitting the user the option of structuring his program into convenient segments.

For example, we can select label A whose function will be nothing other than to store the value of a into memory register 1. It is a very short segment indeed, consisting of the following three lines:

f LBL A
STO 1
h RTN

At the same time, label B can be reserved for storing the value of b into R2, while label C can define a function whose role is simply to store c into R3. These segments may be written as shown:

f LBL B   f LBL C
STO 2   STO 3
h RTN   h RTN

The rest of the program may now be incorporated into a fourth function, say D, in which the area of the triangle is calculated using the previously stored values of a, b, and c.

What we have outlined is a method of breaking up the program into four functions or routines, each one of which is headed by its own label and is terminated by a return instruction. These four routines are keyed into the calculator, and once they are all resident in its memory, any desired values of a, b, and c may be keyed in (in any order) followed by the pressing of the appropriate label key. Once these three values have been keyed in and their corresponding label keys pressed, the area of the triangle may be calculated by simply pressing the [D] key. Here is the complete program.

Program HP-67-4: Modified Area of a Triangle

Step Number	Instruction	Comments
001	f LBL A	Defines function A, which stores the value of a in register 1
002	STO 1	
003	h RTN	
004	f LBL B	Defines function B, which stores the value of b in register 2
005	STO 2	
006	h RTN	
007	f LBL C	Defines function C, which stores the value of c in register 3
008	STO 3	
009	h RTN	

Program HP-67-4 (cont'd)

Step Number	Instruction	Comments
010	f LBL D	
011	RCL 1	
012	RCL 3	
013	+	
014	RCL 2	
015	+	
016	2	
017	÷	
018	STO 4	
019	RCL 1	
020	−	Defines function D, which calculates the area of the triangle given the three sides a, b, and c stored in registers 1, 2 and 3, respectively
021	RCL 4	
022	X	
023	RCL 4	
024	RCL 2	
025	−	
026	X	
027	RCL 4	
028	RCL 3	
029	−	
030	X	
031	f √x	
032	h RTN	

It is pointed out that the order of keying in routines A, B, C, and D is not important since they are identified by their label names and not by their particular locations in memory.

Schematic HP-67-4

S	1	2	3	4	5
K	switch to	press	key in steps	switch	5
D	W/PRGM	f CL PRGM	of Program	to RUN	5.
	mode		HP-67-4	mode	
C					a

S	6	7	8	9	10
K	A	4	B	3	C
D	5.00	4.	4.00	3.	3.00
C		b		c	

Schematic HP-67-4 (cont'd)

S	11	12	13	14	15
K	D	10.1	A	9.6	B
D	6.00	10.1	10.10	9.6	9.60
C	area	a		b	

S	16	17	18	19	20
K	13.8	C	D	15	B
D	13.8	13.80	48.47	15.	15.00
C	c		area	b	

S	21	22	23	24	25
K	20	C	10	A	D
D	20.	20.00	10.	10.00	72.62
C	c		a		area

Successive Factorial Program

On the HP-67, one can readily compute the factorial of any positive integer up to 69 simply by keying in the number and pressing the [h] [N!] keys. We shall use this factorial function key to illustrate the following important programming techniques:

1. Implementing a counter within a program.
2. Use of the unconditional branch (GTO) instruction.
3. Use of the pause instruction.

What we propose to do is to calculate within a program the factorial of the integers 1, 2, 3, . . . , 69, pausing each time for about one second to display the result. The reader will thus be able to see in a graphic manner the exponential growth of the factorial function.

The flowchart in Fig. 8-7 illustrates the logic employed in implementing this strategy. This flowchart is unusual in that no provision has been indicated for terminating the program. This is quite deliberate since, as will shortly be seen, the factorials of the numbers 1 through 69 will be calculated successively. The calculator will automatically come to a halt when an attempt is made to calculate the factorial of 70, which causes overflow to occur. This method may be criticized as lacking somewhat in elegance, but in a short while we shall show a way to terminate the program in a more orthodox manner.

The Pause Instruction [h] [PAUSE]

For those situations where the programmer wishes to keep a visual check on particular data during the course of execution, he may include a PAUSE instruction in the program wherever it is needed. When the PAUSE instruction is encountered during program execution, the program is

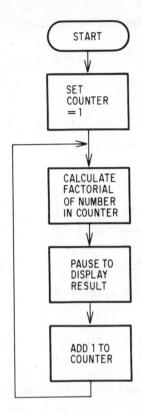

Fig. 8-7 Flowchart HP-67-5:
Successive Factorials

temporarily halted for a period of about one second so that the contents of the x register at that point may be viewed. At the end of the PAUSE, execution of the program resumes in the normal way. Of course, should it be desired to have a pause of more than one second, this may be arranged by inserting a sequence of pause instructions in a program. In a sense the PAUSE instruction is analogous to the print instruction usually associated with large computers, the only difference being that the latter provides a permanent record of the results.

As we mentioned earlier, the companion desk top calculator to the HP-67, known as the HP-97, does, in fact, have a printer associated with it. The [f] [-x-] instruction on the HP-67 is interpreted on the HP-97 as being a print instruction. On the HP-97 this may be regarded as a "print the contents of the x register (display)" instruction. The HP-67 treats this as a *five* second PAUSE instruction.

Unconditional Branching

As has been apparent in previous programs, instructions are generally executed sequentially. For special situations, however, it is desirable to make a jump to another part of the program somewhere else in memory. This may be accomplished on the HP-67 by using the "go to" instruction labeled [GTO]. Jumps can be made only to instructions containing labels, as shown in the following examples:

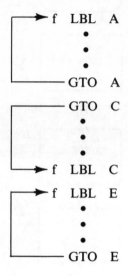

These examples clearly show that jumps may be made in a backwards as well as a forward direction. In addition to the labels A through E, one is at liberty to jump to labels a through e. In fact, the choice of labels is even wider since one also is permitted to jump to labels 0 through 9.

It is pointed out that when setting up a label name a through e, one must use the key sequence, for example,

[g] [LBL f] [a]

Here are some more examples of valid uses of the GTO instruction:

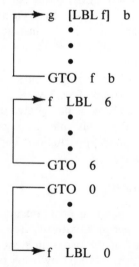

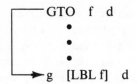

Each time a GTO instruction is encountered, control is sent immediately to that label referenced by the "go to." Execution resumes from this label in the ordinary way.

Here is a program to compute and display all the factorials 1 through 69.

Program HP-67-5: Successive Factorials

Step Number	Instruction	Comments
001	f LBL A	
002	1	Sets up counter in register 0 with initial value of 1
003	STO 0	
004	DSP 0	Fixes display for no decimal places
005	f LBL 1	Defines transfer point labeled 1
006	RCL 0	Recalls counter to display
007	h N!	Calculates factorial of value in display
008	h PAUSE	Pauses for one second to display result
009	1	Adds 1 to counter
010	STO + 0	
011	GTO 1	Transfers control to location 005

Schematic HP-67-5

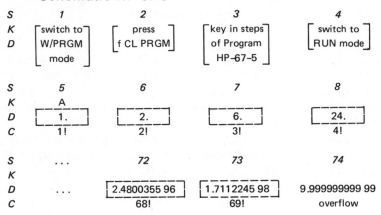

S	1	2	3	4
K				
D	switch to W/PRGM mode	press f CL PRGM	key in steps of Program HP-67-5	switch to RUN mode

S	5	6	7	8
K	A			
D	1.	2.	6.	24.
C	1!	2!	3!	4!

S	...	72	73	74
K				
D	...	2.4800355 96	1.7112245 98	9.999999999 99
C		68!	69!	overflow

As will be apparent from this program, two separate labels are involved, label A and label 1. The program is initiated by storing 1 in register 0. Since we are dealing with integer numbers exclusively, we can suppress the two decimal places that would ordinarily be seen by including the instruction DSP 0. After the factorial has been displayed for one second, 1 is added to the contents of register 0 using the STO + 0 instruction, which you will recall from our discussion of register arithmetic. When the GTO 1 is executed, we set up a loop to statement 005 where subsequent factorials are computed.

Sum of Consecutive Integers Problem

It is the famous mathematician Gauss who is credited with having arrived at the formula for adding up the consecutive integers 1 through n in his head. In the event that you are not familiar with his formula, which is a paragon of simplicity:

$$Sum = n(n + 1)/2$$

For example, the sum of the integers 1 through 10 is 55:

$$Sum = 10(10 + 1)/2$$
$$= 55$$

Since this formula sums the digits from 1 to n, it would have to be amended somewhat were we to require the sum of the integers from some arbitrary starting point, say k, through n. The amended formula becomes:

$$Sum = [n(n + 1) - k(k - 1)]/2$$

The sum of the integers say, from 7 through 10, would be calculated by substituting the value 7 for k and 10 for n:

$$Sum = [10(11) - 7(6)]/2$$
$$= 34$$

We can arrive at this same result by adding up the numbers k through n by the "brute force" method, without resorting to the formula itself. For the sake of illustration, this brute force method is accomplished by means of a loop, in which the successive integers are generated and added to register 2. Naturally, we want this process to stop once all the additions have been completed. This is accomplished by comparing the stored value of n in the y register with the most recent integer generated in the x register. This comparison is effected by using one of the eight conditional test instructions available on the HP-67.

Conditional Branching

One of the great advantages of the HP-67 is the rich variety of conditional test instructions that are available. We have already encountered the "go to" instructions, which transfers control to another part of the program "without any questions being asked." The eight conditional operations we are about to discuss permit special action to be taken, depending upon the contents of the x and y registers. They are:

Conditional Test	Explanation
1. g x = y	Asks if the contents of the x and y registers are equal
2. g x ≠ y	Asks if the contents of the x and y registers are *not* equal
3. g x ≤ y	Asks if the contents of the x register are less than or equal to that of the y register
4. g x > y	Asks if the contents of the x register are greater than that of the y register
5. f x = 0	Asks if the contents of the x register equal zero
6. f x ≠ 0	Asks if the contents of the x register are *not* equal to zero
7. f x < 0	Asks if the contents of the x register are less than zero
8. f x > 0	Asks if the contents of the x register are greater than zero

Each of these eight conditional branches behaves in essentially the same manner. If the answer to the particular question being asked is YES—that is, the test proves to be *true*—execution of the program continues normally with the next instruction in sequence. However, if the answer to the question is NO—that is, the test proves to be *false*—then the next instruction immediately following the conditional test in program memory is automatically *skipped,* as illustrated in the following diagram.

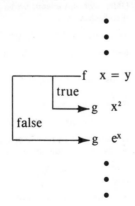

When the f x = y instruction is encountered during program execution, the question asked is "Are the contents of the x and y registers equal?" If the contents of the x register are, in fact, equal to the contents of the y register—that is, the test proves to be true—then execution continues in the normal manner with the next instruction in memory where the value in the display is squared. If, on the other hand, the contents of the x and y registers are not identical—that is, the test proves to be false—then the next instruction in memory, the g x^2 instruction, is automatically *skipped*. Execution resumes with the instruction contained in the *second* location following the conditional test instruction where the exponential function e^x is calculated.

If the instruction immediately following the conditional test instruction happens to be a GTO instruction, we have, in effect, set up a *conditional* go to instruction. For example, the sequence of instructions

$$g \quad x = 0$$
$$GTO \quad f \quad a$$

effects a go to to the section of the program identified by a g LBL f a instruction, *if* the contents of the display are equal to zero.

Returning to our problem at hand, its logic may be better understood after an examination of its flowchart shown in Fig. 8-8.

Program HP-67-6: Sum of the Integers k through n

Step Number	Location	Comments
001	g LBL f a	Defines beginning of routine
002	STO 1	Stores keyed in value of k into register 1
003	STO 2	Initializes sum in register 2 to k
004	R/S	Halts program execution to permit value of n to be keyed in
005	STO 3	Stores value of n in register 3
006	f LBL 5	Sets up transfer point for beginning of loop
007	1	Adds 1 to k in register 1
008	STO + 1	
009	RCL 1	Recalls value of k
010	STO + 2	Adds k to sum in register 2
011	RCL 3	Recalls value of n to display, lifting value of k from the x register to the y register
012	g x ≠ y	Asks if the x and y registers are not equal in content
013	GTO 5	Yes; then branch to beginning of loop
014	RCL 2	No; then recall sum to display
015	h RTN	Halts program execution with sum in display

Schematic HP-67-6

S	1	2	3	4	5
K	⎡switch to⎤	⎡press ⎤	⎡key in steps⎤	⎡switch⎤	7
D	⎢W/PRGM⎥	⎢f CL PRGM⎥	⎢of Program⎥	⎢to RUN⎥	7.
	⎣mode ⎦	⎣ ⎦	⎣HP–67–6 ⎦	⎣mode ⎦	
C					k

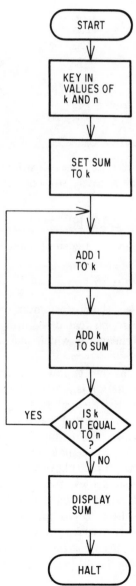

Fig. 8-8 Flowchart HP-67-6:
Sum of the Integers k through n

Schematic HP-67-6 (cont'd)

S	6	7	8	9	10
K	f	a	10	R/S	1
D	7.	7.00	10.	34.00	1.
C		program halts to permit keying in of n	n	$\displaystyle\sum_{i=7}^{10}(i)$	1

S	11	12	13	14	
K	f	a	100	R/S	. . . etc.
D	1.	1.00	100.	5050.00	
C			n	$\displaystyle\sum_{i=1}^{100}(i)$	

Indirect Addressing

On the HP-67, as you will recall, one can store information from the display *directly* into a memory register, say register 9, by means of the following keystrokes:

[STO] [9]

By the same token, data stored in, say register 6, may be recalled directly to the display by the key sequence

[RCL] [6]

In each of the cases cited above, the corresponding registers are accessed directly. However, among the sophisticated features of the HP-67 is one called *indirect addressing,* by means of which registers may be accessed indirectly using the I register.

In order to illustrate this most powerful feature, Table 8-2 is provided. It assumes that information is stored in each of the 26 available storage registers R0 through R9, Rs0 through Rs9, R_A through R_E, and the I register. In fact, it is strongly suggested that the reader key these values into his calculator so that we may talk realistically about the operations to be performed on these registers. You will remember that to load a value from the display into the I register the [h] [STI] keys are used. Of course, to load values into the secondary registers they must first be loaded into their corresponding primary registers and interchanged with the [f] [P≥S] keys.

After these values have been keyed in, they may be checked by utilizing the automatic register review feature of the HP-67 ([h] [REG]). Once they are confirmed to have been correctly keyed in, recall the contents of the indexing register I by using the [h] [RCI] keys. The value 5.00 should now appear in the display.

Table 8-2 Register Layout for the HP-67

Register Name	Register No.	Contents
*R0	0	[21.]
R1	1	[4.567 −09]
R2	2	[2.]
R3	3	[−68.9273]
R4	4	[7.]
R5	5	[16.]
R6	6	[55.]
R7	7	[0.]
R8	8	[1.0598326 23]
R9	9	[0.]
†Rs0	10	[13.3789]
Rs1	11	[4]
Rs2	12	[24]
Rs3	13	[55]
Rs4	14	[2.718281828]
Rs5	15	[0.]
Rs6	16	[3.141592654]
Rs7	17	[3.]
Rs8	18	[0.]
Rs9	19	[25.]
‡R_A	20	[0.]
R_B	21	[0.]
R_C	22	[6.3297]
R_D	23	[−13.38516]
R_E	24	[921.0365]
ξI	25	[5.]

*   Primary Registers: R0 – R9
†   Secondary Registers: Rs0 – Rs9
‡   Additional Primary Registers: R_A – R_E
ξ   Indexing Register

If we now press the keys

[RCL] [(i)]

the contents of the register number contained in the I register will be brought to the display. In other words, the number 5 contained in register I is used as the address for the register being accessed. As you will observe from the chart, register 5 contains the value 16. It is this value that is sent to the display in this indirect manner.

To interchange the value of the I register with that of the display, press the [h] [x ≳ I] keys. The I register will now contain the value 16. Pressing the [RCL] [(i)] keys once again will indirectly recall to the display the contents of the register referenced by the I register—that is, register 16. From Table 8-2 it will be observed that register 16 contains the value π, which is now displayed.

We would now like to change the contents of register I to illustrate further examples of indirect addressing. Now store the number 23 in the I register. Recall the contents of register 6 in the normal (direct) manner using the [RCL] [6] keys. The value 55 will then be sent to the display. To store the value 55 (currently in the display) into the memory register indirectly referenced by the I register, press the keys

$$[STO] \ [(i)]$$

This will have the effect of storing the displayed value into the register number contained in register I. In this case, 55 will be stored into register 23 (register R_D).

Indirect addressing may be further exploited when performing register arithmetic. Here are some examples, together with explanations of indirect register arithmetic operations.

Example A:

$$STO + (i)$$

The effect of this sequence of keystrokes is to add the current value of the display to the memory register indirectly referenced by the I register. That is to say, if the I register contains the number 0, for example, then the current contents of the display will be added to register R0 after keying in the above sequence.

Example B:

$$STO \div (i)$$

Keying in this key sequence has the effect of dividing the value in the display by the contents of the memory register referenced by the I register.

In a similar fashion, subtraction and multiplication operations may be performed indirectly on any of the 25 memory registers by using the STO – (i) and STO $\times$ (i) instructions, respectively.

We have by no means exhausted the variety of instructions that may be combined with the powerful indirect addressing feature. These others will, however, be discussed at the appropriate time.

Finding the Minimum Value in the Registers

For the purpose of the next problem, let us assume that during the course of calculation of a problem, n intermediate results (where n may be as large as 24) are stored successively in registers 1 through 24, the value of n being stored in the I register. You will recall that the primary registers R0 through R9 are designated 0 through 9; the secondary registers Rs0 through Rs9, 10 through 19; registers R_A through R_E, 20 through 24; and the I register, number 25.

Once registers 1 through 24 have been assigned their values, we wish, within the program, to find the minimum value.

To help the reader follow the logical flow of the program we shall soon present, a flowchart is shown in Fig. 8-9. A few explanatory notes regarding the I register and the notation used is probably in order. Remember, the I register can act just like any other register for storing and recalling a value. When used in this manner, its indirect addressing capability is ignored. However, as we have explained, the contents of the I register may be used to specify any one of 26 registers. This, of course, is the basis of indirect addressing. What we have, in effect, is a register specifying another register. On occasions, we want to refer to register I itself and at other times to the register being referenced by the I register. In order to avoid ambiguity, the flowchart that follows is documented with (i) to indicate the register being referenced by the I register, and I, for the I register itself. This convention, incidentally, is used also by Hewlett-Packard in the labeling of their keys.

The DSZ and ISZ Instructions

In addition to the various branching instructions available on the HP-67 are two special branch instructions, both of which may be exploited to advantage when writing complex programs, particularly those that are iterative in nature.

The DSZ instruction, when encountered during program execution, first decrements the contents of the I register by 1—that is, subtracts 1 from it. Then it asks the question: Is the resulting value in the I register equal to zero? If it is, then the next step in sequence is automatically skipped. If the contents of the I register is not equal to zero, then execution continues in the normal manner with the next instruction in sequence. It is for this reason that the instruction is called Decrement and Skip on Zero (DSZ).

The Increment and Skip on Zero is very similar to the DSZ instruction, except that the I register is first incremented, rather than decremented, by 1. Once again, the instruction immediately following the ISZ is automatically skipped if the resulting value of the I register is zero. This instruction may prove useful when counting *up* from some negative starting value to zero.

By the way, one is not confined to decrementing or incrementing the I register. The HP-67 provides the flexibility whereby one may use the I register to decrement or increment another register. For example, if the number 5 is in the I register, one can indirectly perform a decrement and

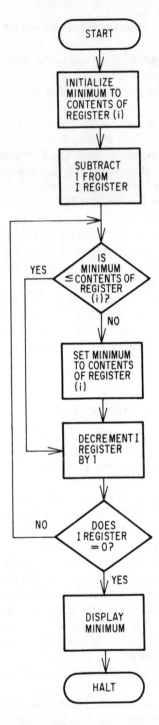

Fig. 8-9 Flowchart HP-67-7: Finding the Minimum of a Set of Values

skip on zero operation on register 5 by incorporating the following keys into a program:

$$[g] \ [DSZ \ (i)]$$

Similarly, to include an increment and skip on zero instruction for register 5 into a program, the key sequence

$$[g] \ [ISZ \ (i)]$$

can be used.

Program HP-67-7: Finding the Minimum of a Set of Values

Step Number	Instruction	Comments
001	f LBL E	
002	RCL (i)	Recalls first value to display
003	STO 0	Initializes minimum in register R0 to this value
004	h RCI	Recalls value of n to display
005	1	
006	−	$n - 1$
007	h STI	Stores adjusted value of n into I register
008	f LBL 1	
009	RCL (i)	Recalls value contained in memory register referenced by register I
010	RCL 0	Recalls current minimum to display
011	g x ≤ y	Is minimum ≤ contents of register (i)?
012	GTO 2	Yes; then continue with next value
013	h R↓	No; rolls down stack to bring contents of register (i) back into the display (Note: RCL (i) instruction would serve the same purpose.)
014	STO 0	Updates value of minimum
015	f LBL 2	
016	f DSZ	Decrements the I register by 1; if the contents of register I now equals 0, then skip the next instruction
017	GTO 1	Loop back to label 1 to continue processing
018	RCL 0	Recalls minimum value to display
019	h RTN	

According to the schematic that follows, five numbers are loaded into registers 1, 2, 3, 4, and 5. To find the minimum of five numbers, one would not ordinarily resort to an expensive machine such as the HP-67. One would simply look at the numbers and select the minimum by using powers of observation rather than any intellectual skills. But we want to show how the method works. So we key in the five numbers directly. What applies to these five numbers will apply equally to any value of n not greater than 24.

Schematic HP-67-7

Find the minimum of –12.7, 13.89, 9.8, –13.6, 27.

S	1	2	3	4	5
K	⌈ switch ⌉	⌈ press ⌉	⌈key in steps⌉	⌈ switch⌉	12.7
D	to PRGM	f CL PRGM	of Program	to RUN	12.7
	⌊ mode ⌋	⌊ ⌋	⌊ HP-67-7 ⌋	⌊ mode⌋	

S	6	7	8	9	10
K	CHS	STO	1	13.89	STO
D	–12.7	–12.7	–12.70	13.89	13.89
C	1st			2nd	
	value			value	

S	11	12	13	14	15
K	2	9.8	STO	3	13.6
D	13.89	9.8	9.8	9.80	13.6
C		3rd			
		value			

S	16	17	18	19	20
K	CHS	STO	4	27	STO
D	–13.6	–13.6	–13.60	27.	27.
C	4th			5th	
	value			value	

S	21	22	23	24	25
K	5	5	h	STI	E
D	27.00	5.	5.	5.00	–13.60
C		n = 5			minimum
					value

Sorting Numbers on the HP-67

If you are in any doubt as to the power of the HP-67, let it be said that by taking advantage of the many sophisticated features one can duplicate the processes that until now have been the sole preserve of computers, whose costs run into the thousands and sometimes millions of dollars. One of the needs that repeatedly emerges in both business programming and advanced mathematics is that of sorting a set of values into either ascending or descending order. There are a great number of programming methods that have been devised to sort values, and a good deal of literature has been written on this subject. What we propose to do here is to sort, in ascending order, up to 23 values that have been stored in registers R1 through Rn (where n ≤ 23). The particular method (algorithm) we have selected is known as the bubble sort. It is so called because with each pass the latest maximum is pushed down to the bottom of the list.

Suppose we have the following five numbers to sort into ascending order:

Element Number	Value
1	4.3
2	2.6
3	6.5
4	3.8
5	2.4

If we were to start with the last value on the list, we could compare it with its neighboring fourth element. If this value is greater than the fifth element, indicating that *these two* elements are not in order, then we switch these two values.

Since 3.8 is indeed greater than 2.4, the positions of these two values in the list are exchanged. We now have:

1	4.3
2	2.6
3	6.5
4	2.4
5	3.8

The fifth element is now compared with the third element in the list, and since this latter value of 6.5 is greater than the former value 3.8, their positions in the list also are switched as follows:

1	4.3
2	2.6
3	3.8
4	2.4
5	6.5

Similarly, the fifth element is compared to the second element and finally with the first element on the list. Since neither of these two values is greater than 6.5, no switches are made and the first pass through the sort is complete. The effect of this first pass is to have "bubbled" the largest value in the list down to the fifth and last position.

The second pass of the sort consists of comparing the fourth element in the list with the third, second, and first elements in the list, making any necessary switches, as described above. By the end of the second pass, the

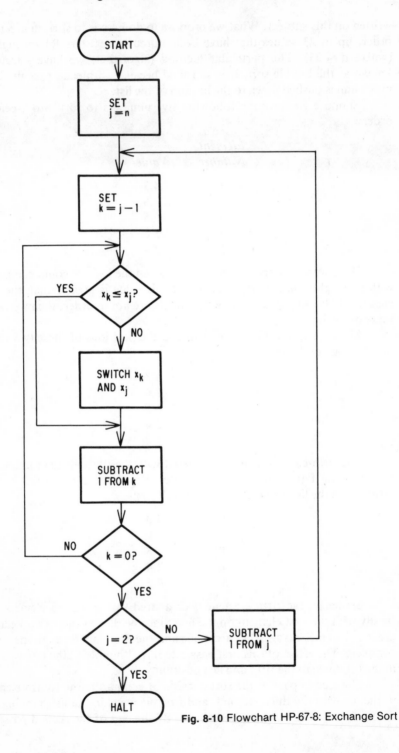

Fig. 8-10 Flowchart HP-67-8: Exchange Sort

second largest value in the list has been sorted into the fourth position. The
list of elements now appears as follows:

1	3.8
2	2.6
3	2.4
4	4.3
5	6.5

The third and fourth passes complete the sort, and the final sorted list of
values becomes:

1	2.4
2	2.6
3	3.8
4	4.3
5	6.5

It is worth noting that the simple bubble sort as outlined requires
$(n - 1)$ passes to sort an n element list of values.

The method described is, in fact, precisely that used in the program
that follows. To further clarify the way in which the sort is implemented on
the HP-67, a flowchart is shown in Fig. 8-10, which assumes that the value
of n is keyed into the I register.

Program HP-67-8: Sorting Numbers

Step Number	Instruction	Comments
001	f LBL B	Exchange Sort
002	h RCI	n
003	STO 0	Sets $j = n$
004	f LBL 3	
005	RCL 0	
006	1	$k = j - 1$
007	—	
008	STO E	
009	f LBL 1	
010	RCL 0	j
011	h STI	
012	RCL (i)	x_j
013	RCL E	k
014	h STI	
015	h R↓	Rolls down stack to put value of x_j back into display
016	RCL (i)	x_k

Program HP-67-8 (cont'd)

Step Number	Instruction	Comments
017	g x ⩽ y	$x_k \leqslant x_j$?
018	GTO 2	Yes; don't switch values
019	h x ⩾ y	No; switch values; bring x_j into display
020	STO (i)	$x_j \rightarrow$ register k
021	RCL 0	j
022	h STI	
023	h R↓ h R↓ }	Brings x_k back to display
024	STO (i)	$x_k \rightarrow$ register j
025	f LBL 2	
026	2 }	Places 24 (number of register E)
027	4	in I register
028	h STI	
029	g DSZ (i)	Decrements register E by 1 and tests for equality with zero
030	GTO 1	$R_E \neq 0$, continue looping
031	RCL 0	$R_E = 0$, finished pass, see if done with sort
032	2	
033	g x = y	j = 2?
034	h RTN	Yes; then program execution is terminated
035	1 }	No; subtract 1 from j and continue with
036	STO −0	next pass
037	GTO 3	

Schematic HP-67-8

S	1	2	3	4	5	6
K	[switch	[press	[key in steps	[switch	4.3	STO
D	to PRGM	f CL PRGM]	of Program	to RUN	4.3	4.3
	mode]		HP–67–8]	mode]		
C					x_1	

S	7	8	9	10	11	12
K	1	2.6	STO	2	6.5	STO
D	4.30	2.6	2.6	2.60	6.5	6.5
C		x_2			x_3	

Schematic HP-67-8 (cont'd)

S	13	14	15	16	17	18
K	3	3.8	STO	4	2.4	STO
D	6.50	3.8	3.8	3.80	2.4	2.4
C		x_4			x_5	

S	19	20	21	22	23	24
K	5	5	h	STI	B	RCL
D	2.40	5	5	5.00	2.00	2.00
C		n			sort	

S	25	26	27	28	29	30
K	1	RCL	2	RCL	3	RCL
D	2.40	2.40	2.60	2.60	3.80	3.80
C	smallest element					

S	31	32	33
K	4	RCL	5
D	4.30	4.30	6.50
C			largest element

Using Subroutines on the HP-67

For those situations where it is necessary to execute the *same* sequence of instructions from several different points in a program, one cannot use the GTO instruction since this would work for the first time only, not on succeeding occasions. If that sequence of instructions is included in subroutine form, it may be accessed as often as is needed and each time it returns control to the instruction *following* that which called it.

A subroutine on the HP-67 is characterized by a header label and a terminal RTN instruction. But this does not differ at all from any of the programs that we have already presented in this section. True. The subroutine is invoked, however, by a special instruction called the GSB (go to subroutine). When the RTN instruction is executed, control is returned to the "main" program that called it, in particular, to the instruction following that which invoked the subroutine. Generally speaking, writing a program in subroutine form considerably minimizes the length of the program, and indeed this might be a crucial factor in determining whether a particular program can fit into the 224 available program locations.

Returning to Program HP-67-8, the exchange sort program, let us assume that we have recorded it on a magnetic card, as discussed earlier. The illustration in Fig. 8-11 suggests a reasonable way of identifying the card.

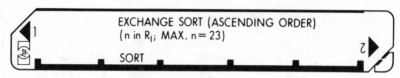

EXCHANGE SORT (ASCENDING ORDER)
(n in R$_I$; MAX. n = 23)

SORT

Fig. 8-11

Suppose at some subsequent point in time we have devised a program (labeled A), which generates some set of values and stores them into registers R1, . . . , R23. Now let us assume that it is necessary for the program to sort these values into ascending order. We could incorporate into the program itself the sequence of instructions necessary to sort them. An alternative and perhaps better solution to the problem is simply to insert into the required point of the program a

GSB   B

instruction (assuming that label B is not defined elsewhere in the program). Prior to inserting this instruction into the program, it is necessary to first store the value of n into the I register, as required by the sort routine.

Use may now be made of the sort routine stored on the magnetic card in the following manner:

1. Determine the program location of the last instruction in the program resident in memory (this will normally be the terminating h RTN instruction). Assume this is location number xyz.
2. In RUN mode, press the keys
[GTO] [·] [x] [y] [z]
This has the effect of positioning the program pointer to location xyz.
3. Press the keys
[g] [MERGE]
This signals the HP-67 to *merge* the next program passed through the card reader into program memory starting with location xyz + 1.
4. Select the sort card and pass it through the reader slot of the HP-67. Since the sort program required fewer than 113 locations of memory, it is only necessary to read in side 1 of the card.
5. Program A may now be executed in the normal way. When the GSB B instruction is encountered during program execution, control will be sent to the sort routine. This will sort the values in the registers into ascending order and then return control to the calling routine upon execution of the h RTN instruction.

By using this technique of merging programs, the sort routine can be merged into a resident program whenever it is required.

The g MERGE instruction can be used to merge more than one program into memory. Thus a library of routines can be stored on *separate* magnetic cards and routines loaded as necessary by using this powerful MERGE instruction.

Flags

The next program introduces us to the concept of *flags,* of which there are four on the HP-67, referred to as F0, F1, F2, and F3. These flags may be set to an on or an off position and may subsequently be tested to determine their status.

In order to set a flag to the on position, that is, to true, the instruction SF (set flag) is used, followed by one of the four digit keys 0, 1, 2, or 3.

To clear a flag, that is, to make it false, the CF (clear flag) instruction is used, once again followed by the appropriate digit key 0 through 3. Incidentally, whenever the HP-67 is switched on or the [f] [CL PRGM] keys are pressed, the four flags are automatically cleared.

Once a flag has been set either true or false, its status may subsequently be tested by making use of the F? instruction, followed by a digit 0 through 3. If the result of the test is true, that is, the flag is on, then the next instruction in sequence is executed in the normal manner. If, however, the test proves false, that is, the flag is off or cleared, the instruction immediately following the flag test instruction is automatically skipped. Thus it becomes obvious that the F? instruction behaves in much the same manner as the conditional branch instructions previously encountered.

It is worth noting that flags 2 and 3 are special in that they behave differently from flags 0 and 1. Whenever the status of either of these two flags is tested by the F? instruction, they are automatically turned off after the test has been made, *regardless of the result of the test.* Thus flags 2 and 3 may prove useful in those instances where it is necessary that a flag be cleared after it has been tested.

Flag F3 is further distinguished from the other three flags, which are available on the HP-67, in that this flag is automatically set *whenever a number is keyed into the display.* This special flag is referred to as the *data entry flag* and can prove very helpful indeed for those situations where a decision is to be made based on whether or not a value was previously keyed into the calculator.

Use of this data entry flag feature will be made in Program HP-67-9, the compound interest program that follows immediately.

Compound Interest Problem

The standard formula for computing the compound interest is

$$S = P(1 + r)^n$$

where

S = total compound sum
P = principal invested
r = interest rate per compound period
n = number of compound periods

For example, if $1,000 is invested at 8% interest, compounded quarterly, we can calculate the total compounded amount after two years by substituting into the formula the values:

$$1000 \text{ for } P$$
$$0.08/4 = 0.02 \text{ for } r$$
$$2 \times 4 = 8 \text{ for } n$$

$$S = 1000(1 + 0.02)^8$$
$$= 1000(1.02)^8$$
$$= \$1,171.66$$

In the above case we solved for the value S given the other three values of P, r, and n. At times it is useful, if not necessary, to solve for *any* one of these four variables given the other three. By algebraic manipulation we can derive the formulas to express any variable in terms of the other three variables:

$$P = S/(1 + r)^n$$
$$r = (S/P)^{1/n} - 1$$
$$n = \ln (S/P)/\ln (1 + r)$$

In the program that follows, the three known values are keyed in according to the following scheme:

Variable	Associated Key
S	A
P	B
r	C
n	D

After the value of each known variable is keyed into the display, its associated label key A through D is pressed. This may be done in any order. Pressing the key associated with the unknown variable subsequently sends its calculated value to the display.

The strategy employed in this program exploits the use of the data entry flag F3. As each of the functions is invoked, flag F3 is tested. If the flag is set, indicating a value has been keyed in immediately prior to invoking the function, the value is stored in a memory register. If, on the other hand, flag F3 has not been set, this means that no value was keyed in, implying that this is the variable whose solution is required. The function then solves for the unknown variable in terms of the other three previously keyed in values.

Program HP-67-9: Compound Interest

Step Number	Instruction	Comments
001	f LBL A	S
002	h F? 3	Is flag 3 set, i.e., was the value of S keyed in? (Note: test operation automatically clears flag)
003	GTO 1	Yes; go to label 1
004	RCL 2	No; solve for S in terms of P, r, and n; recalls value of P to display
005	RCL 3	$1 + r$
006	RCL 4	n
007	h y^x	$(1 + r)^n$
008	X	$S = P(1 + r)^n$
009	h RTN	
010	f LBL 1	Value of S has been keyed in
011	STO 1	Stores S in R1
012	h RTN	
013	f LBL B	P
014	h F? 3	Was the value of P keyed in?
015	GTO 2	Yes; go to label 2
016	RCL 1	No; solve for P; recalls value of S to display
017	RCL 3	$1 + r$
018	RCL 4	n
019	h y^x	$(1 + r)^n$
020	÷	$P = S/(1 + r)^n$.
021	h RTN	
022	f LBL 2	Value of P has been keyed in
023	STO 2	Stores P in R2
024	h RTN	
025	f LBL C	r
026	h F? 3	Was the value of r keyed in?
027	GTO 3	Yes; go to label 3 No; solve for r in terms of S, P, and n
028	RCL 1	S
029	RCL 2	P
030	÷	S/P
031	RCL 4	n

Program HP-67-9 (cont'd)

Step Number	Instruction	Comments
032	h 1/x	$1/n$
033	h y^x	$(S/P)^{1/n}$
034	1	
035	—	$r = (S/P)^{1/n} - 1$
036	h RTN	
037	f LBL 3	
038	1	
039	+	$r + 1$
040	STO 3	Saves $(r + 1)$ in R3
041	h RTN	
042	f LBL D	n
043	h F? 3	Was value of n keyed in?
044	GTO 4	Yes; go to label 4 No; solve for n in terms of S, P, and r
045	RCL 1	S
046	RCL 2	P
047	÷	S/P
048	f LN	ln(S/P)
049	RCL 3	$1 + r$
050	f LN	$\ln(1 + r)$
051	÷	$n = \ln(S/P) / \ln(1 + r)$
052	h RTN	
053	f LBL 4	
054	STO 4	Stores value of n in R4
055	h RTN	

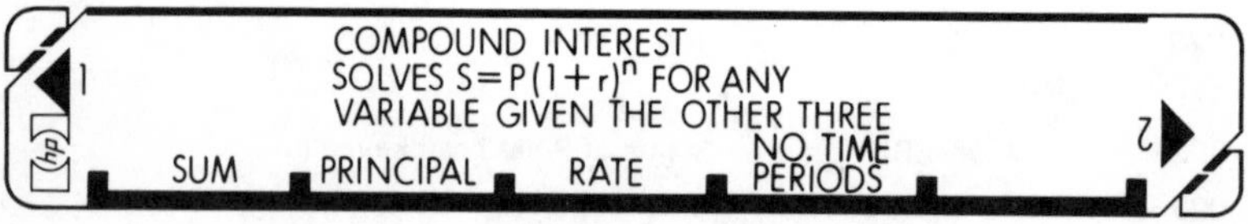

COMPOUND INTEREST
SOLVES $S = P(1 + r)^n$ FOR ANY
VARIABLE GIVEN THE OTHER THREE
SUM   PRINCIPAL   RATE   NO. TIME PERIODS

Fig. 8-12

A point worth mentioning about this program is that when the value of r is pressed, the value of r + 1 is stored into register 3 for ease of computation.

Should it be desired to record this program on a magnetic card, it is recommended that it be marked as shown in Fig. 8-12 and inserted in the window slot to remind the user of the association between the variables and the label keys.

Schematic HP-67-9

1. Solve for S given P = 1,000; r = 0.02; n = 8
2. Solve for n given S = 5,639.24; P = 4,500; r = 0.01625

S	1	2	3	4
K	⎡ switch ⎤	⎡ press ⎤	⎡key in steps⎤	⎡ switch ⎤
D	⎢to PRGM⎥	⎣f CL PRGM⎦	⎢of Program⎥	⎢to RUN⎥
	⎣ mode ⎦		⎣ HP-67-9 ⎦	⎣ mode ⎦

S	5	6	7	8
K	1000	B	.02	C
D	1000.	1000.00	.02	1.02
C	P		r	r + 1

S	9	10	11	12
K	8	D	A	5639.24
D	8.	8.00	1171.76	5639.24
C	n		value of S is	S
			computed	
			automatically	

S	13	14	15	16
K	A	4500	B	0.01625
D	5639.24	4500.	4500.00	0.01625
C		P		r

S	17	18		
K	C	D		
D	1.02	14.00		
C	r + 1 (display	value of n		
	rounded to	calculated by		
	two decimal places)	program		

Further Uses of the I Register

1. *DSP (i).* These keystrokes have the effect of setting the display to the number of rounded decimal places specified by whatever value is contained in the I register.

Example 13

S	1	2	3	4	5
K	5	h	STI	DSP	(i)
D	5.	5.	5.00	5.00	5.00000
C			5 now in		
			I register		

2. *GTO (i)*. If the I register contains a value from 1 to 19, then an unconditional transfer to the label specified is effected. Usually, of course, such a number will be an integer. If it is not, transfer is made to the label specified by the integral portion of the value in the I register. Labels 1 through 9 represent none other than themselves. The values 10 through 14 refer to labels A through E, respectively, while 15 through 19 refer to labels a through e. For example, if the I register contains the value 17, and the GTO (i) instruction is encountered during execution of the program, then an unconditional transfer is made to g LBL f c. If such a label does not exist, the program is halted with the word *Error* in the display.

If the value in the I register is a negative number between −1 and −999 and the GTO (i) instruction is executed, transfer of control during execution is sent back in program memory the number of steps specified by that negative value in the I register, wrapping around the memory if necessary.

3. *GSB (i)*. These keystrokes have an effect analogous to the GTO (i) instruction, which was just described. For example, executing a GSB (i) instruction with a value of 3 in the I register has the effect of calling the subroutine identified by an f LBL 3 instruction.

The Smart Card Reader

In our description of the manner in which one can record a program on a magnetic card, the reader may have been left with the impression that it is the program steps only that are stored on the magnetic card. In point of fact, other information besides the program is recorded automatically onto the card. This includes the current status of the four flags F0 through F3, the current trigonometric mode, and the current display format. When this card is read into the calculator on a subsequent occasion, all of these settings are automatically effected.

In addition to storing a program onto a magnetic card, the contents of the primary storage registers and register I, as well as the contents of the secondary storage registers may be recorded for subsequent use onto a magnetic card by means of the W/DATA instruction.

Debugging and Editing Programs on the HP-67

One would be guilty of excessive wishful thinking if one believed that a program written to solve a particular problem on the HP-67 will work the first time it is tried. It might, but the chances are awfully great that it won't. And it is not necessarily any reflection on the programmer. It is just in the nature of programming to make mistakes, some subtle and others not so subtle. In order to find and correct errors—to "debug" the program as the professional programmers describe it—the calculator has features that greatly assist the user in making any necessary modifications. In general it is not required to rekey in the program each time a correction is needed.

The HP-67 is equipped with the following editing features:

1. Each instruction in any of the 224 program memory locations may be displayed. This is done by pressing the [GTO] and [.] keys, followed by the three digit program memory address in RUN mode and then switching to W/PRGM mode.
2. A program may be stepped through sequentially in either a forward or backward manner to examine successive memory locations by using the [SST] or [h] [BST] keys in W/PRGM mode.
3. An instruction stored in a program location in memory may be replaced by a new instruction.
4. An instruction may be deleted from program memory by using the [h] [DEL] keys.
5. Programs may be merged into memory by using the [g] [MERGE] keys.

A useful debugging technique is to incorporate a PAUSE instruction into the program at critical junctures so that intermediate results can be examined and verified.

Pressing the [SST] key in RUN mode displays the current instruction and its location number as long as the key is held down. When the key is released, that instruction is executed.

Some Final Remarks on the HP-67

As will be quite apparent, a calculator as sophisticated as the HP-67 cannot be adequately treated in a book in which so many other calculators are included. It is clear that a sizable book could easily be devoted entirely to this one calculator. For pragmatic reasons, we shall have to conclude our discussion of the HP-67 and respectfully refer the reader to the 341 page Owner's Handbook and Programming Guide, which is supplied free with the purchase of the calculator.

CHAPTER NINE
THE HEWLETT-PACKARD 19C AND 29C

Probably as a result of the popularity achieved by the continuous memory feature of the HP-25C, Hewlett-Packard introduced in the latter part of 1977 two new advanced programmable calculators, both of which had this continuous memory feature. One of these calculators, the HP-19C, represents a milestone in the development of programmable pocket calculators in that, in addition to its continuous memory, it has a built-in thermal printer that may be used to print out results or to list an entire program. In addition to the fact that it prints silently on heat-sensitive paper, the complete unit—calculator and printer combined—slip easily into a shirt pocket. For those individuals who do not need the printing feature, Hewlett-Packard released, at the same time as it did the HP-19C, a model without a printer called the HP-29C. Programming both calculators is identical except for the printer functions, which are available only on the HP-19C. For this reason, both models will be treated identically in this chapter, except that the special features relating to the printing mechanism on the HP-19C will be treated separately at the end of the chapter.

Pictures of the HP-19C and HP-29C are shown in Fig. 9-1 and Fig. 9-2 respectively. Both the HP-19C and HP-29C permit a program to be 98 steps long. Each memory location, however, may take 1, 2, 3, or even 4 keystrokes, thereby providing greater memory efficiency. Of the 30 addressable storage registers that are available for the storage of data, 16 of them are supported by continuous memory along with the complete 98 steps of program memory, the display, and the format of the display.

Both calculators are rich in useful scientific functions including trigonometric functions, polar-rectangular conversions, decimal and nondecimal hour conversion, three angular modes, logarithmic functions, and a variety of statistical functions.

To facilitate ease of writing sophisticated programs, both models have six conditional branch instructions, in addition to an increment/decrement and skip-on-zero instruction. Addressing may be done by referring to labels, which may also be indirectly addressed. Three levels of subroutines are possible on both models, in addition to a variety of useful editing features.

Fig. 9-1 HP-19C (*Courtesy* Hewlett-Packard Company)

Programming the HP-19C/29C

A textile manufacturer has a series of orders on hand for a particular fabric. Each of the lengths of fabric ordered is specified in lengths of *feet*. The textile manufacturer, however, has to set up his machinery in units of *yards* and tenths of a yard. In view of this fact, the manufacturer must calculate for each order expressed in feet the equivalent length in yards and tenths of a yard. For example, if a bolt of cloth measured 124 feet, he would have to calculate the required number of yards according to the following schematic:

Fig. 9-2 HP-29C (*Courtesy* Hewlett-Packard Company)

Example 1

S	1	2	3	4	5	6
K	f fix	1	124	ENTER↑	3	÷
D		0.0	124.	124.0	3.	41.3
C	fix the display					124 ft = 41.3 yd
	to one decimal					
	place					

Steps 1 and 2 in Example 1 fix the display to one decimal place accuracy, since we are interested only in yards and tenths of a yard.

Steps 3 through 6 would have to be keyed in each time it is desired to convert a length of fabric expressed in feet to its equivalent length in yards and tenths of a yard. On a programmable calculator such as the HP-19C/29C, a sequence of instructions can be stored in the calculator's memory in the form of a program and accessed each time it is required without having to undergo the tedium of having to key it in each time.

Program HP-19C/29C-1: Feet to Yards Conversion

Instruction	Comments
ENTER↑	Copies length expressed in feet from the display or x register into the y register
3	
÷	Calculates length in yd = length in ft/3

Keying in the Program

1. Switch the calculator into program mode; that is, slide the switch to PRGM.
2. Press the [f] [PRGM] keys. This has the effect of clearing the program memory.
3. Key in the instructions of Program HP-19C/29C-1 in exactly the same sequence as shown.
4. Slide the switch to RUN mode.

Running the Program

1. Press the [f] [fix][1] keys to set the proper display format.
2. Press the keys marked [g] [RTN].
3. Key in the value of the length expressed in feet.
4. Press the Run/Stop key marked [R/S]. The program will automatically be executed from its beginning, and the length expressed in yards will appear in the display.
5. Repeat steps 2 through 4 for each new value to be converted.

Schematic HP-19C/29C-1

S	1	2	3	4
K	⌈slide switch⌉	f PRGM	⌈key in steps⌉	⌈slide switch⌉
D	⌊ to PRGM ⌋	00	of Program	⌊ to RUN ⌋
			⌊HP–19C/29C–1⌋	
C		clear program memory		

S	5	6	7	8	9
K	f FIX	1	g RTN	124	R/S
D		0.0		124.	41.3
C			position program at its beginning	length in feet	length in yards

S	10	11	12	
K	g RTN	197	R/S	. . . etc.
D	41.3	197.	65.7	
C			197 ft = 65.7 yd	

Thus we see that 124 feet is equivalent to 41.3 yards, and 197 feet is equivalent to 65.7 yards.

It may seem to the reader that very little if anything at all has been gained by keying in the program for repeated use. This may indeed be the case for the illustration we have presented, but it is atypical of the vast variety of programs that have to be solved in everyday life. This will become apparent in our next program, which is of a slightly more sophisticated nature.

The Effective Annual Interest Rate

Banks across the nation regularly advertise for would-be investors with slogans such as "5% savings account compounded quarterly—effective annual interest rate 5.09%." The reason why the effective rate is higher than the nominal rate is that when an account is compounded, interest is made on the interest as well.

The effective annual interest rate E may be calculated from the formula

$$E = [1 + (r/t)]^t - 1$$

where

r = nominal rate of interest, e.g., 5%

t = number of times per year interest is compounded, e.g., quarterly = 4, semiannually = 2

Thus to calculate the effective annual interest of a 5% savings account compounded quarterly, we simply substitute the value 0.05 for 5, and 4 for t in the above formula.

$$E = [1 + (0.05/4)]^4 - 1$$

Example 2: Evaluate $[1 + (0.05/4)]^4 - 1$

S	1	2	3	4	5	6
K	f fix	4	.05	ENTER↑	4	÷
D		0.00	0.05	0.0500	4.	0.0125
C			r		t	r/t

S	7	8	9	10	11	12
K	1	+	4	f y^x	1	−
D	1.	1.0125	4.	1.0509	1	0.0509
C		1 + (r/t)	t	$[1 + (r/t)]^t$		$E = [1 + (r/t)]^t - 1$

When a program is run the instructions are ordinarily executed in sequence, one instruction after the next. On occasions, however, it is desirable to deviate from this sequential processing by jumping to some other point in the program. For this purpose, a label may be used to define such a point. On the HP-19C/29C there are ten such labels, which are referred to as LBL 0 to LBL 9. Whenever a label is required, the keystrokes [g][LBL], followed by a digit key 0 – 9 is inserted in the appropriate place in the program. This label instruction merely serves as a marker and has no other effect on the program.

When a jump to a particular label is required in a program, the go to instruction (GTO) is used. If a jump is required to label 5, for example, the unconditional transfer to the label is effected by a GTO 5 instruction. When the GTO instruction is encountered during execution of the program, control is sent directly to the location containing the f LBL 5 instruction—wherever it may be located in the program—and execution resumes in the normal sequential fashion from that point.

In the program we are about to present, the g LBL 1 instruction is used as a marker for the beginning of the program so that the program may be reinitiated by a simple GTO 1 instruction, which is the last instruction in the program. This obviates the need to press [g] [RTN] each time the program is re-executed, as was the case in our first simple example.

The Run/Stop key stops execution of the program. This allows the user to not only view the contents of the display but permits him to key in any data items that may be needed by the program. Once the data item has been keyed in and/or the contents of the display observed, the program can be restarted by pressing this same [R/S] key in RUN mode.

As mentioned earlier, the formula that calculates the effective annual interest rate requires that the interest rate r be expressed as a decimal fraction. Therefore, for a 5% interest rate, a value of 0.05 must be used. Similarly, an interest rate of 6 1/4% requires the value 0.0625 to be used as the value of r in the formula. In order to lighten the burden of the user, the program that calculates the effective annual interest rate permits him or her to key in the interest rate as a percentage. That is, a 5% interest rate would be keyed into the calculator simply as a 5; similarly, a 6 1/4% interest rate would be keyed in as 6.25. In order to convert this value of r into a form suitable for use in the formula, all that is necessary is that the value keyed in be divided by 100.

For similar reasons, the final effective annual interest rate E as calculated by the program is multiplied by 100 before the program halts with this value in the display. Thus, an effective annual interest rate of 5.09% will simply be displayed as 5.09 by the program.

Program HP-19C/29C-2: Effective Annual Interest Rate

Instruction	Comments
g LBL 1	Defines label 1
1	
0	Divides the interest rate keyed in by 100 for
0	use in the formula
÷	

Program HP-19C/29C-2 (cont'd)

Instruction	Comments
R/S	Halts program execution to permit the value of t to be keyed in
STO 1	Saves t in register 1
÷	r/t
1	
+	1 + (r/t)
RCL 1	Recalls the value of t to the x register, pushing the value 1 + (r/t) into the y register
f y^x	Calculates $[1 + (r/t)]^t$
1	
-	Calculates $E = [1 + (r/t)]^t - 1$
1	
0	Multiplies the resulting interest rate by 100
0	and halts the program to permit the final
X	value to be read
R/S	
GTO 1	Transfers control unconditionally to LBL 1 so that the next value of E can be calculated

Schematic HP-19C/29C-2

S	1	2	3	4	5
K	slide switch	F PRGM	key in steps	slide switch	f fix
D	to PRGM	00	of Program HP-19C/29C-2	to RUN	

S	6	7	8	9	10
K	2	g RTN	5	R/S	4
D	0.00	0.00	5.	0.05	4.
C		resets program to its beginning	r		t

S	11	12	13	14	15
K	R/S	5	R/S	365	R/S
D	5.09	5	0.05	365.	5.13
C	E	r		t	t

S	16	17	18	19	
K	6.25	R/S	2	R/S	...etc.
D	6.25	0.06	2.	6.35	
C	r		t	E	

    It is necessary to press the [g] [RTN] keys only once to reset the program to its beginning in RUN mode. This is because immediately after the program has been keyed in the program pointer points to the last instruction of the program. To commence execution of the program from that point would be a fruitless exercise. The [g][RTN] keys set the program pointer to the beginning of program memory, where our program to calculate the effective annual interest begins. The GTO 1 instruction of the program serves this very same purpose for the second and subsequent runs of the program.

The person who has the chore of calculating the effective annual interest rate for a large number of transactions at various times throughout a work period may reap the advantages of a continuous memory calculator, since once keyed in, the program resides in memory continuously even when the calculator is shut off. It may be switched on at any time thereafter, and results can be obtained immediately without having to rekey in the program.

Evaluating a Function between Limits

In many disciplines it is sometimes necessary to evaluate a given function between certain limits. In the simplest case we might have a function of x that has to be evaluated for all values of x between a certain minimum value of x and a certain maximum value of x, in steps of a given increment.

The program that follows permits a user to key in the minimum value, followed by the maximum value and then by the increment. The function being evaluated is:

$$f(x) = (e^x + 1)/5$$

In each of the programs presented so far in this chapter, each and every instruction in the program was executed in sequence. At times, however, it becomes necessary to execute a given sequence of instructions, only if certain conditions are met, and if so, to branch around them. This concept of conditional branching forms the basis of sophisticated programming in that it allows for an elaborate network of decisions to be made during execution of the program.

The program that follows introduces us to the means by which decisions are made on the HP-19C/29C calculators. There are a total of eight conditional branch instructions. These eight instructions allow the following questions to be asked during program execution:

Comparisons between the x Register and Zero

1. Are the contents of the x register equal to zero? (g x = 0)
2. Is the x register not equal to zero? (g x ≠ 0)
3. Is the x register greater than zero? (g x>0)
4. Is the x register less than zero? (g x<0)

Comparisons between the x Register and the y Register

5. Are the contents of the x register equal to the contents of the y register? (f x = y)
6. Is the x register not equal to the y register? (f x ≠ y)
7. Is the x register greater than the y register? (f x>y)
8. Is the x register less than or equal to the y register? (f x≤y)

Whenever a decision has to be made in a program, one of the eight tests cited above must be selected. Of course, one would select that which is most convenient for the given situation. Whichever one is selected, however, the comparison is made, and if the comparison is true then execution continues in the normal sequential fashion with the instruction contained in the memory location immediately following the conditional branch instruction. However, if the condition is not satisfied, then the calculator automatically skips the instruction contained in the following memory location, and execution continues in the normal manner with the *second* instruction following the conditional branch instruction.

The following diagram illustrates the manner in which each of these conditional branch instructions operates.

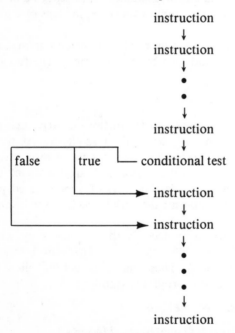

It is necessary to employ a conditional test in the next program to determine if the end limit of the interval has been reached and to terminate the program if it has.

As an alternative to the R/S instruction, which stops execution of the program during RUN mode, the user may opt to use the PAUSE instruction. Unlike the [R/S] key, which must be pressed again to resume execution of the program, the PAUSE instruction, when encountered in the program, stops execution temporarily—for one second to be exact. During that time the contents of the display may be viewed and recorded if necessary. If the user feels that one second is not long enough, several PAUSE instructions in succession may be included.

The operation of Program HP-19C/29C-3 is rather straightforward. The start and end points of the interval together with the value of the increment are keyed in by the user at the beginning and are stored by the program into data storage registers R0 through R2 respectively. The starting point of the interval represents the first value of x to be evaluated by the function. After this value is displayed, the function is evaluated and its result also is displayed. The next value of x is then calculated by adding the increment to the current value of x. If this new value is within the bounds of the interval—that is, it is not greater than the end point value—then we are not done processing and the function must be evaluated once again. However, if the new value of x is greater than the end value, the program will have run its course, and execution is automatically halted—when the R/S instruction is encountered.

When keying in a program, the observant user will notice the rather unique format of the display when the calculator is switched to PRGM mode. This format reflects both the location of the instruction within the memory (00 to 98) along with the instruction contained in that location. The leftmost pair of digits in the display represents the location of the instruction, while the remaining digits represent the instruction itself in coded form. When the [f] [PRGM] keys are depressed, the complete memory is cleared and the instruction pointer is set to location 00, as is evidenced by the display. To say that the memory has been "cleared" on the HP-19C/29C means that an R/S instruction has been stored in all 98 available program locations. As a matter of fact, if the single step key, marked [SST], is repeatedly pressed the display will show the same instruction in the right hand of the display in each successive memory location. On the HP-29C this instruction is coded as 74, while on the 19C it is coded as 64. In each case these numbers refer to the same instruction, namely the R/S.

Whenever an instruction is keyed into program memory, a number appears in the display. This number uniquely locates the key associated with that instruction by row and by column. For example, on the HP-29C keying the R/S instruction into a program sends the number 74 to the display. This number 74 should be read as: seventh row down from the top of the calculator, fourth column across from the left. Similarly, the [CHS] key, which is in the third row, second column, is coded as 32. The code for the log key is 14 43, since the [f] prefix key, which is located in the first row, fourth column, is needed to access the log function, located in the fourth row, third column. The instruction STO 7 is coded as 23 07, where the digit keys 0 – 9 are represented by themselves. Familiarity with these codes often proves helpful when debugging and editing programs.

In all succeeding programs in this chapter, we shall include the location for each instruction.

It is time now to return to our program that evaluates a function between given limits.

Program HP-19C/29C-3: Evaluating a Function between Limits

Location	Instruction	Comments
01	g LBL 0	Defines label 0
02	STO 0	Stores starting value in the display into R0
03	R/S	Halts program to allow user to key in the ending value
04	STO 1	Stores ending value in R1
05	R/S	Halts program to allow for the keying in of the increment
06	STO 2	Stores increment in R2
07	RCL 0	x
08	g LBL 1	Defines label 1 – the beginning of the main processing loop
09	f PAUSE	Pauses to display current value of x
10	g e^x	
11	1	
12	+	Calculates the value of $f(x) = (e^x + 1)/5$
13	5	
14	÷	
15	f PAUSE	Pauses to display the result
16	f PAUSE	
17	RCL 2	Adds increment to current value of x
18	STO + 0	contained in R0
19	RCL 1	
20	RCL 0	Compares the current x value to the ending value and loops back to label 1 if we are not yet done
21	f x ≤ y	
22	GTO 1	
23	R/S	Halts program execution
24	GTO 0	Transfers to label 0 if the program is to be run again

Schematic HP-19C/29C-3

S	1	2	3	4	5
K	slide switch	f PRGM	key in steps	slide switch	f fix
D	to PRGM	00	of Program	to RUN	
			HP–19C/29C–3		

S	6	7	8	9	10
K	2	GTO	0	1	CHS
D	0.00	0.00	0.00		−1.
C			sets up program pointer to		
			label 0, which is the beginning		
			of the program		

S	11	12	13	14	15
K	R/S	.5	R/S	.25	R/S
D	−1.00	0.5	0.50	0.25	
C	start point		end point	increment	

S	16	17	18	19	20
K					
D	−1.00	0.27	−0.75	0.29	−0.50
C	x	f(x)	x	f(−.75)	x

S	21	22	23	24	25
K					
D	0.32	−0.25	0.36	0.00	0.40
C	f(−.5)	x	f(−.25)	x	f(0)

S	26	27	28	29	30
K					
D	0.25	0.46	0.50	0.53	0.75
C	x	f(.25)	x	f(.5)	

For an initial value of −1.00, a final value of 0.5, and an increment of 0.25 we find that the function has been evaluated for all the included points. These may be summarized as follows:

x	f(x)
−1.00	0.27
−0.75	0.29
−0.50	0.32
−0.25	0.36
0.00	0.40
0.25	0.46
0.50	0.53

Notice that in steps 7 and 8 of Schematic HP-19C/29C-3, the [GTO][0] keys are pressed manually in order to set the program pointer to label 0. Of course, the function we used is only one of an infinite number of different functions that could have been used. The reader may wish to substitute his or her own function for evaluation.

The Sum of the Cubes of the Digits

An appreciation of the programmable calculator as a "number cruncher" may be realized when it is put to work to solve the following problem. Are there any three-digit numbers between m and n such that the sum of the cubes of the digits in that number is equal to the number itself? In other words, is there a number abc such that $a^3 + b^3 + c^3 = abc$?

The following program permits a user to key in the starting number and the finishing number. All the numbers between (and including) these two limits are then tested to determine whether the sum of the cubes of its digits is equal to the number itself. To process a problem like this by hand is tedious, to say the least. On the calculator it is reduced to a joy.

The approach adopted to determine whether the sum of the cubes of the three digits is equal to the original number is to repeatedly isolate the rightmost digit from the number being examined. Suppose, for example, we are examining the number 321. We wish to calculate the sum

$$3^3 + 2^3 + 1^3$$

and compare the sum with the number 321. However, in order to do so, it is necessary to isolate each digit of the number individually. This may be done by dividing the number by 10, and isolating the integer portion of the result.

$$321/10 = 32.1$$

The integer portion of this result is 32. If now we multiply this by 10 ($32 \times 10 = 320$) and subtract the result from the original number 321, the difference will be the rightmost digit, namely 1.

The integer portion of the 32.1 is now treated in exactly the same way in order to isolate *its* rightmost digit, namely 2:

$$32/10 = 3.2$$

The integer portion of $3.2 = 3$

$$3 \times 10 = 30$$
$$32 - 30 = 2$$

The procedure for extracting the rightmost digit of any integer number may be summarized by the formula:

$$\text{Rightmost digit} = \text{number} - \text{Int (number/10)} \times 10$$

This formula can be applied repeatedly to any given number to isolate its digits. For each successive application of the formula, the new number to be used is the integer portion of the number divided by 10, which was calculated in the previous iteration.

$$
\begin{aligned}
\text{number} &= 321 \\
\text{right digit} &= 321 - \text{Int}\,(321/10) \times 10 \\
&= 321 - 320 \\
&= 1 \\
\text{number} &= 32 \\
\text{right digit} &= 32 - \text{Int}\,(32/10) \times 10 \\
&= 32 - 30 \\
&= 2 \\
\text{number} &= 3 \\
\text{right digit} &= 3 - \text{Int}\,(3/10) \times 10 \\
&= 3 - 0 \\
&= 3 \\
\text{number} &= 0
\end{aligned}
$$

In the program that follows advantage is taken of the INTeger function, which extracts the integer portion of the number in the display. This function is accessed by means of the [f] [INT] keys.

The companion function to INT is the FRAC function, which extracts the fractional portion of the number in the display. This function is accessed by means of the [g] [FRAC] keys.

Program HP-19C/29C-4: The Sum of the Cubes of the Digits

Location	Instruction	Comments
01	g LBL 0	Defines label 0
02	f fix 0	Sets the display for zero decimal places
03	STO 0	Stores starting number in R0
04	R/S	Halts program execution to permit the user to key in the final number to be tested
05	STO 3	Stores terminating value in R3
06	g LBL 1	Defines label 1
07	RCL 0	Copies current number to be tested into R1
08	STO 1	
09	CL x	Initializes the sum of the cubes of the digits, which will be maintained in R2 to zero
10	STO 2	

Program HP-19C/29C-4 (cont'd)

Location	Instruction	Comments
11	g LBL 2	Defines label 2
12	RCL 1	Recalls test number to the display
13	RCL 1	Pushes the value into the stack for later use
14	1	⎫
15	0	⎬ Divides test number by 10
16	÷	⎭
17	f INT	Extracts integer portion of test number divided by 10
18	STO 1	Stores this value back in R1
19	1	⎫
20	0	⎬ Extracts rightmost digit of number originally in R1 according to:
21	×	⎬ Rightmost digit = number − Int
22	−	⎭ (number/10) × 10
23	ENTER↑	Copies digit into stack
24	g x^2	⎫ Calculates digit^3 = digit × digit^2
25	×	⎭
26	STO + 2	Adds the cubed digit in the display to the accumulated sum in R2
27	RCL 1	⎫ If all digits have not yet been extracted
28	g x ≠ 0	⎬ from the test number, go to label 2 to
29	GTO 2	⎭ extract the next digit
30	RCL 0	Original test number
31	RCL 2	Accumulated sum
32	f x = y	Are they equal? i.e., does the sum of the cubes of the digits in R2 equal the number itself in R0?
33	R/S	Yes, then halt the program to permit this number to be noted
34	1	⎫ Increment the current test number by 1
35	STO + 0	⎭
36	RCL 3	Ending number
37	RCL 0	Current test number
38	f x ⩽ y	If current test number is ⩽ ending number then we are not done, so loop back to label 1
39	GTO 1	
40	CL x	⎫ Halts the program with a zero in the display
41	R/S	⎬ to indicate the program has completed execution
42	GTO 0	Loops back to label 0 to permit a new range of numbers to be tested

Schematic HP-19C/29C-4

S	1	2	3	4
K	⌈slide switch⌉	f PRGM	⌈ key in steps ⌉	⌈slide switch⌉
D	⌊ to PRGM ⌋	00	of Program	⌊ to RUN ⌋
			⌊HP–19C/29C–4⌋	

S	5	6	7
K	GTO	0	350
D			350.
C			starting value

S	8	9	10
K	R/S	450	R/S
D	350.	450.	370.
C		ending value	$3^3 + 7^3 + 0^3 = 370$

S	11	12	13
K	R/S	R/S	R/S
D	371.	407.	0.
C	$3^3 + 7^3 + 1^3 = 371$	$4^3 + 0^3 + 7^3 = 407$	done

Thus we see that after keying in a starting value of 350 and a terminal value of 450, the program determines that only three numbers in this interval satisfy the criteria. These numbers are 370, 371, and 407.

Choosing the Most Profitable Pipe

Suppose that a businessman has a need for a length of metal pipe for a given project. He is offered two pipes of differing lengths and different internal and external diameters but both made of the same metal. Both lengths of pipe turn out to be suitable, and the cost for each pipe is the same. The businessman has to make a choice of which one to buy. He decides that, in view of the fact that he can dispose of the pipe once he has completed his project, he will purchase the pipe with the greater amount of metal since a junk dealer with whom he does business, buys according to weight. In order to calculate the thickness of each pipe, we need only calculate the volume of the *cylinder* with the larger diameter and subtract from this value the volume of the cylinder with the smaller diameter. (See Fig. 9-3.)

Volume of the material = Volume of larger cylinder – Volume of smaller cylinder

$$= (\pi D^2 l)/4 - (\pi d^2 l)/4$$

$$= [\pi l(D^2 - d^2)]/4$$

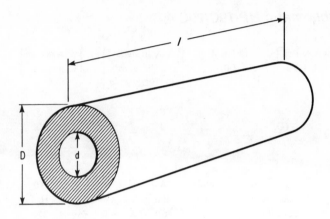

Fig. 9-3

This formula calculates the volume of the material in a pipe of length *l* and diameters D and d, where D represents the external diameter of the pipe and d represents the internal diameter.

The values of *l*, D, and d are keyed in for each of the two pipes in question and the volume of the material calculated for each. These two values are then compared: if the first has the greater amount of material, the number 1 is sent to the display, while if the second is the greater, 2 is sent to the display. In the event that the volume of material in both pipes is the same, zero is displayed.

For ease of programming the expression

$$V = [l\pi(D^2 - d^2)]/4$$

is written as a subroutine. The subroutine is invoked twice, once for the calculation of the first pipe and next for the calculation of the second pipe. A subroutine is identified by use of the f LBL instruction in the same fashion as used previously. The subroutine may be called or invoked by incorporating the GSB instruction followed by a digit key 0–9 in the appropriate place in the program. When the GSB instruction is encountered during program execution, a branch is made directly to the label specified by the GSB instruction in exactly the same manner as is made by the GTO instruction. The distinction here is that the calculator automatically remembers the location in program memory from where the subroutine was invoked.

When all of the instructions of a subroutine have been executed, the g RTN instruction is used to return control to the instruction immediately following the call to the subroutine.

Program HP-19C/29C-5: Choosing the Most Profitable Pipe

Location	Instruction	Comments
01	g LBL 0	
02	GSB 1	Calculates V1 = the volume of the material in pipe 1
03	GSB 1	Calculates V2 = the volume of the material in pipe 2
04	f x > y	V2 > V1?
05	GTO 2	Yes
06	f x ≠ y	V2 ≠ V1?
07	GTO 3	Yes
08	C /x	V1 = V2; halts with zero in the display
09	R/S	
10	GTO 0	
11	g LBL 2	
12	2	V1 < V2; display a 2
13	R/S	
14	GTO 0	
15	g LBL 3	
16	1	V1 > V2; display a 1
17	R/S	
18	GTO 0	
19	g LBL 1	Defines beginning of subroutine
20	g x^2	D^2
21	R/S	Halts program to permit the value of d to be keyed in
22	g x^2	d^2
23	—	$D^2 - d^2$
24	R/S	Halts program to permit the value of l to be keyed in
25	X	$l(D^2 - d^2)$
26	gπ	
27	X	$l\pi(D^2 - d^2)$
28	4	
29	÷	$V = [l\pi(D^2 - d^2)]/4$
30	R/S	Halts program to display results
31	g RTN	Returns control to the calling routine

From Schematic HP-19C/29C-5 it is clear that in the first case, the pipe with diameters 6 and 4 and of length 130 has the greater amount of

material and therefore would be the better buy. In the second illustrative case (see steps 22–34), the two pipes under consideration are shown to contain the same amount of material.

Schematic HP-19C/29C-5

S	1	2	3	4
K	slide switch to PRGM	f PRGM	key in steps of Program HP-19C/29C-5	slide switch to RUN
D		00		

S	5	6	7	8
K	f fix	2	GTO	0
D		0.00	0.00	0.00

S	9	10	11	12
K	7	R/S	5	R/S
D	7.	49.00	5.	24.00
C	D		d	

S	13	14	15	16
K	100	R/S	6	R/S
D	100.	1884.96	6.	36.00
C	l	V1	D	

S	17	18	19	20
K	4	R/S	130	R/S
D	4.	20.00	130.	2042.04
C	d		l	V2

S	21	22	23	24
K	R/S	4	R/S	3
D	2.00	4.	16.00	3.
C	V2 contains more material	D		d

S	25	26	27	28
K	R/S	9	R/S	5
D	7.00	9.	49.48	5.
C		l	V1	D

S	29	30	31	32
K	R/S	4	R/S	7
D	25.00	4.	9.00	7
C		d		l

S	33	34
K	R/S	R/S
D	49.48	0.00
C	V2	volumes are identical

The Month of Birth Problem

Suppose the students of a class are polled for the month of the year in which they were born. A tally is then made of the number of students born in January, the number born in February, and so on. The totals are now examined to determine if there is any particular month that has a disproportionate number of births.

This tallying operation may be done quite easily on the HP-19C/29C by making use of its *indirect addressing* feature.

The HP-19C/29C has a total of 30 data storage registers. Sixteen of these registers have continuous memory and may be accessed directly with instructions such as

STO   4
RCL   8
         •
         •
         •

         etc.

Registers 0–9 may be accessed in this manner, while the remaining six registers (registers 10–15) must be accessed by pressing the period or decimal point key followed by a digit key from 0 through 5. For example, the instruction [STO] [.] [5] stores the contents of the display into memory register . 5 (R.5). Similarly, the instruction [RCL] [.] [0] recalls the value contained in register . 0 (R.0) to the display.

In addition to these 16 registers there are 14 registers that are volatile, meaning that when the calculator is switched off any data stored in them are lost. The only way in which data may be stored into or recalled from these registers is through indirect addressing. The entire layout scheme of the memory registers in the HP-19C/29C is shown on the next page.

It will be noticed from this layout that the 14 volatile storage registers may be addressed only indirectly by the numbers 16–29. The 16 nonvolatile storage registers, however, may be addressed using either direct or indirect addressing techniques.

In order to address a data register indirectly, the indirect address for the particular register to be accessed must first be stored in register 0. The lower case key marked [(i)] can then be used to address the desired register referenced by R0. For example, to store the value 5 into register 20, which must be addressed indirectly, the following keystrokes must be used:

[20]
[STO] [0]
[5]
[STO] [(i)]

The key sequence [STO] [(i)] may be read as "store the contents of the display into the memory register referenced by register 0."

Direct Address	Indirect Address		Indirect Address	
0	0		16	
1	1		17	
2	2		18	
3	3		19	
4	4		20	
5	5		21	
6	6		22	
7	7		23	
8	8		24	
9	9		25	
.0	10		26	
.1	11		27	
.2	12		28	
.3	13		29	
.4	14			
.5	15		* 14 Volatile Storage Registers	

16 Nonvolatile Storage Registers

* These registers may be addressed only indirectly.

To recall the contents of register 8, the conventional key sequence

[RCL] [8]

could be used to directly recall its contents to the display. Alternatively, the key sequence

[8]
[STO] [0]
[RCL] [(i)]

will perform the equivalent task using the indirect addressing feature of the HP-19C/29C. While the advantages of this feature may not yet be apparent, when writing complex programs indirect addressing gives the programmer extra versatility in that a register number does not have to be explicitly incorporated into the program but can be calculated by the program, stored in register 0, and then referenced indirectly.

This indirect addressing feature also is available for use by the GTO and GSB instructions. The instruction

GTO (i)

will transfer control to the label referenced by R0. This value should, of course, be a number from 0 to 9. The sequence of instructions

3
STO 0
GTO (i)

will cause the program to branch to label 3. Similarly, the sequence

2
÷
g FRAC
1 0
×
STO 0
GSB (i)

will take a number, divide it by two, extract the remainder, multiply it by 10, and then store the result in R0. A subroutine will then be invoked depending upon the contents of R0. If the original number in the display were an integer, executing the above sequence of instructions would have the effect of calling subroutine 0 if the number were even (i.e., evenly divisible by 2), while subroutine 5 would be invoked if the number were odd. (It is suggested that the reader verify that this is the case.)

The effect of storing a negative value from –1 to –99 into R0 and then executing a GTO (i) instruction is to cause the program to branch *backwards* the number of locations specified by this value. The sequence of instructions

Location	Instruction
•	•
•	•
•	•
10	9
11	CHS
12	STO 0
13	GTO (i)

causes the program to branch from location 13 back 9 steps to location 4 when the GTO (i) instruction is encountered. The GSB (i) instruction also can be used in a similar fashion to invoke a subroutine located back in memory the number of steps specified by the contents of R0.

Program HP-19C/29C-6: The Month of Birth Problem

Location	Instruction	Comments
01	g LBL 0	
02	f Fix 0	
03	f Reg	Clears all 30 data storage registers
04	g LBL 1	

Program HP-19C/29C-6 (cont'd)

Location	Instruction	Comments
05	STO 0	Stores the month (1–12) into R0 to use indirect addressing
06	9	
07	9	If 99 was keyed in, branches to label 2 to display results
08	f x = y	
09	GTO 2	
10	1	Adds 1 to one of R1–R12 depending upon the particular month which was keyed in and stored in R0
11	STO + (i)	
12	STO + .3	Adds 1 to counter of number of birthdays keyed in in R.3 and recalls this value to the display
13	RCL .3	
14	R/S	Halts for next month to be keyed in and loops
15	GTO 1	
16	g LBL 2	Display results in R1–R12
17	1	Initializes the month number in R0 to 1
18	STO 0	
19	g LBL 3	
20	f PAUSE	Displays month
21	RCL (i)	Displays number of birthdays in that month
22	f PAUSE	
23	1	Increments month counter
24	STO + 0	
25	1	
26	2	
27	RCL 0	If we have not yet displayed the results for all 12 months, then loop
28	f x ≤ y	
29	GTO 3	
30	RCL .3	Or else recall total to display and halt
31	R/S	
32	GTO 0	

Schematic HP-19C/29C-6

S	1	2	3	4
K	slide switch	f PRGM	key in steps	slide switch
D	to PRGM	00	of Program HP-19C/29C-6	to RUN

Schematic HP-19C/29C-6 (cont'd)

S	5	6	7	8
K	GTO	0	7.	R/S
D			7.	1
C			July	
S	9	10	11	12
K	2	R/S	4	R/S
D	2.	2.	4.	3.
C	February		April	
S	13	14	15	16
K	5	R/S	9	R/S
D	5.	4.	9.	5.
C	May		September	
S	17	18	19	20
K	12.	R/S	12	R/S
D	12.	6.	12.	7.
C	December		December	
S	21	22	23	24
K	1	R/S	3	R/S
D	1.	8.	3.	9.
C	January		March	
S	25	26	27	28
K	4	R/S	6	R/S
D	4.	10.	6.	11.
C	April		June	
S	29	30	31	32
K	7	R/S	7	R/S
D	7.	12.	7.	13.
C	July		July	
S	33	34	35	36
K	8	R/S	1	R/S
D	8.	14.	1.	15.
C	August		January	
S	37	38	39	40
K	8	R/S	99	R/S
D	8.	16.	99.	
C	August		terminate entry of data	

Schematic HP-19C/29C-6 (cont'd)

S	41	42	43	44
K				
D	2.	2.	1.	3.
C	2 birthdays in January		1 in February	

S	45	46	47	48
K				
D	1.	4.	2	5.
C	1 in March		2 in April	

S	49	50	51	52
K				
D	1.	6.	1.	7.
C	1 in May		1 in June	

S	53	54	55	56
K				
D	3.	8.	2.	9.
C	3 in July		2 in August	

S	57	58	59	60
K				
D	1.	10.	0.	11.
C	1 in September		none in October	

S	61	62	63	64
K				
D	0.	12.	2	16.
C		none in November	2 in December	total

A g LBL 0 instruction is used at the beginning of the program to mark the start of the program. Since we are dealing only with integer numbers, the calculator is fixed at zero decimal places. All of the 30 data storage registers are cleared by means of the single instruction f REG. The registers R1–R12 are used in the program to store the frequencies of the occurrence of the months 1 through 12 in the corresponding registers. Immediately following the f REG instruction is another marker g LBL 1, which defines the start of the main processing loop. Within this loop, the user keys in the particular month of birth as an integer from 1 to 12 and then presses the [R/S] key. The program first checks to see if this number is equal to the number 99. This arbitrarily selected number is used as a signal that no more data is to be keyed in. If the number keyed in is not 99, then it is stored into register R0 so that one of the registers R1–R12 may be indirectly addressed. The sequence of instructions

$$1 \text{ STO} + (i)$$

has the effect of adding 1 to the register specified in R0. Thus, if the value 3 were keyed in, indicating the month of birth is March, then after storing this value in R0 the two instructions listed above would increment the contents of R3 by 1.

After the appropriate frequency counter is updated, the program adds 1 to the contents of register R.3. This register is used to maintain a running count of the number of data items keyed in thus far. This value is recalled to the display at each pass through the loop. The reader is alerted to the fact that register R.1, for example, could not have been used to maintain this count since R.1 is really register 11, which is used to maintain the frequency count of the number of birthdays in November, the eleventh month.

When the number 99 is keyed in, indicating the end of data, a branch is made to label 2. At this point we are ready to display the frequency count for all of the months 1–12. To initiate this process, 1 is stored in register 0. The PAUSE instruction permits this 1 to be viewed perliminary to the display of the frequency count for this month, which is recalled indirectly to the display. Another PAUSE instruction permits this value to be noted.

Register R0 is then incremented by 1 and compared with the number 12. If 12 has not yet been reached—that is, we have not yet displayed all of our results—control is sent to label 3 where the next month is displayed followed by its corresponding frequency count.

Once the frequency for all of the twelve months has been displayed, the total number of data items is recalled to the display and the program halted.

Additional Features of the HP-19C/29C

The DSZ and ISZ Instructions. When programming certain types of problems, it is frequently necessary to iterate through a loop a specific number of times. For ease of programming such problems, the instructions DSZ and ISZ are provided.

The Decrement and Skip on Zero (DSZ) instruction performs a twofold task. Whenever a DSZ instruction is encountered during program execution, the contents of register R0 is first decremented by 1. Next a test is made to determine if the resulting contents of R0 is zero. If it is, the next instruction in sequence is automatically skipped, and execution continues with the second instruction following the DSZ instruction. If, however, the contents of R0 is not zero then execution continues in the normal sequential fashion with the instruction immediately following the DSZ instruction. As an example of the use of the DSZ instruction, suppose it were desired to execute a given set of instructions exactly 9 times. Enclosing the set of instructions by the following set of instructions will accomplish the task efficiently.

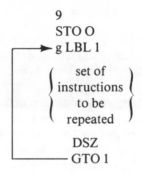

9
STO 0
g LBL 1

{ set of instructions to be repeated }

DSZ
GTO 1

The value 9 is stored into R0 since this is the number of times we wish to execute the loop. The label 1 is used to identify the beginning of the loop. The DSZ instruction is placed after the last instruction of the set to be repeated. When this instruction is encountered, the contents of R0 will be decremented by 1 and a branch made back to the beginning of the loop at label 1, only if its contents are not zero. This process would be repeated exactly 9 times until the value in R0 is decremented from a 1 to a 0, at which point the GTO 1 instruction will be skipped.

The Increment and Skip on Zero (ISZ) instruction performs in a similar manner to the DSZ instruction. As the name of the instruction implies, the role of the ISZ instruction is to first increment the contents of register R0 by 1 and then skip the following instruction if the resulting contents of R0 are zero. This instruction is useful when it is desired to count up from a negative value to 0.

The Printing Feature of the HP-19C. As mentioned earlier, one of the more significant advances in programmable pocket calculators is incorporated in the HP-19C, which has a built-in thermal printer. Not only is it possible to make it print out a complete program (using the PRT PRGM instruction) but, in addition, intermediate results may be printed as well as the contents of the stack registers, the contents of the 30 storage data registers, and the contents of the statistical data storage registers. These are used by the statistical functions on the HP-19C.

In each of the programs described in this chapter, where a PAUSE instruction has been used to permit the viewing of the contents of the display, it may be replaced by a PR x instruction. This will have the effect of sending the contents of the display or x register to the printer, thus providing a hard copy of the results.

To print and label the contents of the stack, the PRT STK instruction is used. The contents of the data storage registers may be printed and labeled by the PRT REG instruction, while the PRT Σ instruction prints and labels the contents of the statistical storage registers. In order to space the paper a single line (i.e., to print a blank line) the instruction SPC is used. Naturally, several SPC instructions may be used in succession to skip multiple lines on the printer.

Debugging and Editing Programs on the HP-19C/29C

The HP-19C/29C calculators provide the user with many state-of-the-art tools, which aid greatly in the debugging of programs. For example, a user might wish to execute his program one step at a time in order to watch the progress of the program during the course of its execution. In RUN mode, pressing the Single STep key marked [SST] has the effect of displaying both the location and the instruction stored in the location in program memory for as long as the key is depressed. Releasing the [SST] key causes that particular instruction to be executed. This [SST] key may be pressed to monitor the execution of successive instructions of the program.

The pause key may be used in RUN mode to slow down execution of the program sufficiently to enable the user to view the changing contents of the display. This slow motion remains in effect for as long as the pause key is depressed.

One should not be surprised to find that a first attempt at writing a program does not succeed. Invariably the program has to be amended before it runs in precisely the manner intended. When an error has been detected in a program or where a sequence of instructions is found that needs to be amended or edited, the program need not be keyed in again in its entirety, but rather advantage may be taken of the editing features that are provided on the HP-19C/29C.

To insert an instruction or a set of instructions in a given portion of a program, the calculator must first be positioned at that point. This may be done in one of several ways. In PRGM mode, the [SST] key can be used to successively step through the program memory. This key can be used until the desired location or instruction appears in the display. Similarly, the Back STep key [BST] can be used to back step through the program to the desired location.

If the precise location for the modification is known in advance, the calculator may be positioned directly to that location by pressing the [GTO] and [.] keys followed by the two-digit location number in RUN mode. [GTO] [.] [2] [5], for example, will position the calculator at location 25. In a similar fashion, to position the calculator at a specified location, the [GTO] key followed by a digit key 0–9 in RUN mode will achieve the desired result. Pressing the keys [GTO] [6], for example, has the effect of positioning the calculator at label 6.

Once the desired location has been reached, the instruction in that location can be deleted by simply pressing the [g] [Del] keys in PRGM mode. All of the instructions following the deleted instruction are automatically moved up a location in program memory.

To insert an instruction before the current instruction in the display, simply key in the desired instruction or instructions in the normal manner in PRGM mode. The portion of the program following the inserted section will have been pushed down automatically.

CHAPTER TEN
THE HEWLETT-PACKARD 33E

In May 1978 Hewlett-Packard announced and released its E-series of calculators: the HP-31E, HP-32E, and HP-33E. The sleek looking HP-33E is a scientific pocket programmable calculator that supercedes the HP-25 and has a much larger display, making for considerably easier reading. It has 49 program locations, each of which may contain up to three keystrokes. In addition to the 49 line program memory, the HP-33E has eight addressable data storage registers. The 10-digit display is different from all previous Hewlett-Packard models in that commas are automatically inserted at the appropriate places when displaying numbers greater than 999 in the standard fixed format.

Another first time feature is a self-checking routine by which the user can be perfectly confident that the calculator is functioning properly. By pressing the keys

$$\boxed{\text{STO}} \quad \boxed{\text{ENTER↑}}$$

an internal self-checking routine is activated. If all the internal circuitry is in order, there will be a delay of a few seconds, after which the display will contain the code

$$-8,8,8,8,8,8,8,8,8,8,$$

The HP-33E is a sophisticated calculator containing a wealth of scientific and statistical functions. A picture of the HP-33E is shown in Fig. 10-1.

The HP-33E with its 49 lines of fully merged program memory has a variety of specialized functions that make the calculator a veritable workhorse. To enable the programmer to make quick and easy decisions in a program, the HP-33E has eight conditional branch instructions, which seems to be the standard adopted on almost all of the Hewlett-Packard models.

On the HP-33E greater program efficiency is gained by the use of subroutines, which may be nested three levels deep.

The HP-33E provides the user with the option of displaying data in one of three different modes. In addition to the standard fixed place decimal and scientific notation formats, the HP-33E permits numbers to be

Fig. 10-1 HP-33E (*Courtesy* Hewlett-Packard Company)

displayed in engineering notation. In this mode, all exponents are shown as a multiple of three. A special MANTissa key allows the user to temporarily override the current display format and view the entire 10 digit accuracy of the mantissa in the display for as long as the key is held down or for a period of about one second. The calculator "wakes up" in fixed four decimal place format when switched on.

Programming the HP-33E

F to C Temperature Conversion

In most of the United States, temperatures are still given in the Fahrenheit scale even though there is much pressure exerted to convert to the metric system, which expresses temperatures in the Celsius scale, sometimes called the Centigrade scale. Let us suppose that a college student has the task of converting a temperature expressed in the Fahrenheit scale to its equivalent in the Celsius scale. To carry out such a conversion, the student resorts to the following formula that may be used for converting any Fahrenheit temperature to its equivalent Celsius temperature:

$$C = (F - 32)/1.8$$

Example 1: Convert 29.8°F to °C

S	1	2	3	4	5	6
K	29.8	ENTER↑	32	−	1.8	÷
D	29.8	29.8000	32.	−2.2000	1.8	−1.2222
C	°F			F − 32		°C

From this schematic it is clear that 29.8°F is equivalent to −1.2222°C.

If our hypothetical student had the onerous task of having to convert a list of 100 temperatures from Fahrenheit to Celsius, he would have to repeat the above sequence of keystrokes for each temperature to be converted. This would mean that over 600 keystrokes would be necessary in order to convert the 100 temperatures in the list. Much time and effort could be saved, however, by utilizing the programmability of the HP-33E. When this calculator is switched into the special PRGM (program) mode, any keystrokes that are subsequently keyed in are automatically stored into the calculator's memory and are remembered by the calculator until either they are replaced by new ones or the machine is switched off.

Program HP-33E-1: Fahrenheit to Celsius Temperature Conversion

Instruction	Comments
ENTER↑	Copies the temperature expressed in Fahrenheit from the x register into the y register
3 2	} Enters the number 32 into the display
−	F − 32
1 • 8	} Enters the number 1.8 into the display
÷	C = (F − 32)/1.8

In Example 1 on the previous page, each of the keystrokes in the sequence from step 2 to step 6 would have to be repeated for each temperature to be converted. This sequence therefore becomes the body of Program HP-33E-1 that converts a temperature keyed into the display from Fahrenheit to Celsius.

Keying in the Program

1. Switch the calculator into program mode by sliding the PRGM-RUN switch to PRGM.
2. Clear the memory of any previous programs by pressing the keys [f] [PRGM].
3. Key in the instructions of Program HP-33E-1 exactly as shown.
4. Slide the switch to RUN to exit from program mode.

Running the Program

1. Press the keys marked [GTO][0][0]. This causes the program pointer to be positioned at the beginning of the program.
2. Key in the temperature to be converted to Celsius.
3. Press the Run/Stop key marked [R/S]. The program will automatically be executed from its beginning, and the converted temperature will automatically appear in the display.
4. Repeat steps 2 and 3 for each new value to be converted.

Schematic HP-33E-1

S	1	2	3	4
K	⌈slide switch⌉	f PRGM	⌈key in the steps	⌈slide switch⌉
D	⌊ to PRGM ⌋	00	of Program	⌊ to RUN ⌋
			⌊ HP–33E–1 ⌋	

S	5	6	7	8
K	GTO	0	0	29.8
D	0.0000	0.0000	0.0000	29.8
C		resets program pointer to the beginning		F

S	9	10	11	12
K	R/S	32	R/S	40
D	−1.2222	32.	0.0000	40.
C	C	F	C	

S	13	14		
K	CHS	R/S	. . . etc.	
D	−40.	−40.0000		
C	F	C		

As we have already pointed out, the HP-33E has 49 locations in which to store the program. These locations are numbered consecutively from 01 through 49. There is a location 00 but this location is an automatic halt. The HP-33E has been designed so that should a program be keyed in that does not use up all of memory, the instruction following the last acts as a "halt." Initially, all of the locations from 01 to 49 are automatically filled with a "go to 00" instruction. This is the case whenever the machine is switched on or the [f] [PRGM] keys are pressed while the calculator is in PRGM mode. Therefore, whenever a program is keyed in, it "overwrites" these "go to" instructions (abbreviated GTO) for the length of the program itself. All subsequent locations therefore would still contain these GTO 00 instructions. Advantage is taken of this feature in Program HP-33E-1. The instruction that follows the last instruction of the program is the GTO 00 instruction by default. This has the effect of transferring control to location 00 that has the effect of not only halting the program so that the results may be viewed in the display, but also positions the program pointer at the beginning of the program for the next temperature to be converted.

The Odd-Even Task

The next program is admittedly somewhat contrived but is intended to illustrate how elementary decisions can be made on the HP-33E.

Normally, program instructions are executed in sequence, one after the other. However, by means of a GTO instruction control can be set *unconditionally* to any other part of the program. We have already seen how the instruction GTO 00 transfers control unconditionally to location 00. In a similar fashion, the instruction GTO 16, for example, sends control directly to memory location 16, where execution continues with whatever particular instruction is stored in that location.

There are altogether eight *conditional* instructions to enable the programmer to make decisions within a program. Four of them compare the contents of the display (or x register) to zero while the other four compare the contents of the x register with the contents of the y register. This arrangement permits the following questions to be asked within a program. (Each question is followed by the required keystrokes.)

Comparison's between the x Register and Zero

1. Are the contents of the x register equal to zero? (g x = 0)
2. Is the x register not equal to zero? (g x $\neq$ 0)
3. Is the x register greater than zero? (g x > 0)
4. Is the x register less than zero? (g x < 0)

Comparison's between the x Register and the y Register

5. Is the x register equal to the y register? (f x = y)
6. Is the x register not equal to the y register? (f x $\neq$ y)

7. Is the x register greater than the y register? (f x > y)

8. Is the x register less than or equal to the y register? (f x ≤ y)

Whenever one of these eight conditional branch instructions is encountered during program execution, the following sequence of events occurs:

1. A comparison is made between the x register and zero or the y register, depending upon the particular instruction used.

2. If the condition is satisfied—that is, the answer to the question is YES—execution continues in the normal sequential manner with the next instruction in sequence.

3. If the condition is not satisfied—that is, the answer to the question is NO—the instruction immediately following the conditional branch instruction is automatically *skipped*, and execution continued with the second instruction following the conditional branch instruction.

Each of the 49 memory locations 01–49 is capable of storing an instruction. In program mode (i.e., with the switch at PRGM) the location numbers are included with the code for the instruction itself. For example, the instruction

$$03-\quad 71$$

means that the third location contains the instruction whose key is located in the seventh row, first column. This is none other than the divide instruction. The instruction

$$01-\quad 23\quad 1$$

means that in location 01 (the dash is for cosmetic reasons only) the keystrokes stored are: (1) the key in the second row, third column (STO) and (2) the digit 1. This is the keycode representation of the STO 1 instruction. The instruction

$$04-\quad 15\quad 33$$

specifies the contents of location 04. The instruction referred to relates to the key in the first row, fifth column (the prefix key [g]), while the 33 refers to the key in the third row, third column. Since it is prefixed by [g] it is the FRAC function that is being used.

The instruction $\sqrt{x}$, for example, which is accessed by pressing the keys [f] [0] has the keycode

$$14\quad 0$$

All the digit keys and any of their associated functions have keycodes that are the digits themselves.

The [FRAC] function key extracts the fractional portion of the number in the display, replacing it with the fractional portion. For example, pressing the [g] [FRAC] keys with the number 51.2345 has the effect of sending the fractional portion, namely .2345 to the display.

Incidentally, the FRAC function has a companion instruction that can be used to extract the integral portion of a number in the display. It is accessed by the [g] [INT] keys. Pressing these keys has the effect of truncating the value in the display, replacing this value by the number without its fractional portion.

Let us now return to the odd-even task. Suppose that you are presented with a list of positive integer numbers. Your task is to take each number individually and determine if it is odd or even. If it is odd, the number is to be multiplied by 3 and 1 added to the product. If the number is even, it is simply to be divided by 2.

How can we get a calculator to decide if a number is even or odd? Intelligent human beings need only look at the unit's digit of the number. If it is 0, 2, 4, 6, or 8 it is even; otherwise, it is odd. On the calculator this odd-even test can be made by dividing the number by 2. If there is a remainder, the number is odd. If the remainder is zero, the number is even. In order to test for a zero remainder on the HP-33E, the fractional portion of the quotient is extracted by using the [g] [FRAC] function mentioned earlier. This value can then be compared for equality with zero by using the g x = 0 conditional branch instruction. If the number in question is even, the remainder after dividing by 2 will be zero, and the g x = 0 test will prove true. However, if the number in question is odd, the g x = 0 test will fail and the instruction immediately following the g x = 0 test will be automatically skipped.

In the program that follows, the user keys in each number to be tested and presses the [R/S] key. The program will determine if the number is odd or even and automatically display the appropriate result.

Program HP-33E-2: The Odd-Even Task

Location	Instruction	Comments
01	STO 1	Saves the number in the display in data register R1
02	2	Divides the number by 2 to determine if it
03	÷	is even or odd
04	g FRAC	Extracts the fractional portion of the value in the display. If the original number was even the contents of the display will now be zero
05	g x = 0	Is x equal to 0? or Is the remainder 0?
06	GTO 13	Yes; the number is even — branch to location 13
07	RCL 1	No; the number is odd. Recall it to the display

Program HP-33E-2 (cont'd)

Location	Instruction	Comments
08	3	
09	X	
10	1	Multiplies by 3 and adds 1
11	+	
12	GTO 00	Branches to location 00 to halt the program and display the results
13	f LAST x	The number is even; this instruction recalls the contents of the display before the last operation. In this case, the number divided by 2 was in the display before the g FRAC was performed. This is the value we wish to display
14	GTO 00	
•	•	These are automatically included
•	•	and do not have to be keyed in by
•	•	the programmer
49	GTO 00	

Schematic HP-33E-2

S	1	2	3	4
K	[switch to	f PRGM	[key in the steps	[switch
D	PRGM]	00	of Program HP–33E–2]	to RUN]
C		clear program memory		

S	5	6	7	8	9
K	f fix	0	GTO	0	0
D	0.0000	0.	0.	0.	0.
C	sets the display for no decimal places		resets the program to its beginning		

S	10	11	12	13	14
K	5	R/S	6	R/S	1024
D	5.	16.	6.	3.	1,024.
C		$(3 \times 5) + 1 = 16$		$6/2 = 3$	

S	15	16	17
K	R/S	97	R/S
D	512.	97.	292.

Ulam's Conjecture with Iteration Counter

A Polish-American mathematician named Stanislav Ulam pondered the problem posed in Program HP-33E-2. If we treat the original number keyed in as a starting number, we could repeatedly rerun the program with the result obtained in the previous run by simply pressing the [R/S] key. To clarify this, let us select the number 5 as our starting number. Running Program HP-33E-2 with this value gives a result of 16. Pressing the [R/S] key with this value in the display has the effect of reexecuting the program. Since 16 is even, the value 8 is displayed. This in turn goes to 4, then to 2 and then to 1. Ulam conjectured that any positive integer when treated in this manner would eventually reach 1. The fact of the matter is that so far as is known no one has been able to prove or disprove this conjecture.

The purpose of the following program is to test Ulam's Conjecture for any keyed in positive integer. Each intermediate result is displayed for a period of about one second by making use of the PAUSE instruction. The f PAUSE instruction has the effect of momentarily halting execution of the program so that results may be viewed in the display.

To enhance the program, a count is kept of the number of times the process is repeated until the number finally reaches 1. If the number keyed in is 5, for example, the intermediate results of

$$16, 8, 4, 2, 1$$

would be displayed in succession. As will be seen, it took five steps to reach the number 1. In the program an iteration counter is kept in register R0 and is incremented by 1 each time the process is repeated. The final value of this counter is displayed at the end of each run.

Program HP-33E-3: Ulam's Conjecture with Iteration Count

Location	Instruction	Comments
01	f FIX 0	Displays integers only
02	STO 1	Stores starting number in data register R1
03	0	Initializes iteration count to zero
04	STO 0	
05	1	Is the number 1 yet? (i.e., are we done?)
06	RCL 1	
07	f x = y	
08	GTO 26	Yes; then branches to location 26
09	2	No; then test if the number is odd or even by first dividing it by 2
10	÷	
11	g FRAC	Then extract the fractional portion

Program HP-33E-3 (cont'd)

Location	Instruction	Comments
12	g x = 0	Remainder = 0?
13	GTO 20	Yes; number is even
14	RCL 1	No; number is odd
15	3	
16	×	
17	1	
18	+	
19	GTO 21	Branch to location 21 to display the results
20	f LAST x	Program branches here if the number is even and the f LAST x instruction recalls the halved number to the display
21	f PAUSE	Pauses to display the results
22	STO 1	Stores this as the new number for the next iteration
23	1	Adds 1 to the iteration counter in R0
24	STO + 0	
25	GTO 05	Branches to location 5 to perform the next iteration
26	RCL 0	Program branches here when 1 is reached to display the number of iterations and to stop the program
27	GTO 00	

Schematic HP-33E-3

	1	2	3	4
S K D	[switch to PRGM mode]	f PRGM 00	[key in the steps of Program HP–33E–3]	[switch to RUN mode]

	5	6	7	8	9
S					
K	GTO	0	0	5	R/S
D	0.0000	0.0000	0.0000	5.	16.
C				starting number	3n + 1

	10	11	12	13	14
S					
K					
D	8.	4.	2.	1.	5.
C	n/2	n/2	n/2	n/2	number of iterations

Schematic HP-33E-3 (cont'd)

S	15	16	17	18	19
K	7				
D	7.	22.	11.	34.	17.
C	starting number				

S	20	21	22	23	24
K					
D	52.	26.	13.	40.	20.
C					

S	25	26	27	28	29
K					
D	10.	5.	16.	8.	4.
C					

S	30	31	32
K			
D	2.	1.	16.
C			number of iterations

The Wind Chill Temperature

During the winter season the meteorological office often includes with its weather forecasts an index known as the *wind chill* temperature. This is how cold the air feels when the wind is blowing. As you are probably well aware, the stronger the wind, the colder it feels. The wind chill temperature may be calculated by means of the following somewhat forbidding-looking formula:

$$W = 33 - (10\sqrt{V} - V + 10.5)(33 - T)/23.1$$

where

V = wind velocity in meters per second
T = outside temperature in °C
W = wind chill temperatures in °C

Since many of us are still not used to temperatures in the Celsius scale and are probably even less familiar with wind velocities expressed in meters per second rather than in miles per hour, we can assign to the calculator the task of doing these conversions for us.

The formula for converting a Fahrenheit temperature to one on the Celsius scale was utilized in Program HP-33E-1. It is

$$C = (F - 32)/1.8$$

To convert a wind velocity from miles per hour to meters per second the formula

$$Vmps = 0.447 \times Vmph$$

is used where Vmps is the velocity in meters per second.

In the program that follows, the user keys in the outside temperature in degrees Fahrenheit. Upon pressing its [R/S] key, the program stops with the equivalent temperature on the Celsius scale. At that point the wind velocity expressed in miles per hour is keyed in and the [R/S] key pressed again. The program comes to a halt with the wind chill temperature in degrees Fahrenheit in the display. The temperature is converted to Fahrenheit within the program by the formula:

$$F = C \times 1.8 + 32$$

Program HP-33E-4: Wind Chill Temperature

Location	Instruction	Comments
01	3	
02	2	
03	−	
04	1	Converts keyed in temperature from Fahrenheit to Celsius and stores the result in register R2
05	•	
06	8	
07	÷	
08	STO 2	
09	R/S	Halts program execution so that the wind speed, expressed in miles per hour, may be keyed in
10	ENTER↑	
11	•	
12	4	
13	4	Vmps = .447 Vmph
14	7	
15	×	
16	STO 3	Saves Vmps in R3
17	3	
18	3	
19	ENTER↑	
20	1	
21	0	

Program HP-33E-4 (cont'd)

Location	Instruction	Comments
22	RCL 3	Vmps
23	f $\sqrt{x}$	$\sqrt{\text{Vmps}}$
24	x	$10\sqrt{\text{Vmps}}$
25	RCL 3	Vmps
26	—	$10\sqrt{\text{Vmps}} - \text{Vmps}$
27	1	
28	0	
29	•	
30	5	
31	+	$10\sqrt{\text{Vmps}} - \text{Vmps} + 10.5$
32	3	
33	3	
34	RCL 2	T
35	—	$33 - t$
36	X	$(10\sqrt{\text{Vmps}} - \text{Vmps} + 10.5)(33 - T)$
37	2	
38	3	
39	•	
40	1	
41	÷	$(10\sqrt{\text{Vmps}} - \text{Vmps} + 10.5)(33 - T)/23.1$
42	—	$W = 33 - (10\sqrt{\text{Vmps}} - \text{Vmps} + 10.5)(33 - T)/23.1$
43	1	
44	•	Converts W to its equivalent in degrees
45	8	Fahrenheit. The program automatically
46	X	halts after the instruction in location 49,
47	3	the highest location in the calculator's
48	2	memory, is executed
49	+	

It will be noticed that this program utilizes all of the 49 memory locations available on the HP-33E. If a program is longer than 49 steps, it could still be accommodated by storing constants such as 1.8, 32, and 0.447 in data storage registers before the program is executed and recalling them to the display as they are needed. When constants are included as part of a program, each digit and decimal point takes up a location of its own, and this can prove to be extremely consuming of memory space.

Schematic HP-33E-4

S	1	2	3	4
K	switch to	f PRGM	key in the steps	switch to
D	PRGM mode	00	of Program	RUN mode
			HP-33E-4	

S	5	6	7	8
K	GTO	0	0	50
D	0.0000	0.0000	0.0000.	50.

S	9	10	11	12
K	R/S	15	R/S	35.
D	10.0000	15.	38.1911	35.
C	$50°\,F = 10°C$	Vmph	Wind Chill	
			Temp $= 38.2°\,F$	

S	13	14	15	16
K	R/S	20	R/S	5
D	1.6667	20	14.5890	5.
C	$35°\,F = 1.67°C$	Vmph	Wind Chill	
			Temp $= 14.6°\,F$	

S	17	18	19
K	R/S	40	R/S
D	−15.0000	40.	−39.1528
C	$5°\,F = −15°C$	Vmph	brrrrr!

Permutations and Combinations

In problems involving the concept of probability, one often encounters the notions of permutations and combinations. The mathematical function associated with these concepts is the factorial function. The factorial of the number 6, written (6!), for example, is the product of all the digits from 1 through the number 6, that is,

$$6! = 6 \times 5 \times 4 \times 3 \times 2 \times 1$$
$$= 720$$

In general,

$$n! = n \times (n-1) \times (n-2) \times \ldots \times 2 \times 1$$

In order to clarify the difference between permutations and combinations, let us suppose that we want to wager a bet on a horse race in which eight horses are running. For the sake of convenience, let the individual horses be named

A, B, C, D, E, F, G, and H

Let us assume that each horse has an equal probability of winning the race.

Many racetracks offer a particularly large bonus to the bettor who can accurately forecast horses that will finish first and second. With this kind of a bet it is not only necessary to pick the two winning horses but also to specify which one will be first and which one will be second.

Computing the probability of selecting the winning combination is a problem of permutations. The number of possible winning combinations may be calculated by the formula

$$_n P_r = \frac{n!}{(n-r)!}$$

where

      n = the number of objects
      r = the number of objects selected at a given time

In the horse race cited above, n is equal to 8, which is the number of horses, and r is equal to 2, which is the number of horses selected:

$$_8 P_2 = \frac{8!}{(8-2)!} = 56$$

From the above it is clear that the chances against correctly forecasting the first and the second winning horses is 55-to-1.

The problem of predicting which two horses will finish either first or second is not the same as the problem of predicting precisely which horse will finish first and which will finish second. The former task is obviously much easier than the latter. To predict which two horses will be the winners (either first or second) is a problem of combinations rather than permutations. Combinations may be calculated from the formula

$$_n C_r = \frac{n!}{(n-r)!r!}$$

where

      n = the number of objects
      r = the number of objects selected at a given time

$$_8 C_2 = \frac{8!}{(8-2)!2!} = 28$$

Thus we see that the odds of selecting the two winning horses has been reduced to 27-to-1.

The program that follows enables the user to key in the value of n followed by the value of r. The program then calculates in succession the permutations and combinations for these values, pausing briefly between the displaying of the results.

A perusal of two formulas will quickly lead the reader to the conclusion that frequent use is made of the factorial function. However, since the HP-33E is not equipped with a factorial function key, the factorial function must be programmed.

In view of the fact that the factorial function is required at various points when evaluating the formulas, it need be written once and once only and accessed as often as is necessary provided it is written in the form of a *subroutine.*

A transfer to a subroutine is initiated by the instruction GSB nn where nn is a memory address from 01 to 49 inclusive. This instruction may appear anywhere within the program, and when it is encountered a branch is made to the specified location. When the branch is made, a record is automatically made of the location that initiated the subroutine call. A subroutine is terminated when the g RTN instruction is encountered. At that point control is sent back to the location *following* the GSB instruction that invoked the subroutine.

By utilizing subroutines one is able to shorten the overall length of a program as well as promote the idea of disciplined structured programming.

Program HP-33E-5: Permutations and Combinations

Location	Instruction	Comments
01	STO 2	Saves n in R2
02	GSB 20	Invokes subroutine which begins at location 20 of program memory. This subroutine calculates the factorial of the value n in the display
03	STO 3	Saves n! in R3
04	R/S	User keys in the value of r at this point
05	STO 4	Saves r in R4
06	GSB 20	Branches to subroutine which calculates r!
07	STO 5	Saves r! in R5
08	RCL 2	n
09	RCL 4	r
10	−	n − r
11	GSB 20	Calculates (n − r)!
12	RCL 3	n!
13	x ≥ y	Since we wish to calculate n!/(n − r)! and not (n − r)!/n!, we must first switch the two operands in the x and y registers before performing the division operation

Program HP-33E-5 (cont'd)

Location	Instruction	Comments
14	÷	Calculates $_nP_r = n!/(n-r)!$
15	f PAUSE	Pauses for approximately 2 seconds so that
16	f PAUSE	the user may view the results
17	RCL 5	r!
18	÷	Calculates $_nC_r = (n/r) = n!/(n-r)!r!$
19	GTO 00	Branches to location 00 to halt program execution
*20	STO 1	Stores the number whose factorial we wish to calculate in R1
21	1	Initialize factorial to 1
22	STO 0	
23	RCL 1	If the number is less than or equal to 1,
24	f x ⩽ y	we have completed the factorial calculation
25	GTO 30	and a branch is made to location 30
26	STO × 0	Otherwise, continue the factorial calculator
27	1	Decrement the number by 1
28	STO − 1	
29	GTO 23	Loop
30	RCL 0	Recalls the calculated factorial value to the display
31	g RTN	Signals the end of the subroutine and returns control to the instruction immediately following the GSB instruction that invoked the subroutine

Schematic HP-33E-5

S	1	2	3	4
K	⎡slide switch⎤	f PRGM	⎡key in steps⎤	⎡ slide switch ⎤
D	⎢ to PRGM ⎥	00	⎢ of Program ⎥	⎣to RUN mode⎦
	⎣ mode ⎦		⎣ HP-33E-5 ⎦	

S	5	6	7	8	9	10
K	GTO	0	0	f fix	0	8
D	0.0000	0.0000	0.0000	0.0000	0.	8.
C						n

---

* Location 20–31 represents a subroutine that calculates the factorial of any positive integer in the display.

Schematic HP-33E-5 (cont'd)

S	11	12	13	14	15	16
K	R/S	2	R/S		8	R/S
D	40,320.	2.	56.	28.	8.	40,320.
C		r	$_8P_2$	$_8C_2$	n	

S	17	18	19		
K	6	R/S			
D	6.	20,160	28.	...etc.	
C		$_8P_6$	$_8C_6$		

Debugging and Editing Programs on the HP-33E

The HP-33E provides the user with several features that facilitate the debugging and editing of programs on the calculator.

In order to trace through the execution of a program one step at a time, the [SST] key is used. The effect of pressing this key while in RUN mode is to first display the current location together with its contents while the key is pressed, and then to execute the particular instruction stored in that location when the key is released. By repeatedly pressing the [SST] key, the entire program can be executed one instruction at a time, a kind of slow-motion execution.

In PRGM mode the [SST] key can be used to step forward through program memory. This is useful when checking a program that has just been keyed in or to advance to a particular location. The [BST] key can be used in PRGM mode to back step through program memory one step each time the key is pressed.

In order to advance the program pointer to a specific location in memory while in PRGM mode, the [GTO] key can be used. The key sequence [GTO] [.] [nn] has the effect of positioning the program at location nn.

It is often necessary to replace a particular instruction in a program with another instruction. This can be accomplished easily on the HP-33E by first positioning the program pointer at the location immediately preceding the instruction to be replaced and then keying in the new instruction. The method of deleting an instruction from a program is to effectively substitute it by a "no operation" instruction (NOP). The program is positioned immediately before the instruction to be deleted and then the [g] [NOP] keys are pressed.

PPC—Formerly the HP-65 Users Club

Writing programs for programmable pocket calculators is an exciting endeavor and represents a formidable challenge for many of us. It is only natural, therefore, that people with similar interests would want to get together, exchange programs and ideas, and discuss future trends.

This need has apparently been satisfied by Richard J. Nelson of Santa Ana, California, who started an HP-65 Users Club in June 1974 as a nonprofit organization entirely independent of Hewlett-Packard.

On January 1, 1978 the club changed its name to PPC, standing for Personal Programmers Club. Each month members are mailed a *PPC Journal* containing calculator programs, diversions, fun and games, suggestions, and ideas on exploiting the calculators' potential to personal advantage.

Since it inception, this club has extended its coverage to include all Hewlett-Packard programmable calculators in addition to the original HP-65.

PPC is the world's first and largest organization devoted to the dissemination of information related to programmable calculators. It currently has about 1000 members and interested readers are encouraged to contact the club and request a copy of their special issue and related literature. A self-addressed 9 by 12 envelope with two ounces of first class postage attached should be mailed to:

> PPC Journal
> 2541 W. Camden Place
> Santa Ana, CA 92704

Any technical questions related specifically to the use of Hewlett-Packard calculators may be addressed to their technical staff, who may be reached by telephone at the toll free number (800) 858–1802.

CHAPTER ELEVEN
IMPLICATIONS OF THE PROGRAMMABLE POCKET CALCULATOR IN SCIENCE, INDUSTRY, AND EDUCATION

It is becoming increasingly clear that the teaching of computer science is a necessity in colleges throughout the United States and overseas. Computers are becoming more visible as each day passes, and although there are still disciplines in which computers have not been used to advantage, the fact remains that the number of such disciplines is getting smaller each year. In science, business, government, the military, banking, industry, and education, computers are playing an increasingly important role, lending themselves to greater efficiency, helping to make reliable decisions based on factual data, and alleviating some of the dull chores that human beings have traditionally carried out.

As a direct result of the exponential growth of computers, the need for computer programmers has correspondingly increased. This accounts to a large extent for the popularity and demand for computer science courses in college and even in high school. There are many institutions that would incorporate computer science courses in their programs but are prevented from doing so because of lack of sufficient funds to buy the necessary equipment. It is felt that the same applies to many primary schools that see the handwriting on the wall and realize the potential benefits of computer programming instruction.

Many schools, if they are fortunate enough, are able to rent a single terminal, which is connected to a remote site and used on a time-sharing basis. Of course, this does reduce the expenses involved but hardly satisfies the needs of hundreds of students, each of whom wants to spend more than just a few minutes at the terminal. It is quite clear that programming is curiously attractive to students at all levels, and few will deny that programming as a discipline offers considerable benefits from a pedagogical point of view. It helps the student to think logically, to gain insight into the solution of problems, and trains him to stick to a problem until it is solved. In this way the computer acts as a kind of a teacher, reinforcing knowledge as it is gained. The student can try as often as he likes to solve a particular problem; the computer will never lose its patience, even if the student loses his. More importantly, computers permit the student to experiment and thereby increase his general understanding as well as to spark his creative ability.

The advent of the programmable pocket calculator provides a solution to the dilemma of the computerless, financially strapped school. With the inevitable decrease in the prices of programmable pocket calculators, they will become available to each student of the class, each of whom will be able to concentrate his complete attention on his personal, portable, programmable, pocket calculator, bought either by the school on a mass purchase basis and loaned to students, or possibly purchased by the student himself as an investment for his entire educational career.

It is more than likely that we shall soon see new, innovative, and challenging college courses evolve around these programmable pocket calculators. It would not be surprising to see improved calculus teaching and better numerical methods courses being taught as a direct result of the emerging programmable pocket calculators.

Not that the use of programmable pocket calculators is restricted to the student. On the contrary, applications for them are abundant in the fields of statistics, finance, surveying, navigation, engineering, physics, and the social sciences. For example, in finance one can write programs to compute mortgages quickly and efficiently; interest rates, savings, discounts and discounted cash flows, and so on. In statistics, programs can be set up to compute linear regression, correlations, probability, and chi-squares, and so on. These programs may be written, entered into the calculator, and subsequently evaluated not only for just one set of data but for an unlimited set of cases. Such is the power of modern computers. Even five years ago programming was restricted to the multi-million dollar computers or those of the desk top variety costing several thousand dollars. With the advent of the programmable pocket calculator, programming is destined to become even more popular. This can hardly be detrimental either to our general intellectual development or to our industrial development.

INDEX